Venture Capital

FOR

DUMMIES®

A Wiley Brand

by Nicole Gravagna, PhD, and Peter K. Adams, MBA

FOR

DUMMIES®

A Wiley Brand

Venture Capital For Dummies®

Published by: John Wiley & Sons, Inc., 111 River Street, Hoboken, NJ 07030-5774, www.wiley.com

Copyright © 2013 by John Wiley & Sons, Inc., Hoboken, New Jersey

Published simultaneously in Canada

No part of this publication may be reproduced, stored in a retrieval system or transmitted in any form or by any means, electronic, mechanical, photocopying, recording, scanning or otherwise, except as permitted under Sections 107 or 108 of the 1976 United States Copyright Act, without the prior written permission of the Publisher. Requests to the Publisher for permission should be addressed to the Permissions Department, John Wiley & Sons, Inc., 111 River Street, Hoboken, NJ 07030, (201) 748-6011, fax (201) 748-6008, or online at http://www.wiley.com/go/permissions.

Trademarks: Wiley, For Dummies, the Dummies Man logo, Dummies.com, Making Everything Easier, and related trade dress are trademarks or registered trademarks of John Wiley & Sons, Inc., and may not be used without written permission. All other trademarks are the property of their respective owners. John Wiley & Sons, Inc., is not associated with any product or vendor mentioned in this book.

For general information on our other products and services, please contact our Customer Care Department within the U.S. at 877-762-2974, outside the U.S. at 317-572-3993, or fax 317-572-4002. For technical support, please visit www.wiley.com/techsupport.

Wiley publishes in a variety of print and electronic formats and by print-on-demand. Some material included with standard print versions of this book may not be included in e-books or in print-on-demand. If this book refers to media such as a CD or DVD that is not included in the version you purchased, you may download this material at http://booksupport.wiley.com. For more information about Wiley products, visit www.wiley.com.

Library of Congress Control Number: 2013942071

ISBN 978-1-118-64223-8 (pbk); ISBN 978-1-118-78470-9 (ebk); ISBN 978-1-118-78473-0 (ebk)

Manufactured in the United States of America

10 9 8 7 6 5 4 3 2 1

Contents at a Glance

Table of Contents

Part II: Becoming Attractive to Venture Capitalists 85

Chapter 6: Positioning Your Company for Funding. 87

Introduction

*I*f you are reading this book, chances are that you own a company or are planning to start one sometime soon. You are probably thinking about raising venture capital. We appreciate that you have come to us in your search for information. It's okay if you don't know a thing about venture capital or private investments at all. We are here to help! We wrote this book for anyone who's considering seeking venture capital. We help nearly 100 companies each year go through the process of seeking investment. All this time, we have been taking notes on what works and what doesn't.

Venture capital and venture capitalists may seem scary and larger-than-life at first. It turns out that VCs are real people, too! In this book, we demystify the venture capitalist so you can get past that "all powerful man (or woman) behind the curtain" feeling.

Venture capital investment is only one of the many ways that you can fund your company.

- ✔ Venture capital investment can help a start-up company attain much larger milestones in a much quicker timeframe than it would otherwise be able to do.

- ✔ Companies that take venture capital get more than money. They also get the expertise of the VCs and VCs' network of advisors and business people.

- ✔ The venture capital track is the fast track. Companies that take venture capital grow large very quickly or are acquired in a few short years. VC-backed companies don't do anything slowly.

After you read this book, you may choose to pursue VC funding, or you may realize that you have other options that better suit your company and your needs. This book can help you grow your company no matter which path you choose.

About This Book

We wrote *Venture Capital For Dummies* for smart people with no prior experience raising money from venture capitalists. Founders with great start-up companies come to us every day asking for advice, education, and introductions to investors. We used our experience to create this book.

Through our work at the Rockies Venture Club, we found ourselves teaching each entrepreneur the same information about venture capital investments. We thought boiling all that knowledge down into one little book — this book — would create a handy reference!

Of course, we wrote this book for entrepreneurs, but angel investors, friends of entrepreneurs, and even consultants who help entrepreneurs grow their companies can find useful information here. When everyone in an entrepreneurial community understands the fundraising process, everyone can help support start-up companies.

If you are an entrepreneur, or know an entrepreneur and want to support his or her company, you can find investors. Everyone knows someone who is an investor or knows an investor. This book can help you uncover the investors in your own network.

As you read this book, keep the following things in mind:

✔ We use the term *venture capitalist* and *VC* interchangeably, reflecting the way the terms are used in everyday conversation.

✔ The sidebars contain extra information that we think supports the main ideas in the book. You can skip them entirely and still get the full facts.

Venture Capital For Dummies is a reference book that you can read in any order you wish. If you are feeling particularly technical one day, you can dive into the chapters about investment structure. If you are more interested in understanding investor psychology, you can read those parts first. Focus on the stuff you want to know.

Foolish Assumptions

In writing this book, we made some assumptions about you, our dear reader. We guess that you are one of the four types of people that we run into through our work in the Rockies Venture Club. You are probably

✔ **An entrepreneur:** Not just any entrepreneur, but one who is ready to get his or her company off the ground, grow it fast, and make some money!

✔ **An investor:** Angel investors and people who invest in their friends' or family members' start-up companies need to understand the future funding pathway for the companies they support.

✔ **An advisor:** Professional consultants and other smart folks (mentors, advisors, gurus, yodas) who donate their time are most helpful when they can give their client companies the best advice possible.

> ✔ **A job hunter:** Jobs are created in start-ups as a matter of course. Venture capital dollars often go to hire key employees. Further, venture capital itself is an attractive industry where both senior and junior VCs can make good money in an exciting job. Either way, this book can help you understand the start-up/VC landscape as a job hunter.

As a member of one of the listed groups, you have come to the right place. We have the information you need to understand venture capital on a level you may not have dreamed possible. If you don't recognize yourself in this list, we welcome you anyway. Have fun. Look around, and we bet you'll find that you learn a thing or two.

Icons Used in this Book

To help you navigate through this book and find the information you're looking for, we've included a variety of icons.

When you're dealing with the future of your company and venture capital, the stakes are pretty high. You'll find this icon whenever you run the risk of losing an opportunity or delaying your company's success.

As experts, we know about and share with you the best shortcuts, work-arounds, and timesavers. You'll find them with this icon.

There's a lot to know and to remember when you're doing all the tasks you need to do to raise funds to help your business grow. Look for this icon to find key concepts and principles.

If you're a detail person, you may appreciate these little nuggets of information. Although interesting, we've included them more for fun. Feel free to skip them if you just want to get to the nuts-and-bolts info. Doing so won't hurt your ability to understand or seek (and hopefully) secure venture capital.

This icon highlights the stories of real business that have already gone down the path you're beginning now.

You can find lots of extra info online related to securing venture capital. This icon points you to these articles.

Beyond the Book

In addition to the material in the print or e-book you're reading right now, this product also comes with some goodies you can access on the web. Check out the free Cheat Sheet at www.dummies.com/cheatsheet/venturecapital for information on things you can do to avoid losing a deal, speed up a deal, and find VCs.

Head to www.dummies.com/extras/venturecapital to find pointers on how to work with team members who are family, find a securities attorney, and dress for your pitch.

Where to Go From Here

Go ahead and browse this book. Follow your interests and instincts. No previous knowledge is required! Start with a chapter that seems new and interesting or maybe even begin with a topic where you feel more experienced. Head to the table of contents or the Index to find topics that you want to know more about immediately. The table of contents is a great map you can use to find information listed chapter by chapter. The index lets you really want to drill down on a topic. If you're completely new to venture capital, why not begin with the chapters in Part I?

Wherever you go, you're sure to find useful information.

Part I

Getting Started with Venture Capital

In this part...

- ✔ Discover the mindset that sets founders of venture businesses apart from other business owners.

- ✔ Get the lowdown on what venture capitalists look for, how venture capital fund works, and the legal restrictions that impact which companies are selected for investment.

- ✔ Determine which funding options — venture capital, angel investors, crowdfunding, and more — can best help your company meet its growth goals.

- ✔ Take the first step to securing venture capital by creating opportunities, online and face to face, to attract the attention of a venture capitalist.

Chapter 1

Nothing Ventured, Nothing Gained: Venture Capital Basics

In This Chapter

▶ Getting familiar with venture capital and venture capitalists

▶ Determining whether you have a venture company

▶ Seeing the whole venture capital process

*I*f you're starting a new business, welcome to the club! Starting a business can be the most exciting, scary, enlightening venture that you embark on. If you've been running a business for a while and are just starting to look for money, you've come to the right place!

Venture capital is often misunderstood and feels like a big cloaked, black box to many people. In reality, venture capital is pretty easy to understand after you've been given the basics. Further, venture capitalists are more open about sharing information than people think. You just need to know where to look for the information.

In this book, you discover which companies benefit most from venture capital, how venture capital works, how to connect with VCs, and when the time comes, how to pitch to investors. We also describe the whole start-up funding landscape and explain how to navigate it wisely. This chapter introduces you to venture capital and provides a general overview. Consider it your gateway to this exciting world.

Understanding Venture Capital and Venture Capitalists

Venture capital is a very specific type of investment for a very unique type of company. Venture capital–backed companies are expected to grow extremely fast — much faster than other companies. In addition, VC-backed companies are sold after five or seven years in an acquisition or on the stock market in an initial public offering (IPO).

VC-backed companies have the potential to make millions (billions?) of dollars for investors and founders. Because of the huge windfall possibilities, a lot of people are interested in creating companies that are attractive to VCs. Nevertheless, venture capital is not a necessary part of building or growing your business. In fact, companies can do very well without venture capital and the involvement of venture capitalists.

Technically speaking, venture capital is just like any other investment, an asset class. Venture capital investments are high risk and also potentially high return. Not all investors want to be involved with venture capital (sometimes called *risk capital*) because of the level of risk involved.

The following sections introduce you to the venture capitalists — the people who invest the money in start-up businesses — and the kinds of companies that are prefect for venture capital.

Introducing venture capitalists

Venture capitalists are the professional investors who give start-up companies money in exchange for equity in the company. They provide both liquid capital and support for a company during a fundamental time in the growth of the business.

Venture capitalists are responsible for bringing together large amounts of money for an investment fund (called *raising a fund)*, which is then used to invest in companies, hand-picked to become part of the VC's (or VC firm's) portfolio. The VC and his team choose companies that are capable of growing very large very fast, earning the VC firm many times its initial investment.

Venture capitalists know that not every company in their portfolio will produce a huge return on investment, and so to tip the hand in their favor, VCs do two things:

- ✔ They invest in companies that have excellent odds of being successful venture-quality companies.
- ✔ They support the companies in their portfolio with resources like mentorship, board members, and strong management.

Companies that work with venture capital give up an element of control in exchange for the opportunity. Most founders find the exchange worth it for the added capital, support, and connections that come with an investment of venture capital.

Knowing what VC firms look for

Venture capital firms tend to specialize. They focus on a specific stage of company and one or two industries. A VC firm may focus on companies in the medical device field, for example, or maybe in clean energy. Because VCs deal with risky investments, they have to make sure that they understand their chosen industry and technologies inside and out. Therefore, your company must fit into the firm's profile before the firm will consider investing. (You can usually find out which industries a VC firm invests in on the firm's website under the About Us tab.)

Focusing on different stages

VCs may invest in seed stage companies (companies with no revenue or little revenue) or stage 2 companies (those with $5 million to 50 million in revenue), or they may fund mergers and acquisitions of larger companies. Companies of different sizes have very different issues and needs. For more on the different fundraising rounds, head to Chapter 9.

Focusing on specific industries

Venture capitalists must be experts in their chosen industries, understanding it completely. This expertise is especially important because the best portfolio companies have game-changing technologies that disrupt markets. Predicting the success of companies that don't have any contemporaries is a very challenging task!

Focusing on the company's progress and potential

Most venture capitalists, even those who invest in seed stage companies, look for the following:

- That the company has a product or has made a lot of progress toward a product
- That the company has a strong team that can execute its plans
- That the company has connected with its target customer and understands its market

These factors impact your company's risk level. Investors have a level of risk that they are willing to accept in a company. Investors interested in later stage companies want you to have removed more of the risk from your company by progressing through necessary milestones. Seed stage investors are more accepting of risk and use a high risk profile as a way to get more equity for the same investment dollars.

Getting familiar with the VC fund lifecycle

Venture capital funds don't last forever. They tend to run on a predictable, ten-year cycle. To give you a better idea of your interactions with VCs, we've paired their activities with yours over the lifetime of the fund.

1. Investors spend the first year raising a fund from high-net-worth individuals (accredited investors), corporations, and institutional investors like pension funds. You aren't involved at this point. If it's a new firm and/or a new fund, you may not even know that the VC exists yet.

2. VCs spend the next few years finding companies to add to their portfolio (called *sourcing deals*). During this period, you'll get introduced to a VC through a mutual contact, or you'll submit your pitch deck to the VC through the VC's website (find out more about pitch decks in Chapter 15.)

3. After the company is given investment and becomes part of the portfolio, the VC proceeds to manage the company. Generally, VCs do this by joining the board.

   VCs are very helpful to entrepreneurs throughout the investment relationship. They tend to act as the voice of experience in the relationship because they've been through company building many times. During this time, you'll be working hard to develop new products, increase revenue, and basically do what you do best — run your company.

4. As the fund nears the end of its lifespan, the VCs work to liquidate the companies through mergers and acquisitions. If the company does very well, it may go public and become a company traded on the open stock market. If the company isn't doing well, it can be shut down and its assets sold separately.

   It's the VCs job to sell your company to a buyer. It's your job to let him. This is how you cash out and take home the spoils of your hard labor.

5. As all the companies in the portfolio are sold, the money is returned to the original investors (limited partners) who entrusted their cash to the VC, and the VC fund closes. At this point, you're free to do whatever you want. Your formal relationship with the VC is over, and you can start a new company, get a 9-5 job in a corporation, or retire.

Choosing the Venture Capital Pathway

Companies that benefit most from venture capital are those that have a disruptive technology or product that they aim to grow very large very quickly. Entrepreneurs who benefit most from venture capital are those who want to create a great new company and do not need to retain full control over it as it grows.

Companies that have a tried-and-true product or service may not benefit from venture capital. Venture capital also may not be right for the company owner who likes to retain primary control or has always dreamed of handing the business down through generations. Chapter 3 is all about determining whether venture capital is right for your business.

When you work with venture capital, you make tradeoffs: You control less of the company and receive less of the total cash after your company sells. On the plus side, you have a support system of smart VCs, and your risk is distributed among more people.

Identifying a good venture business

Your traditional coffee house, clothing store, photography business, landscaping business, restaurant, real estate development company, and filmmaking company don't make sense as venture capital-backed companies. Different kinds of industry-specific investors put money into those types of companies.

Venture capital tends to invest in companies built around software, drug developments, medical devices, engineering devices, and other cutting edge technologies that are considered disruptive to current markets. (*Disruptive technologies* are innovations that could not have been predicted; therefore, their effect on the market as a whole cannot be predicted either.) VCs look for disruptive technologies because the potential for a huge return on investment is greater when the business hinges on very risky technology or market integration. High risk can equal high reward.

Of course, not all technology companies should be venture capital–backed companies. Many of technology companies would do well to grow organically — that is, without large investments of capital — and develop at a slower rate. Organically grown companies can be big winners, too. In fact, if you can get your company to profitability without taking outside investment, you may stand to make more money. Chapter 3 contains all the information you need to start deciding which track your company should take.

Looking at alternatives to venture capital

If you decide that the mega-high growth, high stress, venture-backed start-up company lifestyle isn't what you signed up for, you can grow your company as a small-to-midsized business (SMB). Compared to venture capital–backed companies, SMB companies tend to require a lot less capital, grow more slowly, and remain more stable as they grow.

Smalls business have lots of different ways to raise money, including through bank loans, crowdfunding, friends and family, grants, and franchising. Chapter 4 goes into detail about all your options as a business that ultimately chooses not to raise venture capital.

From Zero to Venture Capital: Knowing What to Do to Secure Venture Capital

The most successful venture capital businesses are not just good at what they do; they are also lucky. Because you can't do anything to improve your serendipity, you can plan your business from the beginning in ways that remove hurdles and increase the possibility of success. Follow these suggestions:

✔ **Start by thinking about the end.** When you look back on this business from the future, what do you want it to look like? Plan for the results that you envision. Chapter 8 tells you what your exit options are and explains how to prepare for your exit.

✔ **Target a huge problem that has a huge market.** VCs want big exits. The best thing that you can do to set your company up for VC funding is to go after a huge problem with a huge market. You can't sell a company for billions if it has an esoteric or limited market. Head to Chapter 6 to find out how to position your business to attract a VC's attention.

✔ **Get your feet under you.** VCs don't fund companies with grand ideas until the company shows a lot of progress toward revenue. This progress is often referred to using the word *traction*. Chapter 6 tells you what key components — business plan, product development, marketing strategies, and more — to focus as you prepare your business for venture capital.

✔ **Become visible.** You can increase the likelihood of getting funded quite a bit by simply meeting the funders. Make friends with investors. Get to know the VCs and the larger start-up community. *Schmoozing* isn't a bad word anymore. Chapter 5 has a number of suggestions for connecting with investors, both online and face-to-face.

✔ **Develop the deal.** Not only do you have to develop the company, but you also have to design a great investment deal. Investors like working with founders who know how to put their due diligence materials together and who have working knowledge of a term sheet. These concepts aren't rocket science, but getting familiar with the process does take time. Get cracking! And go to Chapter 9 for the details.

✔ **Start pitching.** After your company has gained traction, your deal is structured, and VCs know your name (or at least your face), you need to start pitching for investment. Pitching is such an important and involved task, that we dedicate an entire part to it: Part IV.

The following sections delve into more detail on three key points: getting your company ready, designing your investment deal, and approaching investors.

Preparing your company to attract interest

Just as you would prepare your home when you put it on the real estate market, you need to get your company prepared for investors: Gathering the right advisors, making sure your records and certificates are in order, planning your future growth, and really connecting with your customer are all important points when getting ready for investment.

Coinciding fundraising efforts around milestones

One of the hardest things to do in fundraising is to know when to start fundraising. The good news is that you don't have to decide on one particular, set-in-stone date. Instead, one way to ensure you have the funds you need when you need them is to time your fundraising between milestones. Identify all the major milestones that your company must tackle before you achieve profitability, and then plan your fundraising efforts to coincide with the period of time after you've just attained a pretty nice milestone and right before you tackle the next one. Your just-completed milestone will serve as a great story that shows your team's ability to execute.

Notice that this suggestion isn't "begin fundraising after you complete development of your whiz-bang product." You can — and should — begin fundraising rounds earlier than that. The key is to know your business, know your market potential, and be able to show progress toward your goals. Chapter 6 includes information about business plans, product development, promotion strategy, and communicating your future revenue streams before you ever earn a cent from your product. Head to Chapter 14 for a checklist to determine when you should start fundraising.

Polishing your company for investors

Get your company to a point where you feel comfortable having a figurative open house. Many companies are moving and developing so fast that they have ugly loose ends everywhere. You have to polish your company to raise money:

- ✔ Show your market research in ways that investors can follow. Raw data may be okay for you, but the investor is going to want to see well-designed graphs.

- ✔ Revise your business plan and business model regularly so they reflect the new information that you have learned since you originally wrote the documents. Write a two to three page executive summary for investors (they don't have time to read the whole thing).

- ✔ List all the strategic partnerships, mentors, advisors, and other supportive relationships that you have made.

- ✔ Plan out employee needs in the near future and start talking to potential candidates even if you don't plan to hire for 12 months.

Chapter 6 has even more ways to get your company VC ready.

Connecting with customers early

Many companies think that they cannot begin to connect with customers until they have a finished product to sell. Nothing is farther from the truth. You can, and should, be connecting with targeted groups of customers as you develop your product. By the time the product is finished, you will have a small group of happy customers whose excitement you can leverage to promote sales. It's never too early to talk to a potential customer.

Adding expertise to your business

The number of people excited about your company can be indicative of future success, and VCs like to see lots of high-quality people who are willing to put their names on your company.

You can really increase your credibility with VCs by adding expertise to your team in terms of an advisory board or through strong mentors. Don't think you have to pay a ton of employees to have a big team! Chapter 7 is all about relationships and tells you how to get people involved in your company and your deal in many different ways.

Putting together the deal

Developing your business is only one part of raising capital. You have to develop the deal, too. Basically, the deal is the amount of money that you need and the percentage of the company that the investor will get in return for capital under certain conditions. Conditions can include requirements for milestone achievement, involvement of certain industry experts, or many other things. Chapter 9 discusses the deal in detail; following are some key points.

✔ **Lay out your company's plans for the future and determine how many times you'll have to raise capital to achieve your goals;** then coordinate your capital raises with big milestones (refer to the earlier section "Coinciding fundraising efforts around milestones"). Investors would much rather invest when they know a large milestone will be attainable with the capital raised. Matching capital to milestones is akin to raising enough money to put a person through a four-year degree. Nobody wants to invest in something that only gets the job three-quarters of the way done.

Companies raise venture capital after early rounds of angel capital, friends and family investments, or bootstrapping the company for a while. In Chapter 9, you can see what a normal funding pathway looks like. You also find information about the term sheet, differences between equity and convertible debt, and how to avoid pitfalls in early round deal structure.

- ✔ **Identify risks/milestone:** In this book, we use the term *risk* to mean the things that absolutely must go well; otherwise, you cannot achieve your goals. You can communicate the stage of your company, determine the price of your shares, and prove traction all by thoroughly understanding the risks you have overcome and the ones you still have ahead of you. Chapter 10 explores risk and tells you how to use the risks you face as a roadmap to success.

- ✔ **Calculate valuation:** After you have a grasp of risk, you can determine the valuation of your company. Chapter 11 defines multiple ways to calculate valuation and a few ways to discuss the topic with your VC without scaring him or her away!

- ✔ **Be prepared to negotiate:** To negotiate well, you have to understand what you want out of your deal. "A lot of cash" isn't specific enough. Use Chapter 12 to get into the mindset of negotiation. Identify what's important and what can be ignored when you go to the table.

- ✔ **Collect due diligence materials:** One of the best things you can do to help speed along your funding timeline is to get all of your business materials in order for due diligence. Doing so before an investor has shown direct interest may seem premature, but it's really important. Chapter 13 includes a checklist of materials.

Gathering due diligence materials can be a fairly extensive process tat takes weeks to complete. If weeks pass *after* an investor expresses interest in your company, you can lose momentum and subsequently, the deal. Being organized is key!

Making your pitch

In a pitch, you present your company and your deal to investors. These days, the standard way to get money from VCs is to pitch to them using a PowerPoint presentation and a short dialog. The general pitch will go something like this:

1. **You tell investors what you do (software, hardware, device, toy, or business tool, for example) and how you'll make money.**

2. **You discuss just how much money you can make by describing the people or businesses who'll buy this product.**

3. **You tell investors how you will gain access to your customer by detailing the promotional plan and the distribution plan.**

4. **You tell investors about the milestones involved in your company's future development and reassure them that you are capable of running this company by outlining all the milestones that you've already overcome.**

5. **You give financials (these must make sense) and then talk about the investment opportunity.**

Notice anything about this sequence of discussion topics? They all focus on money. If an investor pitch has a theme, that theme is money. You'll talk about your product and how it solves a problem for someone; you'll discuss the market and the investment; but the whole time, you're really talking about money. Head to Chapters 14, 15, and 16 for the details on making your pitch.

Following a few unspoken rules

There's quite a bit of information that you convey nonverbally during a pitch. These unspoken signals are the cues that VCs use to determine whether you're "in the know" about venture capital and how to grow a company. To a VC, working with a founder in the know means that he doesn't have to spend the next three years teaching you how to work with him. Some clues that you're in the know include the following (all of which you'll know after you finish this book):

- **Speaking the language.** It may seem superficial at first, but if you know what a *term sheet* is (Chapter 9), what a *down round* is (Chapter 9), and why an exit is important (Chapter 8), then you are on your way.

- **Understanding the VC's motivations.** It's easiest to do business with someone who understands what you need from the relationship. Find out about this in Chapter 2.

- **Being communicative.** Things aren't always perfect. A VC wants to work with someone who is a forthright partner that can be trusted to share all information in a timely manner.

Most business transactions occur between people who feel like they have a rapport with one another. Before you can ever close the deal, you have to really connect with your investors. Chapter 7 explains how to cultivate relationships with the people you'll come in contact with during your venture adventure.

Planning to do it again!

Fundraising is a process. If you are successful and able to raise money, you will likely raise money again in the future. Fundraising skills are always powerful to have in your back pocket. In addition, the more you pitch, the better and better you get. When a pitch is done well, it's obvious to everyone in the room. Practice your pitch over and over and remember that it can always improve a little more!

Chapter 2

The Venture Capitalist Mindset

*Y*ou may think of venture capitalists mainly as people with money who help companies grow. Although this impression is accurate, there's more to VCs and the venture capital business than that.

Venture capital firms are businesses whose mission is to make money by investing in other rapidly growing businesses. VCs make investments in emerging companies, the most risky investment class known. Although you may believe your company will be the next big thing, most start-ups (80 percent, in fact) lose money and fail. So you can see how venture capital can be a very difficult industry.

In this chapter, we explain what venture capitalists do, how venture capital funds work, why some VCs can work with you and some can't, and more. By the time you're done reading this chapter, you'll know that not all VCs are the same. Understanding the venture capital business in more detail helps you better understand venture capitalists themselves so that you can work with them more easily and effectively. Armed with this info, you'll know what to look for and what to expect from your VC. After all, by finding the right VC, you save yourself time and hassle.

Performing a High-Risk Job: The VC's Role

Venture capital is a financial industry in which institutions (the venture capital firms) raise money from many sources and invest that money in high-risk companies that possess paradigm-changing ideas or technology. By its nature, venture capital is a very high-risk endeavor, and a career in venture capital is intense and often short. Here are a few general things to know about venture capitalists:

- **VCs are not investing their own money in these selected companies.** They invest *other* people's money, which, as you can imagine, is a big responsibility. (If you were investing cash that has been entrusted to you, you would be very careful with it, too!)

- **All VCs run businesses just like you do, except that their businesses are venture capital ones.** Just like all businesspeople, they have to follow through with the agreements they make with their clients — the people who have given them the money to invest. If they don't, they lose their jobs and their careers.

- **Venture capital is the most expensive money you can find to fund your business.** One reason it's so expensive is because of the risks involved (more on that in the next item in this list). Another reason is that making a venture capital investment takes a lot of work. VCs sometimes spend hundreds of hours evaluating and negotiating deals. To secure venture capital, whether you need a couple million dollars or many millions of dollars, you have to give up a lot of equity and control in your business.

Venture capital is not a lifeline, a grant, or a charitable contribution. If your company is having money trouble or is otherwise struggling, a VC wants nothing to do with you. Venture capital is not an alternative to bankruptcy! VCs look for healthy companies.

- **VCs take huge risks with their careers and reputations when they raise venture capital funds.** First, the risk of losing money when investing in start-up businesses is so great that VCs have a difficult time finding the money to invest in the first place. Second, even if a VC does everything right, bad luck alone can result in lost investments. So although the VC doesn't stand to personally lose the invested millions of dollars, he does stand to lose his carefully built reputation, a generous percentage of your final exit when you sell the company, and possibly his career. VCs who fail to make money for their clients don't remain VCs for long.

Clearing up a few myths about venture capitalists

VCs are not out to steal your company, run your company, or otherwise ruin your life. They simply want to ensure that their investment fund makes money. Yet these rather uncomplimentary impressions persist. In this section, we set the record straight.

- ✔ **Myth 1: A more appropriate name would be "vulture capitalists":** Venture capitalists are sometimes called *vulture capitalists,* a nickname that has implies that VCs are opportunistic and pick meat off the bones of sick or dying businesses. Although hedge funds exist that do approach businesses this way, most venture capitalists want to work with healthy, growing businesses to help them develop and mature. The venture capital industry is small, and it doesn't make sense for a VC to do something that might tarnish his reputation with entrepreneurs or other VCs.

- ✔ **Myth 2: They want to steal your company.** Another common misconception is that VCs want to own most of your company. Most VCs don't want to take too much ownership of the entrepreneur's company because the entrepreneur then loses motivation to make the company successful. VCs know that they're actually investing in the entrepreneur, and without their knowledge and energy, the company will be less likely to be successful. VCs with long-term vision understand that a fair deal is in everyone's best interest.

- ✔ **Myth 3: They're unscrupulous.** Venture capitalists have a reputation of being unscrupulous because of stories that they fire companies CEO so that they can gradually take complete ownership and leave the entrepreneur with nothing. In fact, VCs need good companies to come to them with possible deals. If a VC is unscrupulous, and founders start to tell other founders to be wary of her, then the she's not going to be able to make investments in great companies, and her fund will fail to make money.

Most VCs want to manage a series of successive funds. To do so, they need to provide successful returns on their first funds so that they can go back to their investors the next time around. (For more on how VCs find funding, head to the later section "Fundraising — where the investment money comes from.")

When you're seeking and working with VCs, be aware of your own mindset. If you go into the relationship thinking that all VCs are evil and that working with them is an unpleasant necessity of doing business, you may not notice if your VC actually *is* unscrupulous. Keep your mind open so that you can better judge whether the VC you decide to work with is ethical, trustworthy, and an all-around good person; if you discover she's not, find another VC.

Don't fight 'em, join 'em: Working together on the deal

If you get investment, the VC becomes your business partner. As with all business partners, the relationship between founder and VC is an intimate one. You must trust your VC, and she must trust you. This trust is often built during the early stages of the relationship, before the investment is closed.

When you align your desires with your VC's desires, the whole process of working with venture capital goes more smoothly.

Finding a VC you can trust and work with

When you are seeking investment from a VC, do the following:

- ✔ **Determine whether you can trust this person.** Find out who she has invested in and contact those companies. Make sure you get in contact with those who are in business as well as those that are not. Ask around about the VC. It's a small community, and VCs' reputations tend to be well known.

- ✔ **Interview the VC.** The VC isn't the only one who gets to make decisions about whether or not to pursue the relationship. You do, too. Ask questions of the VC about the size of her fund, how much is invested, and what funds are remaining for investment. *Note:* If the VC is raising a new fund, it may be a year or more before she can actually make an investment in your company. Although this is okay, you want to be able to set your expectations accordingly and spend your time approaching other funds that are actively investing.

Also ask whether the VC has a fund. Many people who seem like VCs are actually finders, brokers, and other service providers. Just because they have capital in their name doesn't mean they have capital to invest. Look for telltale signs: exclusive contracts, up-front fees, or requiring you to pay a percentage of the raise amount, for example.

A venture capitalist is not king of the financial world. Instead, she's more like a middle manager who has to answer to a board, partners, and public opinion. This notion may help you get the VC off the pedestal in your mind so you can work with her as an equal and a business partner. Also, when you're going into the pitch and throughout due diligence, think of the VC as a business partner that you can choose to work with or walk away from. Then you'll be more comfortable and more in control going into the pitch and the negotiation. (For information on these aspects of putting together a deal with a VC, head to Parts III and IV.)

You may know of a venture capital fund that is local to you that's fully invested but, for some reason, agrees to see you and have you pitch. Although this is great practice for you, it can be frustrating because a fully invested fund can't invest in your company under any circumstances. However, this VC can give you a very valuable referral to another VC if she thinks your business is appropriate for another fund. The only way you can get money out of this interaction is through such a referral, or if the VC invests her own money as an angel. Chapter 4 has more info on angel investors.

Knowing what to expect

VCs have their own rules of engagement that are based on managing their own time constraints and serving the needs of their limited partners. Although they do need good companies in order to be successful in their business, don't expect the red carpet treatment:

- ✔ **Don't expect easy access:** If you think getting an appointment with your dermatologist is hard, try to get an hour alone with a venture capitalist! VCs are known to be difficult to corner. They have so many demands on their time that they have to fly under the radar sometimes.

- ✔ **Don't expect advice:** VCs rarely give feedback after they reject your deal. First, they don't have the time. Second, they may not have any particular reason for rejecting you; when your job is to screen through hundreds of applications looking for a gem, you are bound to overlook a few rough diamonds now and again. Third, the VC just might not *get it*, in which case she's unlikely to tell you something specific is wrong with your deal; in fact, your deal may be fine. Finally, because VCs don't have time to look into your company very closely before they pass it up, they wouldn't presume to come back to you with deep feedback after only giving your company a glance.

If you want to know why you were rejected, you'll need to figure it out without the VC's help: Ask around. Read up on the VC firm (which you should have done before applying in the first place). Reevaluate whether you are *truly* a good fit; you may discover that you were just really hoping the VC would think you were.

Understanding How a Venture Capital Fund Works

Venture capital funds are entities that exist to manage large amounts of money, put that money in growing companies, and then monitor the companies to protect the investment until what is hopefully a lucrative exit, when the company is at its peak value.

A VC firm is a business in itself that manages a fund which is also an entity within itself. A VC firm can manage more than one fund, either sequentially or simultaneously. In conversation, the words are used interchangeably. Although a limited partner may care which fund his money went into (different terms in each fund perhaps), the entrepreneur cares more about which firm she's working with. The entrepreneur's terms will be dictated by the general partners managing the funds, not by the initial terms of the fund. From the entrepreneur's standpoint, the fund that is investing in her is not relevant. The people she works with in the firm are.

The lifecycle of a venture capital fund has four parts.

- ✔ **Fundraising:** The VC meets with potential limited partners to get them to invest their money in her fund.

- ✔ **Investing:** The VC meets with many companies to find the few that she will invest in.

- ✔ **Managing:** After the fund invests in a company, the VC actively participates on the board of the company, works with the CEO, and makes business connections to make sure that the company is making good business decisions.

- ✔ **Harvesting:** When companies undergo liquidity events such as an initial public offering, merger, acquisition, or a sale of shares to another firm, the VC manages the divvying of funds to all the shareholders.

We explain each of these stages in the following sections.

Fundraising — where the investment money comes from

The *capital* in venture capital comes from wealthy individuals, pension funds, insurance companies, family offices, foundations, and other pools of cash. These entities are looking for higher returns than they can get in the stock market, but they still want to minimize risk. To do so, they look closely at the track record of the venture capitalist in order to pick the funds that are most likely to provide a great return.

The people and organizations that provide the capital are called *limited partners,* because they have limited liability when they participate in the fund. They can lose their money, but they are not at fault if something illegal happens within the venture fund itself or any company that the VC invests in because their participation is limited to investing and not managing the fund.

The venture capitalist has to gather up the total value of the fund, which often exceeds $100 million. VCs do this through a process called *selling the fund*. Basically, they have to convince investors to participate, and to do so, they perform many of the same tasks you'll perform when you seek venture capital yourself: creating a private placement memorandum, putting together a pitch deck, writing up an executive summary, and pitching over and over to potential investors. Selling a fund is a hard job, and it can take a year or more to collect enough money to *close the fund*. After the fund is closed, no more limited partners can participate, and no one is allowed to put more money in.

VCs and their investors enter into a limited partnership agreement, which stipulates things like the kind of company the fund will invest in, the amount of money that will be invested, the phase of development of the company, and the amount of time before the money is to be returned to the limited partners.

Investing — finding companies to fund

After the fund is closed, the VC has to collect applications from companies who want to be funded. Having a constant stream of interested companies is called *deal flow*. If a venture capital firm hopes to fund the best companies, it strives for good deal flow, which means that the firm sees a lot of companies every day. Then the VC firm screens through deal flow, invites companies to pitch, and begins due diligence on the companies it likes.

A typical VC may invest in only one or two deals a year after screening hundreds of deals. So don't get discouraged if you're rejected by the first couple of VCs that you talk to. In fact, one company analyzed its $1 million raise to understand how to make the fundraising process more efficient in the future and discovered that it talked to more than 50 VCs and more than 50 angel investors before closing the round. You can't get discouraged by the first few *no*'s. If your company is making steady progress, then you'll find the right investor eventually.

VCs typically look at 100 or more deals for every one that they invest in. The entire process is a series of go/no-go decisions, and you can fall out of the process anywhere along the line if your company does not live up to what the VC is looking for. In the following sections, we outline the four steps in the process.

Step 1: Screening initial interest

A VC looks for four things:

- ✔ A management team that has the track record and experience to execute
- ✔ A big idea in what will be a very big market
- ✔ A company/product that has the ability to be the leader in the sector
- ✔ Many potential strategic buyers or initial public offering (IPO) potential and a *near term exit* which is a potential for 10X–30X ("10 times" and "30 times" respectively) return in three to seven years.

When the VC finds a company that looks like a good company to fund, she invites the company to meet with the VC firm.

Behind the scenes: VCs and their investors

In addition to working with your company, a VC also has to manage the accounting of the fund itself. Key tasks include

✓ **Timing the collection of money for the fund:** When a VC raises a fund, she doesn't just collect a bunch of checks and put them in a savings account. Instead, investors make commitments to invest certain amounts, and when the VC is ready to invest in a company, she'll call for capital, and the investors will write actual checks to the VC.

The VC collects more than just the investment amount. She also charges a management fee, typically of 2 percent of funds under management, to cover her operating costs as well as the investments she makes.

✓ **Working with outside auditors:** VC funds are typically audited by outside CPAs as a way to ensure investors that their funds are being used properly and according to the limited partnership operating agreement.

✓ **Tracking when and how much money is invested and returned to investors:** VCs provide this information, which can include interim valuations of companies before they reach a liquidation event, to investors, who need it for their own tax reporting.

✓ **Regularly communicating with investors:** VC firms provide regular updates to their limited partners and hold annual or quarterly meetings so that investors can ask questions and be kept up to date on the activities of the fund.

If you don't get through a VC's first round of screening, make sure you understand why. You may be denied simply because of an industry mismatch (your business isn't in the industry the fund invests in; see the later section "Going for an industry match" for details). In this case, there's not much you can do. If you're denied because you need to get more traction — say, growing your revenues to $1 million a year — you can work on achieving that goal and revisit that VC in a year or so when you've turned the corner and are ready to get even bigger.

Step 2: Meeting with companies and seeing their pitch

When the VC finds a company that looks like a good company to fund, she invites the company to meet with the VC firm. If the meeting goes well, the VC firm moves to the next stage: due diligence. For information and instructions on how to pitch your company, head to Part IV.

Step 3: Following up with due diligence

Due diligence is the process of researching a potential investment so well that everything is known about that company. Chapter 13 is devoted to the process of due diligence.

Managing — keeping tabs on the investments

VCs add a lot more value to the companies that they invest in than just capital. They have a huge amount of experience in the industry and have their fingers on the pulse of the latest trends that impact your company. Successful VCs are also very connected to many, many people in the industry. They can provide you with strategic partnerships that help you leverage your success.

Although a VC does not manage your company on a day-to-day basis — that's your job — she will attend your regular board meetings on a schedule ranging from monthly to quarterly. Some VCs get in touch as often as weekly to make sure that things are going well. In addition, the VC firm will periodically ask for information and offer a helping hand when needed. VCs help companies in a variety of ways, ranging from coaching the CEO through challenging issues to making introductions to key contacts in the industry and recruiting key employees.

Harvesting — collecting the final payout

The exit strategy is the most important part of the job for a VC. In most cases, the only way a VC makes money is when the company is sold through an initial public offering (IPO) or is acquired by another company (merger and acquisition, or M&A) or a private equity firm. (This is a key reason why, if your plan for your company is to run it for the rest of your life as a private corporation, a VC will probably not be interested. In this situation, she has no way to return the cash to investors.) But being sold or acquired isn't the sole objective: The key is to be sold for a very high return on investment (ROI).

Looking at ROI

The venture capital model is based on hitting the business equivalent of homeruns. In a portfolio of ten investments, typical VCs can expect more than half to do very poorly. Figure 2-1 shows an example portfolio in which, of ten investments, three are a total loss, three return the initial investment back, three earn between 2X and 6X the initial investment, and one is a "home run" at 30X the initial investment.

This requirement is one of the reasons why deals that are limited to returning only 5X the investment are never in a VCs portfolio. Small ROI deals have all the risk and none of the possibilities.

Many entrepreneurs offer a buy-back of stock as the potential exit strategy. In most cases, this plan is unrealistic. If an investor looks for a 10X return on investment, there is almost no way that a company can return that investment in cash. Here's why: Company value is rarely found simply in cash flow but is typically measured in multiples of EBITDA (earnings before interest, taxes, depreciation, and amortization) that are often many times the company's current cash flow. In this scenario, the company won't have sufficient cash on hand to pay the VC for her equity.

For more information on the kind of return on investment VC firms look for, head to the later section "Making long-term investments for fast growth."

Figure 2-1:
In a portfolio of ten investments, many do poorly. The homerun here is the investment that did 30X returns.

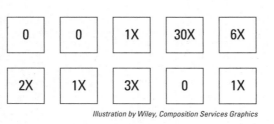

| 0 | 0 | 1X | 30X | 6X |
| 2X | 1X | 3X | 0 | 1X |

Illustration by Wiley, Composition Services Graphics

Planning the exit

Most of the value of the deal comes at the exit, and planning and executing the exit strategy is a key role of the VC. To have a successful exit, several key conditions must exist: rapid growth, a strong and coherent management team, a favorable market and economic conditions for acquisition or IPO, and sufficient traction to justify acquisition by a key player in the market. Understanding that the exit is not just something to be put together at the end, the VC begins planning the exit well in advance, engineering it into the company from the very beginning.

Perhaps even more valuable than knowing how to plan an exit, VCs also know who the strategic acquirers are in your industry, and they probably already have relationships with them. VCs also have the knowledge and expertise to know whether IPO or acquisition is a better strategy for your firm.

Not all companies will have an exit at all, or the exit may be that the company is shut down and liquidated. This can happen when growth doesn't hit projections or when the industry or market changes significantly with new competitive pressures or technologies that eliminate your company's strategic advantage. Other companies, considered the "walking dead," are ones that return a small amount of cash flow to investors, but their chances of being acquired are negligible. Success in a venture capital–backed firm happens less than half the time, so entrepreneurs need to be fully committed while also understanding that failure is an option.

Examining how VCs make money off the deal

VCs make money in three ways:

- **Management fee:** The VC firm earns a management fee that covers its costs for creating deal flow, screening, due diligence, serving on boards, coaching, accounting and reporting, and engineering the exit. The firms typically make 2 percent of the money under management for these services. A $100 million fund, for example, makes $2 million in management fees, which are used to pay all the staff members and keep the lights on in the office.

- **Carried interest at the exit:** VCs make money at the exit through *carried interest,* which is generally called a *carry* in investor lingo. The carried interest is typically equal to 20 percent of the net profit after an exit. If, for example, the fund invested $100 million in ten companies and returned $200 million after all the exits, the VC would be entitled to a carry of $20 million. The carried interest ensures that the VC is focused on developing the greatest possible return for the fund.

- **Interest from investing their own money:** Sometimes VCs get an option to invest their own money into the fund — a big perk for senior staff members (junior staff are often not allowed to invest alongside the firm). Having her own money invested in the fund shows a personal commitment to the fund and ensures alignment between the fund managers and the limited partners because they all share the risk of investment.

When a venture fund loses money, the VC loses not only her own investment, but the opportunity to participate in the carried interest as well. VCs are very motivated not to lose money!

Figure 2-2 shows the VCs' return on investment after a liquidation event and where the money goes.

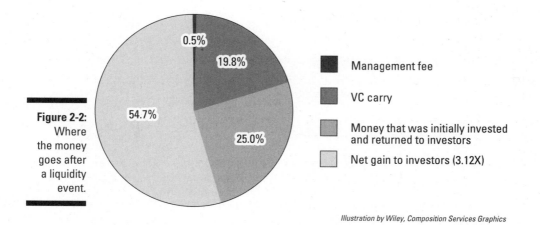

Figure 2-2: Where the money goes after a liquidity event.

- Management fee
- VC carry
- Money that was initially invested and returned to investors
- Net gain to investors (3.12X)

0.5%
19.8%
54.7%
25.0%

Illustration by Wiley, Composition Services Graphics

The history of venture capital

Venture capital has supported risky ventures for centuries. Many of the initial explorations to the New World were funded through a sort of venture capital. More recently, advances in computer technology and medical science have been funded through venture capital.

Georges Doriot is widely considered to be the father of modern venture capital. His company, American Research and Development Corporation (ARDC), was a publicly held company with its shares traded on the stock market. Through ARDC, Doriot is credited with funding and supporting a wide range of companies, more than 100 in total, over nearly 30 years.

Due to U.S. Securities and Exchange Commission (SEC) regulations banning company employees from holding stock in the companies that they were growing and selling, Doriot was unable to compensate his employees as handsomely as they deserved. As a result, ARDC ended up being a university of sorts for new VCs who would work at ARDC to learn the ropes and then leave the company to form their own private venture capital companies.

Although the ARDC model was not sustainable, it pioneered the modern venture capital firm, which uses a limited partnership model that binds multiple limited partners (the silent investors) to a single general partner (the VC). The general partner assumes the control and the liability of the business entity (the VC fund).

In the late 1950s, venture capital moved to Silicon Valley, and the modern venture capital industry was born. Some of the early players were Arthur Rock (Davis & Rock), Tom Perkins (Kleiner, Perkins, Caufield & Byers), and Don Valentine (Sequoia Capital). They invested in companies like Fairchild Semiconductor, Apple, Digital Equipment Corporation, and Genentech, and their early successes led to a thriving Silicon Valley venture capital community.

Although venture capital can be great for society in general by pushing boundaries and supporting new technologies, it can be a devastatingly rough business. The venture capital industry has ups and downs that follow the economy. Like the stock market, it becomes hot, then flat, then goes back up again. Some people lose money, and others make millions. During years of high profitability, venture capital firms with less-than-righteous missions tend to spring up more often. The number of venture capital firms in the U.S. has been over 1,000 in good economic times and wanes to only a few hundred in tight economies.

Generally, a healthy venture capital industry is good for a nation. It stimulates the development of new types of companies and creates jobs. Venture capital invigorates industries as it inspires the next potentially great company to work through the challenges of being a start-up.

Taking a Closer Look VC Investments

You may feel that it is your job as CEO to understand your company, industry, and business like the back of your hand. That's true, but when you are raising capital through VCs, you are expected to understand the VC world, too. If you plan to do business with a VC, then you need to know how venture capital investments work so that you can be an equal partner in the relationship.

Understanding key limitations in the selection process

VCs are tied to their limited partnership agreements, and they have certain investing parameters that they must adhere to. One of the key limitations has to do with what kind of company the fund can invest in. Another is how long the investment period is.

Going for an industry match

VCs get hundreds of applications or pitch decks sent to them every year. Any company that doesn't fit the types of ventures defined in the contracts between the VC and her limited partners is going right in the trash. The reason is that VCs are not legally allowed to fund companies in a different industry than the one specified in the limited partnership agreement. Doing so breaks the contract that the VC has with her limited partners. Bottom line: Some VCs can't invest in your company even if they wanted to.

A company that makes equipment for microbreweries once asked Peter for some advice: It seems that this company had been rejected by a VC known for investing in software companies. The company founder asked whether he should get in contact with that VC again, now that the economy was improving. Peter's answer? No! That VC cannot invest in microbrewery equipment; because of his agreement with his limited partners, he was only able to invest in software companies.

Limiting the amount of time that money can stay invested

A VC is limited in the amount of time that her money can stay invested in your company. She signed an agreement with her limited partners that the fund would liquidate in fewer than ten years. She's banking on the fact that your company can grow fast and get acquired (or go public) before she has to give the money back to her limited partners.

Moving money — and lots of it

The venture capital industry moves lots of money. The average size of a venture capital fund is around $150 million. If you think raising money for your company is hard, imagine how hard raising $150 million with no business idea at all would be! The average size of a VC investment into a company is around $8 million, but some investments are much smaller, and some are much larger. Overall about $20 billion is invested by VCs every year.

Making long-term investments for fast growth

When venture capital firms invest, they intend to keep that company in their portfolios for four to seven years, effectively tying up their money even longer — in some cases for up to ten years. And ten years is a long time for an investor to be separated from his capital. Think about investing in the stock market. You can take your money out whenever you want. If you invest in a certificate of deposit (CD), you leave your money in until the certificate matures, which can be a few months to a few years.

Being VC backed

When a company has sold equity to a venture capital firm, that company is called *VC backed*. During the years that a company is VC backed, it is supported by the firm through business and industry expertise and high-caliber network connections, as well as capital. This relationship can be a very powerful one for a start-up company.

So what is a VC firm looking for in a company? VC-backed companies have quick growth potential, large growth potential, and a smart and flexible team — attributes that the VC believes will generate a large return on investment. The general rule is to aim for at least 10X return on investment in five years.

Achieving 10X return on investment in five years

In selecting companies, VCs look for the kind of growth potential that makes at least 10X return on investment possible. For example, if an investor puts $8 million in your company, she is hoping that you'll be able to give her $80 million back fairly soon. Of course, not all VC-backed companies will return 10X the investors' money in fewer than five years, but it's the benchmark many investors aim for.

To have a growth potential this large, a company must be in a perfect storm of desirable attributes:

- ✔ **Large market:** Are there enough people (or businesses) with enough money willing to buy the product(s) that this company sells?

- ✔ **Growing market:** Is the number of people (or businesses) that will be willing to buy this product in the future increasing?

- ✔ **Game changer:** Is the product or technology going to change the way people or businesses do things?

- ✔ **Team experience:** Is the team able to execute to grow the business at least in the short term?

REMEMBER

Achieving 10X in five years is not a requirement for actual execution. It's more of a lofty goal that has to be possible before the deal will move forward. If a company can return 3X an investor's money in five years, the investor and shareholders will all be thrilled at the company's performance, which would represent an internal rate of return of 25 percent.

The goal: Doing well enough to raise money for their next round

As we explain in the earlier section "Examining how VCs make money off the deal," a significant part of the VC's potential income comes to her when the companies she's invested in have liquidation events. This payment is called the *carry,* and it's contingent on returning money to the limited partners. The better your company performs, the better the fund performs, and the VC's carry will be a larger sum of money.

But more than that, if the VC is unable to return a reasonable sum to the limited partners, she will have a lot of trouble raising another fund when the time comes. The limited partners involved in the last fund won't be interested in working with someone who just lost their money or failed to make their money perform very well.

Keeping current with the venture capital industry

The modern venture capital industry has been around only since World War II. When an industry is so young, it tends to still be in a perpetual state of change. Pressures such as the state of the economy and interest rates have major effects on how many VCs exist in the U.S. at any given time.

The way that venture capitalists do business is also constantly changing. Practices that were standard ten years ago have disappeared. An example of an outdated trend is a high multiple liquidation preference on term sheets in the beginning of 2001; the standard multiple has come back down to 1X. Another trend in the 1990s was to invest large amounts of money in companies that didn't have more than an idea. This trend has passed, and VCs now expect a lot more traction than they did 15 years ago. You have to stay current on trends to keep up with what's considered *normal* when working with VCs.

The National Venture Capital Association (www.nvca.org) is a professional society that keeps tabs on the industry. If you ever need to catch up on trends and the current state of venture capital, you can look to them.

Looking into Other Kinds of Funds and Venture Companies

Venture capital is great for companies that match the profile, but if your company doesn't match, don't worry. Lots of other opportunities are out there:

- **Specialized types of VC funds:** Venture capital funds are allowed to make their own rules about who they fund and who they don't fund. They also can make rules about how much they will put in each company. Industry-restricted funds often follow the industry expertise of the general partner. However, funds can be specialized around a certain mission or geographic region. If you look hard enough, you may be able to find a fund dedicated to support any given type of company. Here are some common specialized fund types:

  - **Geography focused:** Invest in companies that are located in a specific city or region

  - **Impact focused:** Invest in for-profit companies that help the world by furthering a social or ecological cause

  - **University focused:** Invest in companies that are coming out of a specific university or that are started by alumni

  - **Industry focused:** Invest in healthcare IT, clean tech, social media, life sciences, or energy, for example

- **Seed funds:** These are venture capital firms that invest small amounts in very early-stage companies. One might put $25,000 in each of five to ten companies per year. *Note:* Sometimes this term is used for a fund that gifts grants instead of making investments for an exchange of equity. Be careful and know which kind of fund you are talking about to avoid any surprises.

- **Evergreen and rolling funds:** These funds operate differently than the typical model. The evergreen fund is often found in cause-based investments, and every time the fund has an exit, it then rolls that money back into new investments. In rolling funds, the fund manager is constantly seeking investors for the fund. These can be complicated to manage because of the difficulty of setting the value of a fund share at any one point of time when the fund is comprised of illiquid investments with highly indeterminate value.

Chapter 3

Is Working with a VC Right for You?

*V*enture capitalists are highly visible because they work with high-profile companies. Because of this visibility, most people know that they exist and that they help companies grow. Many people also think that the key to growing any business successfully is to involve venture capitalists. It turns out, however, that only a small subset of all companies can benefit from using venture capital to grow. The reason is two-fold: Venture capitalists are extremely selective about the types of companies that they are willing to invest in; and many businesses would do better (for a variety of reasons) by choosing a different method of growth. In addition, entrepreneurs sometimes make a conscious choice to avoid taking venture capital, even if VCs are interested in their companies.

This chapter helps you determine whether your company has the elements that make it attractive to a venture capital firm. We also explain the implications of taking venture capital and give you the information you need to decide whether pursuing VCs to help your company grow makes sense for your situation.

Identifying a VC Investible Company

Some companies are what we call *venture companies* (or *venture-backed companies* after they've taken investment) and some companies are *lifestyle companies*. You need to know the difference between them. Both can be successful, but only venture companies are poised to benefit from venture capital. Lifestyle companies can be highly successful without ever talking to a venture capitalist. They may return hundreds of thousands or even millions of dollars or more per year to the owner, but the company can't be sold for the huge profit that a venture capitalist needs.

Venture capitalists look for companies that are capable of growing very large very quickly. For a company to grow immensely fast, the company must possess certain characteristics in key areas that allow for major growth: scalability, talented management team with a proven history of success, huge and growing market share, and competitive advantage. The following sections provide the details.

Scalability: Understanding your growth potential

Scalability refers to the act of growing larger while keeping intact the ease with which business is done and the business's profitability. Said another way, scalability is how easily your company can increase sales. When investors look at the scalability of a company, they want to see three things: that the business was designed to grow large, that the owners want the business to grow large, and that the owners have the capability to make it happen.

Judging your business's scalability

All businesses are scalable to a point, but some have to make significant changes to their models to grow any further.

If you have a successful consulting company, for example, you may make $1 million per year with five consultants. To grow to $2 million per year, you probably have to add another five consultants, and so on. You can grow your company nicely, but it isn't considered scalable because the incremental costs rise proportionally to revenue. You have to hire and train a lot of people to grow, and your profits will likely never exceed a certain per capita amount.

A venture company may spend a lot of money up front in designing a product, but the returns will rise exponentially as volumes rise. Some examples of this include medical device companies or SaaS (software as a service) software companies where the incremental costs to each sale are almost negligible, but there is a significant up-front cost. SaaS companies are popular with VCs because of the large profit potential if sales grow significantly.

Unlike the consulting company, which can only scale by adding more and more people, a venture company is designed to be scalable from the beginning, and the costs of incremental sales drop sharply as scale increases. Make sure you know the points of scale that will challenge your company's model. VCs look for companies that are able to grow very large easily.

Looking at your desire to grow

Not all entrepreneurs have the desire and capability to scale up to a large organization. Many are satisfied when they make $250–500 thousand per year, and their companies may grow slowly after that.

As an entrepreneur, you need to ask yourself which type of business you're running. Is it a lifestyle company that will yield a comfortable living for you and any other principals, or is it a high stress, high growth venture company that you want to grow to the tens and hundreds of millions?

Lifestyle companies can bring in great profits for the owner(s). The owners tend to control the majority share of the company and therefore have control over the large and small decisions that are made in the company. Owners of lifestyle companies tend to stay involved with their companies for decades or even pass the company down through the family over generations. These companies tend to be low-risk, healthy companies that grow slowly and conservatively. Lifestyle companies are not interesting to VCs.

Venture companies are best for founders who want to grow a company fast, make a lot of money quickly, and then move on to the next thing in their lives. Lifestyle companies are best for founders who want to create jobs and wealth for themselves and their family members over many years.

Management: Assessing the entrepreneurial team

Venture capitalists often say that they "bet on the jockey and not the horse." Translation: The management team is often more important than having a great idea, no matter how great that idea is. VCs point out that they see lots of great ideas but only a few teams that are capable of executing on those ideas. Management teams that are attractive to VCs include people who not only have the skills to succeed in their business but are also entrepreneurs who are more interested in making money than in running a business for life.

The team may be the single most important factor a venture capital investor considers when investing in a company. You can find countless stories of companies that attain huge success after pivoting away from their original idea. Instagram, for example, was originally a location-based social networking app called Burbn; today, it's a photo-sharing app that connects to social media. With Instagram, the investors bet on a team that was able to change quickly to take advantage of rapidly shifting market trends.

Forging a dream team: Forget the titles, focus on skill set

When evaluating the management team, a venture capital investor asks these questions: "Can these people carry out the plan they've described?" "Do they have the skills and experience?" and "Do they have the passion, drive and character to do it?"

That's why the perfect team to run an early-stage company is not necessarily made up of a CEO, CFO, CMO, and so on. Titles at this stage don't mean all that much. A great team is a group of people who are experienced in the tasks and processes that the company is about to undertake.

If, for example, you are proposing to use international manufacturing or sales, your team should include someone who has experience with international manufacturing and business relations. If you plan to sell your product directly to hospitals, your team should include someone who is experienced in the inner workings of hospital purchasing. If your company relies on advanced technology, the team needs to include someone who can manipulate that technology.

Of course, team members with advanced degrees and strong pedigrees are always nice. Teams with experience taking a company all the way through a positive exit are excellent. Teams with PhDs, Harvard MBAs, people with venture capital experience, marketing wizards who built sales up from nothing to $100 million, or a software developer from Google also really stand out. The teams with real-life experience and success will always be more attractive than teams that are packed with academic degrees and no actual experience.

If your team doesn't have the dream pedigree in every area, you still have a chance. Venture capitalists work with young entrepreneurs who can weave a story about their experiences and demonstrate their ability to overcome the obstacles ahead of them. In truth, much of a VC's assessment of the team won't come from your resume; it comes from the passion they see in your presentation (Chapter 16), the thoroughness of your research and thinking (Chapters 6 through 8), and the honesty with which you address the risks inherent in your project (Chapter 10).

A picture perfect team

The perfect team will be different for each company. Each company has different needs, and depending on the available people, you will have to piece together the right experience and skill sets. However, it's even more complicated than that. Your company's perfect team will be different today compared to your perfect team two years from now. Identify your company's needs to determine whom you really need to get on board.

- ✔ **Owners:** Every company will have one or more owners. Sometimes these people are involved in the management team; sometimes they're not.

- ✔ **Management:** The management team is often a group of two to five people who make the majority of the daily decisions in a company. They execute on decisions and steer daily operations. The management team can include cofounders and owners. It can also include hired executives who do not own part of the company. Generally, management is offered stock or stock options as an incentive to work in a high-risk, early-stage company and to make up for the fact that their cash compensation is probably less than they would make at a more established company.

- ✔ **Non-management employees:** Non-management employees are the people hired to handle very specific tasks. They might be collecting data, creating a product, engineering a process, selling the product, or handling customer service. Non-management employees may have stock incentives, or they may be paid in cash without stock options. An alternative to hiring non-management employees is to use third-party consulting, research, or sales firms for your necessary task work.

- ✔ **Advisory board:** Advisory boards are made up of very experienced business people and industry leaders who are interested in steering your company right. They are not involved in daily operations. They meet with management monthly or quarterly to determine whether the company is headed in the right direction or needs to change course. Advisors are often given small amounts of common stock so that they have incentive to come to meetings, give good advice, and make introductions in the industry. The advisory board does not have legal decision-making power.

- ✔ **Executive board:** The executive board has legal decision-making power. This is always an odd numbered group, generally consisting of three to five people who control high-level decision-making. They determine the salary of the CEO who then determines the salaries of the rest of the team. Executive boards approve annual budgets, new strategies, and strategic partnerships. They do not control daily decisions (deciding which candidate to hire for a non-management role, for example, or deciding which shipping company to use for distribution).

- ✔ **Consultants:** Consultants can be considered members of the team in some cases. Interestingly, it is the reputation of the consulting firm that will be vetted instead of the actual individual who is doing the consulting work. If you are working with Deloitte for your growth strategy planning, you would list Deloitte as a team member. The actual name of the consultant won't be as relevant as the well-respected firm.

Market share: Determining how large your market is

Venture capital investors want to be involved in markets that will support the kind of growth they need to be successful. In making an assessment about whether your market is big enough, VCs make a distinction between the size of the market as a whole and the size of the addressable market. The *addressable market* is the part of the market that your company uniquely serves. Your ability to understand this difference will make a huge difference in the credibility you have with your VC.

One reason that VCs want to be in only big markets is because they need many options for a successful exit. If your market is too small to justify going public (usually a threshold of $100 million or more in annual revenues) or doesn't have a significant number of large players with resources to acquire your company, then the VC doesn't have good exit options, and he won't be interested. VCs make big risks and need big payoffs to make it worthwhile.

Defining your addressable market

If your company makes a great new kind of ice cream bar that is exceptionally popular in your test markets, you might say that your market size is based on the $10 billion annual ice cream sales data. But that assertion would be inaccurate, because ice cream novelties (individually wrapped ice cream bars and popsicles) represents only 20 percent of the total ice cream market.

More accurately, you could say that your market size is $2 billion per year. You might even reduce that further by acknowledging that you'll distribute only regionally, as is the trend in the ice cream market. With those parameters in mind, your addressable market is reduced to $500 million per year. If your strategy is to pursue the market through grocery and convenience store sales, your final numbers would need to take into account that the take-home market for ice cream is 67 percent of the market, making your addressable market only $335 million — a long way from your initial claim of $10 billion!

Why do you want to claim a smaller addressable market instead of the whole market? Because VCs will do this reductionist math in their heads anyway. By giving them accurate numbers up front, you demonstrate your in-depth knowledge of your industry, your honesty, and your specific strategy to capture a piece of it.

Gaining traction in the big market

In addition to determining the size of your addressable market, venture capitalists look for companies that have *traction,* the ability to capture a big portion of a big market. Your ability to demonstrate traction in selling into a big market is every bit as important as being in a big market. Big markets are competitive and difficult to break into unless you have an unfair advantage or novel approach. (Big markets often require huge investments to enter and may have extraordinary price pressures that require huge volumes in order to compete. These are often barriers that start-ups cannot overcome.)

Traction is defined in many ways. Traction in a tight-knit field may mean convincing a thought-leader to join your advisory board. Traction in the market means convincing consumers to pay for your product. Traction in a regulatory pathway means that you have gotten through the initial phases of FDA approval. The more traction your company has, the farther you are from simply having an idea, and the closer you come to having a profitable and growing business. Simply stated, the best way to measure traction and market acceptance is your revenue.

Competitive advantage: Foiling the competition

A venture company's success is largely hinged on an unfair advantage. A venture company needs to capture a large portion of the market that might otherwise go to competitors. To do so, it must have an advantage that competitors cannot easily copy, purchase, or develop.

Many entrepreneurs think they can rest easy in the knowledge that their product is a better solution to a market need than anything in existence. Although having a better solution is an advantage, an advantage like that cannot stand alone. Without patent or trade secret protection, other companies can steal your solution and out sell your product in only a few months. Without branding, customers won't recognize your product as a solution to their problem, and they'll purchase the subpar product that speaks to their emotions and desires instead of an unknown and superior product.

VCs love a product that is better and cheaper than the competition, but you must also show that you have ways of preventing other companies from copying your product and selling more of their knock-offs than you can sell of your original.

Patenting your product or technology

One commonly used method to prevent competition from copying a product or technology is by securing a patent. Patents legally prevent other companies from using your product, design, or technology without your consent. Although patents can be expensive, short-lived, difficult to prosecute, and limited in geography, venture capital investors still look for patent protection whenever possible. A patent can be like a watchdog; even when the dog doesn't bite, its presence protects your property.

Patenting has some limitations that you need to consider before you invest the time and money necessary to secure one:

- ✔ Patents don't give you the right to use a product or technology; they only prevent others from using it.

- ✔ Your product/technology must be novel, non-obvious, and previously unpatented.

- ✔ To protect your work with a patent, you must publicly disclose details about your work in a formal patent application. Therefore, any secrets you held before submitting a patent are public after the application is accepted.

- ✔ The legal work and application submission fees required to patent a technology cost between $10,000 and $30,000, and this amount becomes even greater when you consider the annual maintenance fees that must be paid.

- ✔ A patent doesn't actually prevent other companies from copying your product; it only gives you legal grounds to sue.

In a lawsuit over a patent violation, the company with the most money pretty much always wins. Big companies have been known to brazenly copy obviously patented software applications without even bothering to change the text and graphics. In this situation, small companies have little realistic recourse.

✔ A patent is only effective in the country from which it was issued. A United States patent can be legally ignored in China, so to be protected, you need to file patents in multiple countries.

✔ U.S. patents are effective for only about 20 years from the filing date. After that, the technology becomes public domain.

Keeping trade secrets under wrap

Instead of patents, companies sometimes rely on trade secrets. A trade secret is enforced by simply keeping mum about the details. A competitor can't copy the technology or product if it is a total and utter secret. Examples of famous trade secrets are the recipe for Coca Cola, Kentucky Fried Chicken's 11 herbs and spices, the formula for WD-40, and the combination of details that make up Starwood Hotels' luxurious feel.

Unless all future employees can be kept in the dark about the trade secret details, a company runs the risk of losing control of its intellectual property due to a malicious or even accidental slip of the tongue. Companies instate hefty penalties to those who give up the secret, but if the company's success hinges on the secret remaining quiet, once the word is out, it's out. The company has lost its competitive advantage.

Companies sometimes protect against trade secret leaks by preventing any one person from knowing the whole secret. Like requiring two keys at a safety deposit box, splitting secrets in half prevents any one person from spilling the beans. If a company's competitive advantage is hinged on a trade secret, the company would not share the details of the trade secret with a VC. Likely few in the company would even know the whole secret.

Branding: Tying your company to your customer's emotions

A less obvious way to secure market share is through branding. When people think of a brand, they thing of a logo, but really, that's only the beginning. The logo or color scheme is what helps you identify a brand, but true branding is when a company connects with a customer on an emotional level.

Branding is the sense of luxury you feel when you see the BMW symbol and sleek lines on an M Series vehicle. Branding is that down-home comfort of the wood rockers and penny candy kitsch in a Cracker Barrel restaurant. When a company is well branded, you know exactly what to expect from it.

People are creatures of habit and tend to purchase brands that they know and like. A strong brand convinces customers that only one product is the solution to their needs: your product! Customers report that they have a genuine emotional response when they interact with a loved and trusted brand.

Some aspects of a company's branding — things such as clear messaging, attractive design, and identification of the target customer — can be controlled. However, some luck is involved in a viral adoption of a brand. Can you think of a new brand that you started seeing a lot of in a short period of time? In the shoe industry, both Toms and Crocs went viral. This simply means that the brand spread as quickly as any marketing executive could dream about. To go viral with a brand, you have to do a lot of work to create a brand that people will adopt, and then you have to get lucky.

If you are relying on a strong brand to set yourself apart from the competition, then you need to show a trend of quick adoption for your brand before a VC will be interested in your company. Creating a brand can take a lot of time and money. Going viral is never a marketing strategy; it is a rare result. Sometimes it's faster to white label your product and sell it directly to businesses as a plug-in for one of their existing products.

Head start: Being first (or fastest) out of the gate

Rarely, being first to market is sufficient unfair advantage when it would take competitors many months or years to catch up. If being first to market is your only advantage, you've got a very high risk of having another company surpass your sales in year two and put you out of business. VCs do not like to see "First to market" as your only advantage. The history of successful businesses is filled with companies who were second, third, or later entrants to the market. An example of this is Google, who entered the search engine market well after Alta Vista, Ask Jeeves, Lycos, and Yahoo!.

Venture capital mismatch: An example

Roger's Roasted is a local coffee shop with yearly revenues of a half million dollars. When Roger chooses to open a second coffee shop on the other side of town, he realizes he can do this in two ways: He can use his own money to open the new shop, or he can seek outside capital to open the shop. After doing a little research, Roger determines that taking venture capital is not right for Roger's Roasted. Here's why:

✔ **Roger's Roasted has eventual plans for a total of three local stores.** A three-store business in a single town is simply too small of a market share for venture capital. The only way that Roger's Roasted would be interesting to investors is if Roger were to scale the coffee shop into a national chain that could capture a larger portion of the U.S. coffee market.

✔ **Roger only needs $150,000 to open the next store.** The investment need is too small. Venture capital investors have funds of tens or hundreds of millions of dollars, and it can take as much time and paperwork to complete a big deal as a small one. VCs will not enter into a small deal because it isn't worth the time spent on due diligence and market research when the potential investment gain is only around a million dollars.

✔ **After five years, Roger can give investors 2.5X their money back as the best-case scenario.** VCs look for the potential of a 10X return in five years.

✔ **Roger wants to run his coffee shops until he retires.** A VC would encourage Roger to sell the business to increase the VC's return on investment (ROI). Selling the business would also allow the VC firm to extract its money from the business in five to eight years. Roger doesn't want to sell his company, so his plans don't match with those of the VC firm.

Making the VC Decision

Working with venture capital is a choice that changes the path for your company. After you sign documents to sell equity to a VC, your company will never be the same. The clout, resources, and connections that come with a VC can be the necessary push for a small business to really take off. Drawbacks exist, however, and you have to be sure that working with a VC is really the right thing for you and your business.

Venture capitalists are sometimes called "vulture capitalists" because they are focused on the financial bottom line and not on the feelings of the founders. Although this may be a criticism of a VC's tactless bedside manner (which *can* be helped), it is also the nature of the business (which *can't* be helped). Venture capitalists are in the business of making money for their limited partners, themselves, and founders (refer to Chapter 2). When VCs work with entrepreneurs who act on emotional when making decisions that result in a weaker bottom line, the VC is not doing his or her job and can get in serious trouble.

You need to ask yourself whether you want to enter into a relationship with a VC to pursue a large and rapid exit. If you're seeking this relationship for an alternate reason, you may choose not to work with a VC. The reality is that once you involve a VC, it's all about the exit.

Follow these guidelines to determine for yourself whether you and your company are right for venture capital. See Figure 3-1 for a graphical decision tree that can help you decide whether your company should pursue venture capital:

- ✔ **Do you need to raise $3–25 million or more for your project?** The average VC deal is about $7.2 million, and although some VCs provide early-stage seed funding, most won't look at your deal until you need $3 to 25 million. If you need less, you should look toward seed funds, angel capital funding, friends, family and acquaintances, or other avenues such as taking out a second mortgage on your home. Head to Chapter 4 for more on alternative ways to grow your business.

- ✔ **Will your company grow to the point where it will be worth $50 to $100 million or more in an IPO or acquisition?** You can study public offerings and acquisitions in your industry and understand the characteristics of those companies who had liquidity events. If your industry sees exits with 5X ("five times") gross revenues, then you need to grow your company to at least $10 to 20 million in sales within five years. If your company can't support that kind of growth, consider growing your company organically by plowing your profits back into the company and watching it grow gradually over time.

✔ **Is your market large and growing?** When you understand the difference between your industry and your addressable market, ask yourself whether the market is large enough to grow your revenues rapidly and to a large size such that you could be acquired for $50 to 100 million or more. Also determine whether an active public market for stocks exists in your industry, or whether a number of large companies would be likely to acquire your company after it has proven itself a success. If you find yourself in a small or shrinking market, you may want to consider other funding sources, including organic growth more slowly over time.

✔ **Does your company have an unfair advantage?** Does it have something that makes it unique and that will allow it to grow quickly before competitors can become a serious threat? If your company is like others in your industry, you will be competing among many in a crowded market, and you are not likely to achieve venture capital type growth. These companies can still be very profitable but need to look elsewhere for funding.

✔ **Is your team the right one to pursue and attract venture capital funding?** Take a serious look at yourself and your team. Do you have the skills and experience to grow this company fast? Do you have the passion and trustworthiness that venture investors seek? If not, you'll want to recruit talent and create a culture of passion, speed, and trustworthiness. Don't give up! If a team is the only thing your company lacks, you may be ready for venture capital after you address your team issues. (Your VC may help you recruit key missing team members.)

✔ **Are you comfortable with having venture investors highly involved in your company?** This final question is about you and your goals. Venture investors require strict controls on your company and will want to take one or more board seats. They will have the ability to fire you, even though you may be a majority shareholder. They can control how and when you sell the company and when you can issue stock, take on debt, and issue dividends, bonuses, and more. If you are the type who needs total control, then you should seriously think about identifying finance opportunities other than venture capital.

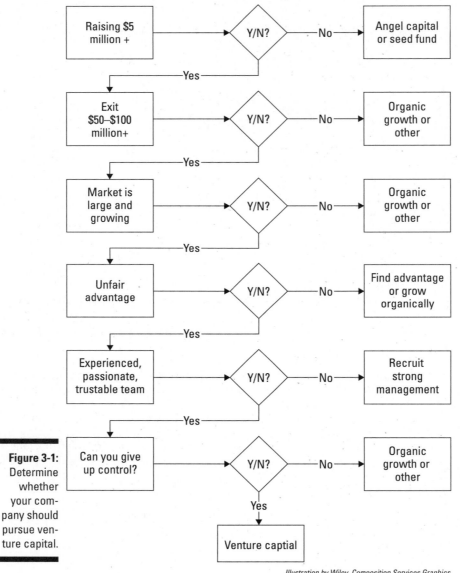

Should my company pursue venture capital?

Figure 3-1: Determine whether your company should pursue venture capital.

Illustration by Wiley, Composition Services Graphics

Chapter 4

Alternatives to Venture Capital Funding

. . . .

In This Chapter

▶ Choosing from a variety of funding options

▶ Identifying advantages and disadvantages of each option

▶ Knowing the difference between accredited and non-accredited investors

▶ Opting to grow your business without outside funding

. . . .

*V*enture capital is not right for every business. If you determined that it's not right for your business (refer to Chapter 3 for help in making that decision), you have plenty of other funding options you can use to grow your business.

In deciding which of the other possibilities is right for you, you want to identify the main reasons you're considering venture capital in the first place because that reason can inform your decision. If you simply need capital to grow your business, consider taking a loan, raising money through people you know, talking to angel investors, crowdfunding, franchising, or writing a grant proposal. If you are looking to add experienced people to your team but can't afford to pay employees, look at finding a cofounder or using venture labor (hiring someone that you pay in equity instead of cash).

In this chapter, we explain all the ways you can grow your business without venture capital and share each option's plusses and minuses so that you can decide which option is best for your company and you.

Taking on Debt

Debt — if you can get it — is a great way to fund your business. It comes in many forms, but the basic arrangement is that someone lends you money that you agree to pay back with interest. You retire your debt by either making monthly payments or by making a balloon payment at the end of a fixed period.

One of the advantages of taking on debt to finance your business is that your relationship with the lender ends as soon as you pay off the loan. The downside is that, if you cannot make your payments, the lender can force you into bankruptcy.

Banks are the first place you may think of for a loan. Most of the time, however, banks simply cannot make loans to start-up companies without some kind of guarantee or security such as a lien on your house. If a bank's business model is to lend money at 8 percent interest, it won't last long lending to start-ups when 80 percent are going to fail. Banks are great to work with after you have steady cash flow and liquid assets such as accounts receivable, but for a start-up loan, you probably want to look elsewhere.

In the following section, we introduce other options designed specifically for start-up businesses and explain what you need to know to secure capital from various agencies.

Investor loans: Debt from individuals

An *investor loan* is exactly what it sounds like: a loan you get from a person (or entity) that wants to invest in your business. How you pay back the loan — principle and interest, or equity in your business — depends on the kind of investor loan you get: straight debt or convertible debt, which we explain in more detail in the following sections.

Investors want some upside for the huge risk they are taking by lending to a start-up company. Convertible debt can improve the upside for investors. Some angel investors will enter into a convertible debt agreement with you.

Going with straight debt

With *straight debt* (also called *hard money*), someone gives you cash, and you agree to pay that person back with interest at a given time in the future.

Because the investor has a lot to lose (the whole debt amount) and only a little interest to gain (probably only a couple of percentage points), finding people who are willing to give you this kind of loan for reasonable terms is difficult. When you do find someone who will give you straight debt, the interest rate will be high, and the loan length will be short.

Friends and relatives are the best source for a straight loan with reasonable rates because they have a personal desire to see you succeed and are less concerned about making money on the loan. So if you have family or friends (or can find other investors) who are willing to give you straight debt with reasonable terms, go with it! Just be sure that you and your lender both put your expectations in writing before any dollars change hands.

Taking the top down: Convertible debt

With convertible debt, the arrangement begins as a normal loan at a particular interest rate (6 or 8 percent, for example), but within the note is a conversion option that states that the debt may convert to equity at some predetermined time, usually when funding is secured through a venture capital firm. In addition, investors typically receive a discount on their equity conversion; they may pay only $0.80 cents on the dollar for the equity purchase. This 20 percent discount compensates the investors for the risk they take in early-stage investing. In other words, you get money for your business now and investors get equity in your business for a discount later.

Convertible debt is not a logical option for all types of business. Convertible debt makes sense only when your company can grow large enough and fast enough to be attractive to venture capitalists in the future. Lifestyle businesses should use straight debt and avoid selling equity if possible.

Convertible debt is one way that you can provide a better upside to investors while taking on a loan. Entrepreneurs tend to like convertible debt for two reasons:

- ✔ **It is much simpler to secure than equity:** To secure equity, you must plan and raise a reasonable round of funding that gets your company to a major milestone; agree on a valuation with investors; develop and get signed a term sheet; and then get a signed stock sale agreement — and you have to do all of this under the watchful eye of your attorney. With convertible debt, you can form an agreement with a single investor over lunch, sign the debt note after a quick phone call to your attorney, and cash the check on the way back to the office. For this reason, the legal costs of raising convertible debt are significantly lower than raising capital through the sale of equity.

- ✔ **It delays the valuation of your company:** Many entrepreneurs have trouble determining the value of their companies. With convertible debt, you can put off the question of valuation until later, when the situation is clearer. Because venture capital investment is often the trigger for conversion, the venture capitalist can help with valuation and set a reasonable price at that time.

If you're considering convertible debt, consult with a securities attorney. An attorney specializing in securities can help you with all kinds of options on convertible debt, including caps, conversion prices, and discounts. A good securities attorney will watch out for the potential unexpected consequences that can occur when you take investments in your company.

Factoring: Accounts receivable finance

Factoring is another debt-based vehicle that is great for start-ups. A *factor* is a person or entity that buys debt. Specifically, a factor buys your accounts receivable at a discount off face value. For example, if you submit $10,000 worth of invoices to a factor who advertises an 80 percent advance, the factor takes a 3.5 percent initial processing fee and gives you $7,650 ($7,650 is 80 percent of $10,000, minus the $350 processing fee). The factor then submits your invoices to your clients, who pay the $10,000 value, and you receive the additional $2,000 at that time.

Bottom line: Factoring is generally more expensive than a bank loan, and it works only for companies that have stacks of invoices that take 30 to 90 days for the clients to pay. As the business owner, you are expecting cash soon, just with a bit of a delay. Factoring is the business equivalent of a payday loan. You can get cash quickly when you need it, but it's going to cost you quite a bit in fees and interest.

Small Business Administration loans

The Small Business Administration (SBA) is a federal agency that supports small business in the U.S. The SBA itself doesn't loan federal money to businesses. Instead, it functions as an intermediary, helping small businesses secure loans with private banks. The SBA guarantees bank loans, thereby lowering the risk of working with small businesses and increasing banks' willingness to go forward with the loans.

Many small businesses are in situations that banks just consider too risky. If a bank has denied you a loan, you may still be able to get an SBA loan. Qualifying for an SBA loan is much easier than qualifying for a regular bank loan. The SBA generally wants a personal guarantee from you as well as demonstrated cash flow as evidence that you can pay the loan back. For more information about the SBA, visit the agency online (http://www.sba.gov).

To qualify for an SBA loan,

- ✔ You must be turned down for a traditional bank loan.
- ✔ You employ fewer than 500 workers.
- ✔ Your company must meet additional lender qualifications such as credit history or revenue.

Tapping into microfinance

If you're a small start-up that doesn't need much money — say, $5,000 to start a hair-braiding studio — microfinance may be a good option. With microfinancing, you form a relationship with the lending organization. Often you are required to take classes or work with a business mentor to help ensure your business success.

The advantage with microfinance is that you get support along with capital. Also, one of the main missions of microfinance is to support communities of people who are at a disadvantage in business. Microfinance is often the only option for those who are accepted into microfinance programs.

Many microfinance organizations are non-profits supported by local economic development offices. To find such organizations in your area, check your local library and community centers. You can also conduct an online search: Just type the word *microfinance* and your state name into the search engine.

Raising Money through People You Know

If you've done a little homework on raising money for your business, you've probably come across the *three Fs*: friends, family, and fools (and which we refer to as "FFF investors" throughout this section). This simply means raising money through people that you know.

Obviously, the designations "friends" and "family" are pretty easy to figure out. The "fool" is anyone — friend, family, or founder — who enters into an agreement without learning what the deal is all about. In the following sections, we tell you what precautions to take and processes to follow to avoid problems and protect your relationships when you raise capital through family members and friends.

Family capital tends to include the whole family

Complicated relationships and prior history in families can play into raising money through family members. Consider this example:

Carol needs $30,000 to launch her business. Her uncle agreed to help her in part because he wanted to make her happy and in part because he felt obligated to support a close family member. The rest of the family thought he should help her, too, but they had different a reason: When Carol's father and uncle were teenagers, their parents sent her uncle to college and her father to the military. Carol's side of the family never made as much money or enjoyed the kind of lifestyle that her uncle's family enjoyed. The extended family feels that Carol's uncle owes Carol's dad many favors because of the imbalance that the grandparents' decision years earlier instigated.

If the business succeeds, the family imbalance won't matter: Everyone will be happy that Carol's business does well and that her uncle makes money, too. But if the business fails and Carol loses her uncle's money, the transaction could bring up a lot of hurt feelings from both sides. Carol's side may feel as though her Uncle can afford to lose the money. Her uncle's side may feel as though he was forced into a losing situation.

Choosing whom to approach

You may love everyone in your personal circle dearly and want to give them all the opportunity to share in your success. But to maintain these relationships heed this advice:

- **Stick to accredited investors:** Take money only from people who can afford to lose it. Accredited investors are legally recognized in a different light than unaccredited investors. Accredited investors own $1 million in assets (not including their homes), or they made $200,000 two years in a row ($300,000 if they're married). If you later raise angel or venture capital money, your capitalization table will be more attractive if you've taken money from only accredited investors.

Many venture capitalists will not enter a deal in which unaccredited investors are involved. The risks of lawsuits from people who are not in a position to lose their investments are often just too high for VCs to justify.

- **Go for fewer rather than more investors:** Because many investments go through several rounds, dragging a large number of small investors through subsequent rounds can be burdensome. In addition, small investors can be disappointed when they can no longer keep up with the increasingly large investments necessary to maintain a reasonable amount of stock in your company.

VCs look for a *clean capitalization table.* Translation: VCs prefer to invest in companies that have just a few investors over those that have ten or more early-stage investors. If you have too many investors, VCs may pass you by.

✔ **Be aware of emotional baggage or previous favors that weight the transaction differently than would be the case if you were dealing with a stranger.** Be very careful that you know all the important history before you enter into an agreement with a family member. Families can have unspoken accounting sheets calculating what is "owed," based on favors and assets transferred between family members. (Head to the sidebar "Family capital tends to include the whole family" for an example of how family relationships can impact business decisions.).

Discussing terms and agreements

Many of the same rules apply when you raise money with friends and family as when you seek venture capital. In both scenarios, you need to be prepared to discuss investment terms and conditions with FFF investors just as you would with an angel investor (explained in the later section "Dancing on the Head of a Pin: Angel Capital") or a venture capitalist. These additional pointers will help you keep your sanity and relationships intact as you grow your business using money from family and friends:

✔ **Set expectations.** Even though you may feel confident in your business idea, you should remember that on average 80 percent of new companies fail in the first few years. Also stipulate what happens if your business fails: Will you pay them back in total? Partially? Will they get your boat as collateral? Be clear about the possibility of failure because underlying assumptions can cause irreparable damage to your relationships.

✔ **Use debt, not equity:** Giving money back with interest is much easier than having your family members continue to own a piece of your company over the long haul. Therefore, when you approach family and friends, ask for loans that you'll repay with interest rather than offer equity in your company.

✔ **Use non-voting, common stock:** If you must give equity because your FFF investor insists on it, make sure that the stock is not tied to a decision making role — or worse, a board seat.

✔ **Tie payments to cash flow:** To avoid a concrete payback plan that may interfere with future growth, create payments that are tied to cash flow. Limit the amount of money that you return to your investor by defining in an agreement a total percent interest that they can expect on their loan. Specify whether you will repay in full with interest, or whether you'll pay them back only after you've reached a specific return on investment.

Qualifying accredited investors

To prevent fraud and protect people from getting in over their heads with private equity investments, which are the highest risk investments that you can make, United States federal law mandates that accredited investors must meet certain asset qualifications. In 2013, there were two main ways to qualify as an accredited investor.

✔ **Income thresholds:** Unmarried investors must have filed tax returns with $200,000 income in the past year with the expectation of having the same income or greater this year. The income requirement is $300,000 for married people filing jointly.

✔ **Available assets:** A person who has over $1 million in assets can be an accredited investor as long as the $1 million total does not include his or her primary home.

These laws are changing, though, so be sure to keep tabs on the current state of private equity investment laws when you are raising capital.

Putting the agreement in writing

People who love each other are likely to leave many concerns — even valid ones — unvoiced. In addition, due to issues like how quickly you can pay back the cash or what happens if the company hits a bump, the investment relationship between loved ones can go sour and drag down the whole company. For these reasons, use a written contract to specify what is expected from each party. By managing your investors' expectations, you can avoid a lot of conflict in the future. Here are your options:

✔ **Memorandum of understanding (MOU):** This fancy term is nothing more than an informal contract. MOUs seem a little friendlier than contracts for no other reason than the word *contract* isn't used. Really. An MOU is just a piece of paper on which you and the other party write down what you understand to be the limits of the relationship. This document is a tangible version of a gentleman's agreement.

✔ **IOU:** An IOU is acceptable but no more legally binding than the MOU. Because an IOU informally acknowledges debt, it's more appropriate to use when you've taken on debt from a friend or family member than when you've offered them stock.

If you sell stock in a friends and family round, work with a securities attorney. A general lawyer will not be sufficient. Using informal agreements when stock is sold turns you both into fools.

Dancing on the Head of a Pin: Angel Capital

Angel investors are different from venture capitalists. First, venture capitalists invest *other* people's money through a fund that they manage (refer to Chapter 2). Angel investors invest their own money. Second, VCs are professionals: They're trained in finance and receive a salary for doing the job. Angel investors are simply high-wealth individuals who are not trained investors and don't necessarily have experience investing in private companies. Angel investors invest in others' companies as a hobby or for fun; they don't typically do it because it's their job. In fact, they may have full-time jobs unrelated to investing, or they may be retired.

No single profile of a "typical" angel investor exists. They're all unique and have different backgrounds, knowledge, and interests. But they do have two things in common:

✔ They invest their own money, not other people's money.

✔ They choose to invest a portion of their wealth in private companies instead of the stock market or real estate.

Angel investors fill an important gap in an early-stage company's funding cycle. Often friends and family cannot raise the $500,000 or more that a company needs to get enough traction to interest a VC for a later round. Angels fill that gap. Each angel typically invests between $10,000 and $200,000 in a single company. A typical angel round will include money from multiple angels and will amount to between $200,000 and $2 million. Sometimes companies stop raising money after the angel round because that funding is all the company needs. In many cases, however, the angel round is just a stepping-stone toward raising institutional investment from a VC.

Raising capital through angel investors

Angel investors may be interested in your deal because they think they can make money by investing in your company. When angels pool their money to invest as a group in a single company, their criteria for investment are often very similar to those of a VC (refer to Chapter 6 for information on what VCs look for). But making money may not be the only reason they want to work with you. Following are a few other reasons that an angel may want to invest:

✔ To provide expertise in your company through an advisory role.

✔ To be part of the company she thinks is cool, even if she knows nothing about the technology.

- ✔ If retired, to buy herself a job to offset boredom.
- ✔ Because she really likes the entrepreneur or the company's mission.
- ✔ To get in on what her best friend just invested in.

You can see from this list of motivations that working with angel investors can be a professional experience, a hassle, or both.

Knowing the roles you have to play

You need an unusually large set of skills to plan, drive, and manage the relationships and activities that need to occur when you try to raise capital from angel investors. The tricks and tips for how to do so is not something that you learn in an MBA program or other formal business class. During the course of closing your angel deal, you will wear many different types of hats. Here are just a few:

- ✔ **Legal:** Know when you can handle the legal implications and know when to call your attorney. Investment laws, tax laws, regulatory laws, and patent laws are just a few of the landmines that you'll need to understand.

- ✔ **Marketing:** You have to get the word out that you are raising money. Depending on current law, you may be limited to networking and word of mouth as your primary methods of advertisement.

- ✔ **Administrative:** You have to be your own secretary by planning meetings, making phone calls, and pushing papers. Extreme attention to detail is necessary as you fill out applications to pitch at investor events and angel group meetings. Creating your due diligence folder (Chapter 13 covers due diligence) is a very large administrative task.

- ✔ **Decision making:** Each time you meet an angel, you have to determine whether you want to accept funding from this person. Walking away from a check takes a strong decision maker, but sometimes doing so is best for the company.

- ✔ **Accounting:** Because investors are primarily investing in your future financial success, you have to produce highly detailed pro formas (head to Chapter 6) and other accounting documents to show you have your thumb on the finances of your business.

- ✔ **Communication:** Pitching to angels is much the same as pitching to VCs. A clear and informative pitch is necessary to further the relationship between your company and an investor. Head to Part IV for details on making your pitch.

- ✔ **Management:** Don't expect angel investors to take care of themselves. They need you to manage your relationship with all of them.

Reading and understanding this book is a great step toward being an angel-savvy entrepreneur because many of the necessary skills are the same when you work with angels or VCs. In the following sections, we tell you what you can do to make sure that your involvement with angel investors is good one.

Choosing your angels carefully

Angel investors are just rich people. There is no guarantee that the angel across the table from you will be an asset to your company. There is a joke among angel investors that they come in three types: smart money, dumb money, and trusting money:

- **Smart money:** These angels know a lot about your company and your field. They can provide capital and a lot of experience.

- **Dumb money:** These investors know nothing about how to run your company. Because of their ignorance, a dumb money investor may become a liability in the future either through litigation (at the worst) or irritating e-mails asking a lot of annoying questions (at the least).

- **Trusting money:** These investors don't know how to run the business and trust you to do a good job.

You want to find someone who can either give you capital and great advice (smart money) or capital and no advice (trusting money). The investor who gives you money and then takes a lot of your time by contacting you and suggesting unhelpful changes to your business model may not be worth her check.

Litigious angels are another problem. Do your homework on people who are interested in investing with you. Find out what kind of relationship the potential investors had with prior companies they've invested in. If they've ever sued anyone over an investment, steer clear!

Driving the relationship throughout

To successfully raise money with angel investors, you have to be able to administrate your own deal. Before the deal is closed, you have to invite the investors to meetings where you pitch your deal. You and your attorney have to provide them with due diligence materials, a term sheet, and other legal documents. You also have to get all your committed angels to sign final documentation and wire their money to your account over the span of a few days.

Large companies have whole departments devoted to investor relations. Little companies need to communicate with their investors, too. One way to keep investors in the loop is to send them a monthly newsletter with the highlights and lowlights of the company.

Connecting with angels

A single angel typically invests between $10,000 to $200,000 in a single company in a single fundraising round. However, the average seed round generates $350,000. Doing some quick math, you see that you have to get 5 to 20 investors together to close your seed round.

In an earlier section, we warned you not to gather more than 10 investors, and now we are saying you might need 20 or more to complete your round. What? It's ideal to get more money from fewer investors, but obviously investment deals are not always perfect. Aim for fewer investors, but you may have to be flexible to get the job done.

Obviously dealing with 20 angels is more difficult than dealing with a single venture capital firm. Working with angels who know one another already through an angel group syndicate can be one way to help ease the burden of managing investors.

According to the Center for Venture Research, 258,000 angel investors were active in the United States in 2010.Compared to the number of active venture capital firms in 2010 (fewer than 500), angels significantly outnumber VCs.

Getting in touch with angel groups

Angels syndicate through angel groups (look to the Angel Capital Association to find the angel groups in your area: http://www.angelcapitalassociation.org.) These groups of angel investors can run the whole spectrum from loose clubs of high-wealth individuals to highly managed organizations run by staff.

To get angel groups to look at your deal, you must submit an application or pitch deck through whatever submission system the group has in place. Many use web portals, such as Gust (http://www.gust.com) or AngelList (https://angel.co/). Each group has its own process for choosing which companies pitch and how to handle due diligence. If you have any questions about the process, just ask someone involved with the group.

Attending angel investor conferences

Angel investors attend investor conferences to see a lot of deals in a short period of time. Most states have one or more investor conferences per year. To get on stage to pitch, you go through an application process and must be accepted. To find conferences in your area, check the Angel Capital Association (http://www.angelcapitalassociation.org) or search online for *angel investing conference*.

Going to trade shows and networking

Investors interested in a specific type of company often frequent trade shows to find investment deals. Investors know that trade shows are a great way to get acquainted with a new industry or meet the up-and-coming companies in an industry in a short time.

Other networking opportunities exist outside of trade shows. Some investors just do a lot of networking in general, hanging out where entrepreneurs hang out, looking to meet the next big entrepreneurial star. Admittedly, this approach is a serendipitous one for an investor, but it's not hard to catch wind of a company that people are getting excited about when you keep your ear to the ground.

The point is that you have to get out and get visible if you are raising money. Let everyone you talk to know that you are interested in meeting investors. Otherwise, you may end up sitting next to the biggest investor in the room and not even know it!

Attracting a Mob: Crowdfunding

Unlike venture capital, where your company has a single investor, crowdfunding allows hundreds or even thousands of people to invest. In crowdfunding terms, the word *investor* is replaced with *backer*. You may have heard some amazing stories of people putting their projects up on a crowdfunding site and receiving millions of dollars in just days.

Although some companies have raised millions of dollars, most crowdfunding portals are limited to $1 million total backing. At this level, crowdfunding is not a replacement for venture capital, but it is an alternative to angel funding for companies that need only a small amount of money to get started or that are on their way to a venture capital round 18 to 24 months down the road.

To get started raising money through crowdfunding, you have to put your company on a crowdfunding platform (website), but that's only the beginning. There is a lot to learn about the information that you add to your crowdfunding profile, the promotion of your page, and the way that you communicate your deal. In addition, new crowdfunding portals are popping up every day, each with its own fees, rules, and types of companies it accepts (be sure to read the fine print). To find out more about crowdfunding, check out *Crowdfund Investing For Dummies,* by Sherwood Neiss, Jason Best, Zak Cassady-Dorion (John Wiley & Sons, Inc.).

Understanding the JOBS Act impact on crowdfunding

The Jumpstart Our Business Startups (JOBS) Act was signed into law April 2012. Basically, this law allows companies to raise money through the Internet and give the backers equity in return. The major difference here is that before the law changed, no equity could be given to backers of companies raising money online or through "general solicitation" (advertising to the public).

This act allows for a new class of Internet funding portals that can be used for general solicitation online. In other words, companies can now generally solicit non-accredited investors through traditional media such as newspapers, newsletters, broadcast media, bulk e-mail, and so on. Previously, such solicitations were illegal because of fears of unscrupulous opportunists tricking kindly retirees out of their pensions.

The ability to use general solicitation to raise funds has had a huge impact for start-ups. Combined with the power of the Internet, companies can now reach millions of potential investors more easily than ever before. Here are some of the key provisions of the act:

- It increased the number of shareholders a company must have from 500 to 2,000 before being required to register with the Security and Exchange Commission (SEC) as a public company.

- It enables companies to now have up to 500 non-accredited investors (individual investors with a net worth of less than $1 million, not including their primary homes, or incomes under $200,000 per year [$300,000 if married]).

Giving perks: Non-equity crowdfunding

With non-equity crowdfunding, you can raise money through backers without giving them equity in return. Often you give them a product or experience in return.

Non-equity crowdfunding sites such as Kickstarter (http://www.kickstarter.com) and Indiegogo (http://www.indiegogo.com) have been extremely popular. These sites expressly prohibit the sale of securities but allow you to give perks to those who send in money. Even though you can't sell equity, these sites are extremely valuable to those who are seeking venture capital.

Consider the following examples. Although they have unusual results, for well-run campaigns, the ability to raise funding without giving up equity is a powerful tool to consider:

- **Ubooly:** This Boulder, Colorado, company makes a cute toy with a software technology element. The company presented to angel investors who liked the concept but were hesitant to invest because they weren't sure that consumers would buy this product. The company listed its project on Kickstarter and raised 113 percent of its $25,000 goal in just a few weeks. Investors got different perks, depending on how much they invested; the perks ranged from a T-shirt to a distribution pack of 100 of the company's products. The company was subsequently accepted as a TechStars company and went on to raise $1.5 million just a few months later, and its product is now sold through retailers everywhere. In this case, Kickstarter definitely kick-started this company by validating market demand and minimizing investors' fears that the product would not sell well.

- **The Pebble E-Paper Watch:** The Pebble E-Paper Watch for iPhone and Android is another story of crowdfunding success. In April 2012, the company launched its campaign to raise $100,000 to help with sending its product to manufacturing. Within a short time, the company had raised over $10 million on Kickstarter with almost 69,000 backers.

Crowdfunding may seem like an entrepreneurs' dream come true, but you should remember that most investment is based on relationships. Using crowdfunding sites alone limits your ability to leverage relationships because sites can't easily replicate real world relationships that are typically a prerequisite for funding.

Using crowdfunding successfully

Because you don't have the opportunity to meet with backers face-to-face when you use a crowdfunding portal, you have to do everything you can to build credibility and drive traffic to the site. To use crowdfunding successfully, do the following:

- **Develop a sophisticated marketing campaign that drives your network of contacts to the crowdfunding portal.** You can do this by enlisting your first-tier connections in LinkedIn, Twitter, Facebook, and other social media sites to help create buzz about your project and send potential investors to the site.

Backers often behave like lemmings in that they'll follow others in investment, but they won't be the first to jump themselves. If you can get your closest social circle to invest and then enlist them to share your opportunity, you are well on your way to a successful campaign.

✔ **Expand your marketing campaign.** Consider sending press releases to any organizations or friendly companies that may be positively impacted by your company's success. Publicize your launch locally so that people in your community are aware of the offering. You can also use e-mail campaigns and traditional print and broadcast media to drive people to your listing.

✔ **Hold a launch party.** Invite all your friends to a party where you describe your campaign. Have fun with it. The more your friends have to drink, the more they might feel inspired to become backers right then and there!

Heeding warnings regarding crowdfunding

Crowdfunding can be a great way to gain exposure and initial funding for your company, but beware of some of the challenges that you may face if you choose crowdfunding:

✔ **Crowded capitalization tables are unattractive to future investors.** After a company has more than 10 or so investors, things begin to get ugly. Although getting funded by VCs isn't impossible when you have a lot of investors involved, it's a lot harder. One technique to lessen this challenge is to create a limited liability corporation (LLC) that your crowd owns. Then, as far as the cap table is concerned, your 500 crowd-funders are now just 1 investor represented by the LLC.

✔ **You're increasing the risk that your intellectual property will be publically exposed.** In some companies, you can't explain the company fully without revealing your "secret sauce" — that is, the trade secrets and processes that comprise the main value in your company When you're dealing with a few trusted professionals such as venture capitalists, you can usually expect your secrets to remain confidential, but if you reveal them to hundreds or thousands of investors, your sauce is no longer secret.

If you do have secrets, make sure that they are not revealed in your crowdfunding project.

✔ **Negotiation is impossible with most current crowdfunding sites.** You may think this is great — just list your project and wait for the money to roll in. Yet if you have an extraordinarily high valuation on your start-up company, you probably won't receive funding. Your failure will be public, and the fact that thousands of people have decided *not* to invest in your company will be clear. Crowdfunding failure may create negative momentum in your funding progress, which may be impossible to overcome.

Accessing Grants to Fund Your Company

Innovative companies can find *non-dilutive capital* in the form of grants (they're called *non-dilutive* because the equity in your company doesn't get diluted since you don't have to give up any equity in exchange for the money). Grants are not loans, either. Assuming you complete the work in the grant proposal and follow the rules of the grant, you never have to pay the money back.

Grants are offered by government agencies, foundations, and commercial entities as an incentive to accomplish (or attempt to accomplish) a goal that the granting organization has identified.

Applying for grants is a lot of work. Federal grants are awarded to applicants at a success rate of only 14 to 25 percent, depending on the year. Writing the grant application requires a lot of preparation and detailed work, which can cost between 1 and 3 months of full-time effort. Also, a lot of time (9 to 12 months) passes between the submission of the application and the time that dollars are actually awarded.

Federal grants: Small Business Innovation Research (SBIR)

The Small Business Innovation Research (SBIR) grant program is offered through the federal government. By law, a percentage of all academic research dollars need to be set aside and given to private businesses for research.

Many different government agencies offer these grants, but the majority of the dollars (81 percent) are distributed through the Department of Defense (DOD) and the National Institutes of Health (NIH). Department of Energy (DOE), National Science Foundation (NSF), and NASA dole out 16 percent, and the rest is parceled through a bunch of small programs in other agencies.

These grants are given to companies that perform research on risky new technologies. In the government's view, companies engaging in low-risk research should be able to get funding through other venues. SBIR grant rules limit the use of funds to research activities only; they cannot be used for marketing, manufacturing, or sales costs.

SBIR grants are broken into two major phases:

- ✔ **Phase I:** In this phase, the grant does not exceed $150,000 and is for a short-term (6 to 9 months) feasibility study. The goal of this phase is to determine whether the technology has any commercial viability and would therefore warrant a full-fledged research and development (R&D) study.

- ✔ **Phase II:** This phase continues the effort that began in phase I. Phase II dollars generally don't exceed $1,000,000 and are expected to drive a project for about 2 years.

Sometimes companies can get grants called *fast track awards* that combine phase I and II applications and dollars into a single transaction.

State grants

Many states have a small fund dedicated to economic development within the state. If your company aligns with the technology or type of company that your state wants to support, you may be able to procure a state grant. Check with your state's office of economic development to see what's currently available.

Foundations and commercial entity grants

Many foundations and commercial entities offer *requests for proposals* each year for commercial companies that are willing to work on projects that support the foundation or entity's mission. Some foundations that award grants to only non-profits make exceptions if the for-profit's project is particularly well aligned with their goals.

Growing Organically: Bootstrapping

When your business grows organically, you don't take outside capital at all; instead, you reinvest your own cash flow into the business, and every dollar comes from revenues that you generate from sales. The phrase *bootstrapping* means the same thing.

Advantages of organic growth

If you are building a company for the long term and don't intend to sell within the next five to ten years, then growing organically is often the best strategy. Here are the advantages:

- ✔ Many companies that bootstrap become highly profitable and never need to raise another dollar.

- ✔ Successful companies learn to create products quickly and get them to market fast. Money is not spent on frivolous parties or perks; instead, it's focused on bringing new revenues in the door.

- ✔ Your time and effort will be devoted to developing your business and increasing sales instead of developing investor relationships.

- ✔ You'll own your whole company outright, which gives you total control and all the financial rewards.

The downside is that your company's growth will be slower.

We have seen many companies who think they need to raise venture capital but who would actually be much better served by taking more time and keeping 100 percent of the equity for themselves and maintaining control of their companies. Some companies are set free by the realization that they don't need to take outside capital at all.

Making organic growth work for you

Companies that grow organically employ a variety of techniques to get a lot of bang for their buck. They may work out of the CEO's garage for years. They employ "guerilla marketing" techniques that get a lot of exposure and sales for almost no dollars. They employ interns, work long hours, and don't pay themselves much at first.

Many CEOs who have bootstrapped say they would never do it any other way, despite the challenges. At least, they say, they are working on growing their company and not blowing the 6 to12 months of distraction that it can take to land a great venture capital deal.

Even if you eventually do end up taking venture capital, you can benefit from taking the organic growth strategy for as long as possible. Here's why:

- ✔ You build traction and therefore value into your company; revenue and profit make you attractive to investors at higher valuation.

✔ You create a culture of discipline and performance. Countless founders got venture capital too early and blew through it before they figured out how to run their companies.

✔ When the time comes to have an initial public offering (IPO) or acquisition, you end up with a greater percentage of the company and will enjoy greater rewards from the exit.

Knowing When Enough Is Enough

Many companies fail, and that's a normal part of entrepreneurship. If you are seeking capital to save a dying business, ask yourself whether your time and energy would be better spent starting an entirely new business or whether this current business still has some life left in it. You may need to seriously consider shuttering your doors if these scenarios seem like they're describing you or your business:

✔ **You have put a lot of time and money into a creating your product, but people don't seem to want to buy it.** Unfortunately, sometimes the market for your product disappears while you are developing it, or it was never really there to begin with. A company with a product no one wants is not going to succeed.

✔ **You've spoken with lots of investors over more than a year and they are all passing on the opportunity.** When a long time passes and you are still pitching the same company to the same investors, you are probably not going to make progress with this company.

✔ **Your employees and co-founders are leaving.** If the rest of the team starts throwing in the towel, then you may be missing signs that it's time to quit.

All companies are not created equal. Most successful entrepreneurs can point to failed and aborted companies in their past. At some point, a founder must simply make the decision to cut losses, close the business, and begin a new chapter in her life. One of the best tenants in entrepreneurship is if you are going to fail, fail fast and move on.

Chapter 5

Connecting with Investors Online and Face to Face

Raising money is all about relationships. You have to make genuine relationships with people in the communities where you hope to be funded. You can't fake this. The trick is to be able to enter into a community quickly, make relationships quickly, and go back to working on your business as soon as possible. You will be richer in the bank after closing your round, and you'll be richer in your network because of all the great people you'll meet.

You have to create a public persona for yourself and a matching one for your company. Fortunately, a lot of social media websites can help with this endeavor. Between Twitter (http://www.twitter.com), LinkedIn (http://www.linkedin.com), Facebook (http://www.facebook.com), AngelList (http://angel.co), Gust (http://www.gust.com), and blogging, you can easily tell people who you are in a way that supports your fundraising goals. In this chapter, we cover the whole process of creating a campaign for yourself and your company to raise money.

We live in a digital world, and people will undoubtedly look you up online after they meet or hear about you. So plan to take a little time to learn social media if you've never used it. Ask around for help if you feel stuck. Being active in social media is no longer optional in the start-up community; it's a must.

Creating an Online Persona for Your Company

When you raise money, the first thing that investors are going to ask is, "Who are these people?" The second thing they'll do is search for your company on the Internet. Investors want to see how you engage your audience even before you have a product to sell.

You can use online tools such as Twitter, LinkedIn, Facebook, and a website to create a public persona before you begin fundraising. Doing so greatly helps people remember who you are and what your company does.

Imagine having hundreds or thousands of people who are excited about the release of your product weeks before it's actually available. Excited crowds don't occur spontaneously; they're created, just like boy bands. You have to cultivate community excitement by connecting with an audience in the ways that the audience members prefer to be engaged. For many audiences, the engagement of choice is intellectual, political, creative, or inspiring.

Whereas in the past, social media may have seemed like a waste of time — something for kids who just want to text, chat, and send pictures back and forth — today, it's a must for business. A business that doesn't have a webpage doesn't seem like a real business. In the following sections, we outline the various online networks you can use to reach out to potential investors and customers.

Twitter, Facebook, and LinkedIn are all free in terms of money, but social media usage doesn't come without a price tag. You have to spend a significant amount of time if you're going to use these methods of connecting with your customer and community. One marketing guru once claimed that 15 minutes per day spent on social media is enough to build an online presence and community. Even at 15 minutes per day, we are talking about a minimum of 5 hours a month on social media. Plus you have to balance your fundraising, product building, team building, and social media time to get everything done.

Creating a website and branded e-mail address

If you do nothing else to build a public persona, get a webpage. Buying a web address and having a page hosted doesn't cost very much — less than $100 per year — but be sure to avoid cheap looking templates that may do more harm than good. For $2,000, you can have a webpage designed for you. You can also use website design services that make putting together a webpage very easy (you don't even need any programming skills). Many easy-to-use and free or inexpensive website building tools are available.

In today's online world, having the right domain name secured can add significant value to your company. If you have a unique name, failing to register it in a timely way demonstrates a casual and risky behavior because you are allowing others to potentially encroach on your brand or to hijack your name and hold it ransom for thousands of dollars. It's far better to spend fifteen minutes and $15 or so per domain and register everything surrounding your name that you can think of.

When you create your website, do the following:

✔ **Pick a name for your site that makes sense, is related to your business, and isn't ridiculous or offensive when read phonetically** (`www.silk-shoes.com`, **for example).** Choosing the web address can be a challenge if your company name is a common word or common name. Above all, make sure that your website name is easy to remember and doesn't have ambiguous or complex spelling that will drive browsers to someone else's site. Follow these guidelines:

• Pick a name that people can remember and spell. If you use a creative spelling for your company, expect that people will first type in the common spelling when searching for you.

• If your site name spelling is ambiguous, be sure to register every possible variation on the name that you can think of and redirect all of those names to your main website.

• Make your web address as short as possible. We have seen addresses that are up to 15 characters, which pretty much assures problems with getting people to remember and access your site. A good rule is to keep it under 10 characters.

✔ **Be sure that your company name is on the website and that your products or potential products are visible.**

✔ **Provide a contact phone number or e-mail address so that people can get in touch with you.** Whether you publicize where your office is located is up to you. Investors will check your website first for contact info when they lose your card.

Most websites come with at least a few free e-mail addresses. You have to set up the e-mail name(s) yourself after you set up the website. When doing so, make sure the e-mail address uses your company name. If your website is `www.silkshoes.com`, for example, your e-mail address would be your-name@silkshoes.com. You should also create a generic e-mail address like info@silkshoes.com that can be used publicly without filling your CEO's inbox. After you create the e-mail address, use it in all of your correspondence, advertising, and print materials.

A generic address, like John@yahoo.com, just won't cut it anymore. Investors cannot take you 100 percent seriously as a founder who is raising money until you use an e-mail address that includes your company business name. If you contact potential investors with a Gmail or Yahoo address, they may have trouble remembering which company you own. Worse, they'll wonder why you aren't totally committed to this business.

Connecting through LinkedIn

If your website and e-mail addresses are the most important public persona your company needs, then LinkedIn (http://www.linkedin.com) houses the most important individual persona that you need. LinkedIn is an online resume that enables you to connect with other business people. This service lets you keep track of the people you've met and attract the people you want to meet. Looking up someone's LinkedIn profile before meeting for coffee or asking him to pitch for investment is now commonplace.

When you set up a LinkedIn profile, you make it easy for potential investors and other business associates to do their homework on you, and you can look up their profiles as well. When you create a LinkedIn profile, make sure that it's complete enough to give people an idea of your track record, but brief enough to avoid forcing them to wade through your high school hockey awards to get to the meat of your experience — assuming, of course, that you don't have a hockey-related company.

The best part about a LinkedIn profile is that you control it in real time. If you begin serving on the board of a non-profit organization and you want to add that to your experience, you can do so right away. If you realize that your past work in a different industry is distracting to people in your current industry, you can delete it from your profile.

Using Twitter

Twitter (http://www.twitter.com) has become a popular way for businesses to connect with their customer bases. Very basically, Twitter is a real-time information network that lets people post *tweets*, short messages (no more than 140 characters) that other members can follow. You can tweet text, links, pictures, and video. The people who are following you will see those tweets and any media attached in their twitter feed.

If you are one of those people who think Twitter isn't important or that you're just tweeting out into thin air, you're wrong! Twitter has become one of the primary ways for individuals and businesses to find and connect to each other. You are able to tweet both individually and as a business; you should do both:

✔ **Tweeting as a company:** Sure, your company isn't a person and doesn't have opinions, but it does have a culture and a brand. Your company should tweet information, news, and links related to the culture and brand.

Leverage your online activities by tweeting whenever you post a new entry to your blog, website, or Facebook page. Tweet when you have a press release. Include your web address in tweets to drive more traffic to your site.

Although anyone in the company can tweet as the company, put one person in charge of the account to make sure that direct Twitter messages (like really short e-mails) are being answered.

✔ **Tweeting as an individual:** You can get your own Twitter username and create your own brand. If you are raising money, then your personal brand should align pretty closely with that of your company. Get your own followers and tweet successful milestones, intriguing thoughts, and informative news to the people who care about your tweets.

When you become active on Twitter, keep these points in mind:

✔ **Twitter is very public.** Assume that everything you write will be sent around the world. Even if you don't have many followers, your few followers can retweet your messages to their followers who may number in the tens of thousands.

✔ **Gathering followers on Twitter takes time.** People have to individually click a button to say that they are interested in your tweets.

After your company has amassed a large number of Twitter followers (hundreds or even thousands), you can proudly claim to have lots of people interested in your company.

Finding friends on Facebook

Facebook (http://www.facebook.com) is another social media system that initially appealed primarily to teens and college students but is now very much for businesses, too. With a Facebook page, you can connect your business with the people who use Facebook (there are over 1 billion of them). Many people now use Facebook for their news and entertainment media. If those people are part of your community, your company needs to have a presence on Facebook, too.

On your Facebook page, post the topics that are important to your brand's community: Post offers, events, information, and news that your customers care about. If you're a coffee company, for example, you'd post on anything related to coffee: coffee breaks, mornings, snack foods to have with coffee, health effects of coffee, art using coffee beans, politics of coffee, and so on. People can "Like" your company's page, which means that they agree to receive your posts in their inbox. When you have a certain number of likes, you have access to more advanced features (like promotions and a memorable custom Facebook address, like www.facebook.com/yourname).

With Facebook, as with any social media, your goal is to engage your community and influence thoughts and actions. Done well (don't just post ads selling your product!), you can expand your community and help create a tight-knit feeling around your product or business. Investors love to see that people care about your company and your product.

Although you use Facebook as an informal marketing tool for your business, make sure your posts are professional. Also keep in mind that amassing a following on Facebook takes time and although it is "free," leveraging it successfully requires significant resources.

Blogging about your company

You can maintain a blog as a highly dynamic part of your website. A blog post is part press release, part editorial, and part entertainment. The best posts include all three elements. Blogs can be articles, videos, photos, or any online mixed media. A blog is a way to convey how you think and what you are thinking about. As such, it can be valuable information for investors who want to get to know who you are and what drives you.

Your blog can be a separate site, using one of the popular blogging platforms like WordPress (http://www.wordpress.org), Blog.com (http://www.blog.com), TypePad Micro (http://www.typepad.com), or Blogger.com (http://www.blogger.com). Most of these platforms are free and can be customized with your brand's images and colors. You can get started in a few hours, and start blogging right away. You may also integrate your blog into your website in order to drive more traffic directly to your site and to minimize the work of maintaining multiple sites in different locations.

You must contribute regularly to a blog, or it loses its purpose — and audience. The point is to keep people coming back to your website as a way to build a community around you. Even if you don't have a product on the shelves yet, you'll have people who care about your company and your product as soon as it is available.

It's not uncommon to see blogs with two or three entries over the first two months that just go blank after that. Make sure that you establish a regular blogging schedule that never has gaps and has posts at least once a week (the ideal). Tools are available that allow you to write five or ten blog posts at one time and to schedule their release on a regular basis so that you can keep your postings spaced out without overwhelming or underwhelming your readers.

Launching a Community Campaign

If you plan to get noticed by VCs by simply contacting the VC, you're missing a bunch of other important channels. Think about fundraising as a presidential campaign: You have to get the word out to as many people as possible — a feat that's especially challenging because of laws preventing companies from advertising investment opportunities publicly in newspapers and online. (Caveat: Laws change, so check current laws.)

How can you get the word out without publicly advertising? By spreading information about your investment through word of mouth channels. In other words, you have to shake a lot of hands and meet a lot of people.

Many towns have start-up communities that rally around new, local companies. Denver, Colorado; New York City, New York; Los Angeles, California; Kansas City, Missouri; Madison, Wisconsin; Austin, Texas; Seattle, Washington; and many other cities have healthy start-up communities. A culture of support exists for start-ups, and you'll be able to find support for your venture if you get outside and connect with the people around you.

You can get 30 minutes of time with almost anyone if you can secure the right introduction. When you begin your campaign of being seen, you're not vying to talk directly to a VC. Instead, you're introducing yourself to all the people who can connect you with investors, advisors, and potential teammates. You're building your reputation as a committed founder and a savvy businessperson. By following this approach, when you do get in front of the VC, he already knows your name.

Having coffee with people

There's nothing like face time to get connected with someone new. An unspoken rule in start-up communities says that anyone will have coffee with an entrepreneur if asked. Sometimes you may have to wait three months and be very persistent, especially if the target is very busy, but the rule holds.

During this coffee meeting, don't pitch your company. Ask questions to find out more about the VC's perspective, his network, and his expertise. Make mental — and real — notes about who this person is and how he fits into the community as a whole. Keep these points in mind:

- **Use your time wisely.** Don't just sit down for a chat about the weather. Make a list of goals that you want to accomplish during the meeting. Busy people appreciate your preparation and focus when meeting.

- **Don't feel shy about asking if someone is an angel investor.** You'd be surprised how many people in start-up communities are investing in the companies around them. If the person is an investor, don't pitch to him immediately. Instead, ask which companies he's invested in recently and put that information in your notes.

✔ **Feel free to ask for an introduction.** You can ask for introductions to specific people, although your meeting partner may not feel comfortable introducing you to people they don't know well. Take this tack: In the general course of conversation, ask whether there is anyone you should meet. Then ask for an introduction to the person whose name they provide. Chances are they're close to the person they suggest. If not, you can add the suggested person to your list of new targets to meet anyway.

When you leave the coffee meeting, at minimum, you should know two things: how this person can help you and how you can help him.

Absolutely send a thank you e-mail to the person you met with. Even better, send a handwritten thank you. No one gets postal mail anymore, but everyone gets between 4 and 400 e-mails every day. A handwritten note will be remembered.

Going to networking events

The best way to meet people is to get out and mingle. Networking events often target a specific topic or field. They generally provide some educational content, showcase an interview with someone interesting, or provide some entertainment. Occasionally, the networking event is nothing more than a time and place designated to allow participants to talk to people in the community.

So many networking events are scheduled in some cities that you could attend one every morning, lunch, and evening. Choose wisely. These events often last a few hours and can absorb a lot of your time. It is wise to attend a particular group's meeting two or three times to see who the regulars are, to develop some relationships, and to truly understand what is going on behind the scenes.

The names of the groups sponsoring the networking events don't always reflect the clientele, so you have to attend to figure out who frequents a particular event. Consider doing a tour of the networking events in your area to see which ones attract the people you want to meet. Smaller "sub-communities" are generally associated with these groups. If you're a software engineer, for example, you can probably choose between the "by-the-book hackers" and the "creative hackers" groups.

Meetup.com (http://www.meetup.com) is the go-to website for everything networking. Most events on Meetup.com are free or come with a small charge to cover food and beverages. Some are formal, and others are haphazard: you never know what to expect until you attend!

Giving non-pitch presentations

During a fundraising campaign, one of your big goals is to get a chance to pitch to investors. But don't assume that an official pitch presentation is your only opportunity to sell yourself. You can get exposure through other kinds of presentations as well. Consider these possibilities:

- ✔ **Universities** are often looking for folks in the community to speak with students or faculty. These opportunities may or may not present themselves to you. If no one approaches you, don't feel shy about offering to give a talk. Find the person in charge of booking speakers and offer a topic you feel comfortable presenting. In general, program planners will be so happy to have an available speaker that they'll try to book you at some point during the semester.

- ✔ **Entrepreneur groups** are always looking for speakers. No matter what your experiences have been so far, chances are you have something to offer.

- ✔ **Community groups** such as Rotary Club, Kiwanis, Lions Club, and others love to connect with the people in their communities. If you have local experience that you'd like to share, you'll almost always be invited to provide their members with an interesting tale.

Some of these potential speaking venues may seem to be off the beaten path when you're looking for investment. After all, do VCs really go to business school talks? Actually, sometimes they do. Moreover, they've likely spoken at the business school themselves and now have a soft spot in their hearts for the program. When the VC sees the e-mail from the business school advertising your talk, he'll feel a subconscious connection with your name.

Online Tools for Real-Life Funding: Investing Sites

As if LinkedIn, Twitter, Facebook, your website, and your community campaigning weren't enough exposure to alert the community and potential investors that you're looking to raise capital, you can post your company on online investor platforms such as Gust (`http://www.gust.com`) and AngelList (`http://angel.co`).

Gust and AngelList are social media sites that allow you to share the details of your fundraising platform. This focus is different from mainstream social media. On mainstream social media sites such as LinkedIn, your goal is to create a persona for yourself and for your company. In contrast, your Gust or AngelList profile is a place to openly share your current fundraising needs, past raises, and past investors (at least those who are also on the site).

Although these platforms have a crowdfunding element, they're not *crowd-funding* platforms per se. Whereas crowdfunding platforms expect you to raise funds directly online, Gust and AngelList encourage you to take the conversation and the investment offline into the real world. Refer to Chapter 4 for more information about crowdfunding.

Looking at Gust and AngelList

Using investor sites like Gust and AngelList is an efficient way to announce your intention to raise capital. New sites are popping up almost daily, in which you can create an extensive profile for your company that includes details about your investment deal as well as all the basic information about your company. Investors all over the world will have access to your profile and will be able to contact you to request more information.

Gust

Gust (http://www.gust.com) is a powerful tool for angels to collaborate and syndicate on deals. You can create a profile on Gust and then submit that profile to angel groups who have accounts with Gust. These groups will then either invite you to pitch with their group or ask for more information.

Gust charges investors a fee, so they don't tend to use the platform as individuals. Instead, angel group administrators manage Gust accounts. They use the service to vet, share, and accept applications based on the group's unique requirements.

Here are some other highlights about Gust:

✔ It's a powerful tool you can use to connect with angel groups.

✔ Its collaborative features allow angels to perform due diligence more quickly.

✔ Investors can share deals with other groups, helping you close your round faster.

✔ Your profile becomes a standard 2-page executive summary that you can print and share with investors in person.

✔ It's free to entrepreneurs.

AngelList

AngelList (https://angel.co) is an online platform for start-ups to connect with investors, mentors, and employees. You can sort by location, market, product, and jobs. AngelList uncovers the otherwise secret world of start-up investing. All you need is a login and a password. AngelList is free to both entrepreneurs and angel investors.

Here are some things AngelList lets you do:

- ✔ Identify the big investors in your region or industry
- ✔ Vet investors based on their experience or reviews
- ✔ Identify companies in your space
- ✔ Find mentors, advisors, and employees
- ✔ Learn how to create a profile from other successful companies
- ✔ Stay informed about the news in the nationwide start-up world

We've found that the best way for investors to understand investment deals is to see a whole lot of them. Entrepreneurs can do a similar exercise with AngelList. Find 20 random investors, read their profiles, and write down your observations. You'll begin to see patterns. How much do they invest per year, and how are the funds distributed? Do they invest alongside other specific investors? What are they looking for? Does their portfolio reflect what they claim to be looking for? And so on.

Signing up for both

When you want to raise money, you should probably use both Gust and AngelList. Why? Because each platform has different investors, and you don't want to ignore either group. Be sure to keep your eyes open for new sites to list on as well, because raising venture capital is a rapidly changing area on the web. Basically, angels fall into one of three basic types: visible angels, angels who invest in organized groups, and invisible angels:

- ✔ **Visible angels:** Some angels are very experienced and totally immersed in the start-up world. Consider investors in this group visible angels because they tend to be visible in the community, either because of their investments or because they are founders of successful ventures. They partner with other visible angels and invest based on referrals from one another.

- ✔ **Angels in groups:** An angel group is a club or entity that handles the sourcing and vetting of deals. An administrator facilitates meetings and sometimes does the legal work of putting the deals together. Angels who prefer angel groups are often less visible than the visible angels. By joining an investment group, investors can get good deal flow (which requires a certain public visibility) but retain anonymity.

- ✔ **Invisible angels:** Occasionally, companies work with individual angels who single-handedly provide the whole seed round for a company. These angels prefer to invest alone, quietly, and without fanfare, working under the radar. The best way to find them is to get the word out that you are raising money and hope they come to you.

When you submit an application through Gust, you'll connect with angel investors who have affiliated into angel groups. In many cases, Gust is the only way to submit your application, as is the case with Robin Hood Ventures, an angel investing group based in Pennsylvania. Gust applications can be made visible to the public (with financial info omitted).

AngelList, on the other hand, connects entrepreneurs with visible angels. The profile you create on AngelList is public, and anyone (investor, entrepreneur, or lurker) with an AngelList login can see your deal. This visibility could attract invisible angels who tend to lurk around looking for deals. Most likely, your audience is made up of visible angels who use AngelList to keep track of the start-up community.

Using investing sites effectively

Getting a profile set up on an investing site is a good start, but don't just post your profile on these sites and sit back waiting for a response. Setting up a profile is just the beginning of your campaign, and you need to work to drive investors to your profile so that they can learn about your company and actively invest.

Preparing to launch on an investing site

Many of the same rules apply in preparing to pitch to investors in person and preparing to launch on an investing site. Immediately after you launch your profile, investors will begin to contact you. You can leverage that initial attention by making sure you're ready to have conversations with investors.

Gust and AngelList vastly increase the number of people that are exposed to your company and your deal. In some ways, you can think about posting on an investment site as instant publicity. So don't make your deal public until you are really ready for it to be publicized. Make sure you've done all the necessary work to prepare your investment deal for primetime. Know how much you're raising, what milestones those funds will help you achieve, how much money you will ultimately need to raise, and how big your company can ultimately become. For help on amassing the info you need to have at your fingertips when talking to investors, head to Chapter 6.

You will likely be contacted by three groups of people: investors in the general public who are seeking basic information, people who are actively interested in investing in your deal, and well-known investors whom you actively want to pursue. It's easy to lose track of conversations you've had over the phone. After 10 or 15 inquiries, you'll forget whom you spoke with if you don't write it down. Plan to keep investor information (name, contact info, type of investor, expertise, amount committed) in a spreadsheet or contact database, along with dates of correspondence.

Mining AngelList profiles

You can learn a lot from reading AngelList investor profiles. These short summaries really get to the bottom of an investor's experience with venture companies and can give you a good idea of their industry interests. David Cohen, founder of TechStars, is a very experienced venture investor. From his AngelList profile, you can see how many companies that he's invested in (approaching 100, but who's keeping track?) and what kinds of companies they are. Because he's invested in SendGrid, TapInfluence, and MobileDay, you can assume that he likes to support technology tools that allow people to communicate more easily. Use this kind of research to find companies like yours and identify the investors who are interested in that space.

Gaining endorsements

Find champions who are willing to endorse you and your deal. Champions are people who will cheer for you even if they can't invest in your company. Here are a couple of options:

- ✔ Ask advisors, investors, and mentors to comment on your online profile and share their support.

- ✔ If you have one or two committed investors (an ideal situation at this point), you can share that information with the new potential investors who make contact. Depending on your desire to engage an individual investor, you can disclose the name and contact information of your committed investors (get permission first!). AngelList and Gust will provide information about who has invested and how much they have invested if the investors decide to post it.

Getting commitments for a round is much like building a snowball: Even if you start with something small, you can grow it quickly. By collecting one or two committed investors early, you're seeding the pot, and you'll find that other investors are easier to gain. Investors are like herd animals, so encouraging your investors to make their actions public really helps to build momentum!

Seeing who is investing

The power behind start-up investing websites is that you can track investors and investments. Investors have profiles, too. You can see who invests in drug development, clean tech, entertainment apps, marketing apps, and more.

You can learn a lot about the way investors think by reading their profiles. Look at the types of companies they invest in. Study their preferred markets and locations. Study how their desired investment industries overlap with their own business experiences.

You can also learn a lot about an investor's reputation by reading the reviews that other people have written. Often you'll find patterns there, too:

- ✔ Three independent reviewers claimed Nicole Glaros of TechStars was "very bright," "smart," and "brilliant." These separate but similar reviews indicate that she is known to have excellent insight and the brainpower to handle a lot of complexity.

- ✔ George Zachary of Charles River Ventures has extensive reviews on his profile. Many reviewers echo a good guy quality and all-in approach to the start-up community and to his investing activities.

- ✔ Andy Palmer of Vertica has a reputation for being exceptionally supportive of the folks he works with. Two reviewers used the word "friend."

Investors on AngelList are only the tip of the iceberg; many other investors prefer to remain less-than-famous and don't post profiles. You can extrapolate what you learn from the angels with profiles and find trends such as, for example, a predisposition toward high growth, high profit SaaS (software as a service) software companies, and a general disinterest in less scalable service or manufacturing firms. Be careful, though, and stereotype only to a point. Remember, people are all unique.

Following the progress of other companies

As a Gust or AngelList participant, you can read profiles from other companies, both in your industry and outside your markets. Doing so gives you a bounty of information.

Think like an investor as you read other companies' profiles: Try to identify the things in the profile that you are attracted to and that put you off. What information do you wish you saw in the profiles? Which teasers make you want to contact the founders? Be critical and use your opinions to make your company profile stand out by conveying the message and calls to action that lead to investment results.

The bar is set high with lots of competition to attract the attention of investors. Try to gauge company stages and put the companies in order from least to most developed in terms of product development, fundraising, and market size. Some of these factors will be hard to judge, but see if you can guess. Don't compete against an unknown quantity; do the homework to make sure that your company is attractive in comparison to everything else that is out there. The best way to work with investors is to understand how they think.

Making Contact with Investors

After you feel comfortable that your company is ready and your deal is mature enough for investors, you will have to actually make contact. Aside from the broad interest and inquiries that you might get from an AngelList profile, all other contact between you and investors will have to originate with you. Plan to do all of the reaching out and following up.

Although you may feel like investors are giving you the runaround and that you have to do all the legwork, it's worth it. Be sure that you focus on time management while you are fundraising. Because closing this deal as soon as possible is in your best interest, it's your responsibility to do all the reaching out.

Creating a hit list

When you plan your fundraising campaign, plan your investor hit list as well. Who would you most like to have on your board, in your deal, and on your side? Make a list of your most likely candidate investors with your team. You and your team should be able to defend why you have added each person's name to the list. This is really important because it enables you to target the right people without wasting a lot of time.

Your VC hit list will change in an iterative way. You may love the blog Redeye VC, written by Josh Koppelman at First Round Capital, and initially put that VC firm on your hit list. Then after doing a little objective research, you discover that First Round Capital claims to be a seed stage-only firm. If your company is in B-round fundraising, you may not be a good fit. Back to the drawing board!

Throughout the process of fundraising, investors will become more or less attractive to work with. Change your hit list as you learn more. Eventually, your hit list will morph into an investor interest list. You will have dropped all the uninterested parties and kept all the interested parties. The investor contact list will be helpful later when you want to update potential investors on progress.

Researching VC firms

VC websites have a lot of information. Generally, they offer an overview of the kinds of investments that the firm makes and include *tombstones,* thumbnail images of the companies in the VC portfolio. Research those portfolio companies to find out whether they're anything like yours.

Pay particular attention to companies that are similar to yours but that would not be competitors. You can use this information to develop a story for the VC about how the decision-making process they used for similar companies would apply to yours. Be careful to make sure that those investments are going well for the VC, though; you don't want to compare your company to a loser!

Getting to know you, VC-style

VCs are funny. If you were to ask VCs how easy it is to get in touch with them, almost inevitably, they'll answer that it's really easy. Ask any entrepreneur whether VCs are easy to get in touch with, and the most likely answer is a negative one. Why the discrepancy? There are probably a number of reasons, but we're guessing it comes down to four basic things:

✔ VCs know a bunch of VCs, so of course they can talk to VCs easily!

✔ Entrepreneurs are intimidated by VCs and therefore don't try as hard as they could to get attention.

✔ Entrepreneurs spam every VC in the country with their pitch deck with a "to whom it may concern" cover letter without bothering to be selective in contacting the right companies.

✔ Miscommunication occurs between VCs and entrepreneurs when the entrepreneur submits an application, the VC quietly rejects it, and the entrepreneur thinks his proposal hasn't been seen.

VCs must set up restrictions for the fund before they can do even a single investment. If your company falls outside those restrictions, the VC firm cannot work with you. Be sure you are contacting appropriate VC firms.

Getting in touch with the VC

You can start making contact after you and the rest of your management team have a few VC firms on your collective hit list. This process is a little like applying for a job: You can paper the world with resumes, but you're more likely to find a perfect fit if you're choosy. The following sections outline your options and offer pointers to getting through the door.

Following the VC's contact rules for application

Before blindly sending in your proposals, make sure you know how the VC firm you're contacting wants material submitted. These days sending in a 200-page business plan via U.S. Mail will likely get your application filed into the trashcan at many VC firms. Most VCs have some text at the bottom of their websites (or on their Contact Us pages) that says to send the deal in e-mail. Pay attention to any caveats: "Send only business plans," "Send only pitch decks," "Send only two pagers," "Be sure your current progress is evident," and so on.

Follow these instructions to the letter. If they say to use a specific subject in the e-mail Subject line, do it! If the instructions tell you not to e-mail the VC but to get an introduction through one of the firm's trusted service providers, do it. If they tell you to meet a man in an overcoat, on a sunny day, by the big rock, guess what? Do it. Okay, maybe not that last one, but you get the point: Follow the directions, or you'll probably be overlooked.

Cold calling after you submit your materials

The best cold call is the follow-up call. Send your application materials to the VC (be sure to follow all the directions) and then call to tell the VC that you've submitted materials. Doing so may seem a little silly, but it's actually very nice to be on the receiving end of that phone call.

By calling, you're letting the admin at the VC office hear your pleasant voice, which will remind him that you're a real person, not just another voiceless business plan. Also, you've saved him the bother of explaining the application process because you've already applied. If you don't get a human on the phone, leave a message saying that you submitted your application. Give your name, company name, and the date you submitted. Then wish the VC a happy day and be done with it.

When you call a VC's office, you will most likely be referred to an administrator or analyst to discuss your application. Depending on the size of the VC firm, you may not get to talk to the VC himself until you have been pre-screened by his team.

Securing a personal introduction if you can

Just as when applying for a job, the best way to get noticed is first to apply and then get a mutual connection to make an introduction. By submitting your application first and then having a friend call on your behalf, you increase the chances that VC will become interested in your deal through the introduction and be motivated to go read your materials.

Contacting angel investors can be a special challenge because they're more difficult to identify; these investors often prefer to be anonymous. For these investors, getting an introduction from someone you both know is key.

This is where networking proves most useful. All those events, meetings, and gatherings you've pursued produce connections galore — connections you can use to secure the introductions that'll move our deal out of the pile and into a VC's hands. For detailed information on how to network, head to Chapter 7.

Providing key information

Although each VC firm you plan to contact may have unique rules about what and how to submit materials, most request that you send one of the following:

- ✔ **The pitch deck:** Most firms request that you e-mail the pitch deck to them. Be sure that you have included all of the points about how you will make money, how much money you can make, and how far you've come.

    If you send a pitch deck, be sure you send the version that has words on it. The wordless pitch deck is powerful when you're presenting and nearly useless when you aren't. To find out more about creating a pitch deck, head to Chapters 14 and 15.

    An alternative that is not commonly requested by VCs but may become more common in the future is a video of you presenting the pitch deck. If you go this route, be sure the audio and video are high quality so that the video enhances and does not distract from your message.

- ✔ **Executive summary:** The executive summary is typically a one to two page document with a brief description of your company, product, market, team, and details of the deal (such as the amount you are raising, pre-money valuation, use of funds, and so on). Many VCs prefer the executive summary as a way to screen the deal because the high-level information tells them whether the deal is in their area, makes sense, and is worth giving a closer look.

- ✔ **Business plan:** Not too many investors require the 50-page business plan anymore. The VC will ask for various portions of your business plan as he goes through the due diligence process, but it's not necessary to send the whole thing as an introduction. Nevertheless, you still should create a business plan in whatever form you like (Chapter 6 has details). It's still useful as a living internal document for you to use with your team. VCs probably would be happier to start with an executive summary or a business model canvas sketch.

Updating VCs on your company's progress

You may not hear anything after you send materials to a VC or angel investor. Months can go by without any word. The best way to handle this is to put each investor that you've approached in a newsletter mailing list. When you have extra special news about progress with your company, send out a short professional newsletter linking to press releases, blog posts, or news articles.

Use a service that allows the investors to unsubscribe if they so choose. VCs who unsubscribe are giving you the message that they are not interested. Everyone else is probably just watching you until your progress reaches a point they are comfortable with. Each VC has a level of risk that he wants in the companies he invests in.

Taking time to building relationships

Chances are no one will fall in love with your deal at first sight. That's why you want to make friends with investors. A VC investment lasts for many years, and investors want to make sure that they like you before investing. If you can get friendly with a VC, you've taken your fundraising potential a step farther. The goal is to stay in touch and show potential investors that you can be a great long-term investment. Here are a couple of suggestions; head to Chapter 7 for more detailed information and strategies on cultivating relationships:

- ✔ **Find opportunities to spend time in the same world with VCs.** Have a mutual friend introduce you, or simply bump into the investor at a networking event. Your goal is to get noticed as a person, not just as a pitch deck.

- ✔ **If you catch up with a VC in a social setting, talk about something other than your deal.** People pitch to VCs all day long. Instead, connect on a personal note about something other than work first. We can tell you from experience that listening to a pitch from someone we already know and like is nice, whereas, having to listen to an unsolicited pitch at a social function is a little off-putting.

Don't water the relationship during the initial phases only to let it wither on the vine later. Take steps to maintain regular contact with news and updates while avoiding so much contact that it seems like spam.

Mum's the Word: Pursuing Non-Disclosure Agreements

Most VCs won't even discuss signing a non-disclosure agreement early on in the conversation and companies that push this issue put themselves at a disadvantage by showing a lack of understanding of the investing environment and norms.

When you first talk with investors, determining what you should share and what you should keep secret can be hard. Let us make it easy: If it's secret, keep it secret. Generally, intellectual property protection covers some aspect of the technology. You really don't need to share the details until you are deeply into due diligence.

Similarly, avoid bumping up against secrets in conversation. You don't want to tease anyone with a sentence that ends abruptly in "Um, never mind, I can't tell you that." Find ways to gloss over the secrets or to describe your technology so simply and at a high level that the secret isn't touched upon.

Frankly, most secrets are pretty specific and rarely does the conversation turn that way. If an investor asks why your therapeutic works better than others, you don't have to tell him that it's because you are using the stereoisomer. You can simply say that you found an important change in the molecule that made all the difference.

Talk with your team about how you'll discuss the secret sauce without uncovering the secret. Generally, initial discussions with investors will revolve around the commercialization of the product and the business model. Investors will trust you that your technology can do what you say it does — at least at first. Your goal is to be able to share that you have secrets associated with a certain aspect of the technology and perhaps that you have them protected with a patent filing. Refer to Chapter 3 for more about patent protection.

Knowing when to ask for an NDA

Investors can't sign nondisclosure agreements (NDA) before they see your pitch or talk to you about your deal. The liability is too great for an investor to agree to nondisclosure until the VC and company enter into full due diligence. Here's why: An investor may see three or four companies with very similar technology or business plans. The companies often do not know that the others exist because all of them are still stealth (code for "haven't put up a website yet"). Later, one company may think that the investor shared its secrets with the second company, when in reality both companies came across the same idea independently. Signing NDAs puts VCs at risk for future lawsuits, so it is not something that they take lightly.

After the VC begins due diligence, an NDA may become part of the agreement. If the company has manufacturing or laboratory space, the investor may sign an NDA before doing a site visit.

Keeping your secret sauce a secret

Even with a signed NDA, you can — and should — keep some secrets under wraps. Consider which secrets are truly protected by patents (and therefore okay to share with investors) and which should simply remain trade secrets until the VC has invested. Talk to your patent attorney to determine which is which.

Part II
Becoming Attractive to Venture Capitalists

Five Vital Relationships to Develop Early On

Venture capital may be about cutting-edge technologies and complicated finance agreements, but it's hinged on real relationships. Until you form true relationships with the other business people in your community, you will be limited in what you can accomplish.

- ✔ **Advisors and service providers:** Advisors are high-caliber mentors who volunteer or are paid a small amount to help your company. Service providers are accountants, attorneys, and bankers. Both can help you connect with venture capitalists.

- ✔ **Strategic partners:** Partners can be your distributors, local government officials, manufacturers, or others that help you grow your company while preserving your resources.

- ✔ **Customers:** It's never too early to talk to your customers. Include early adopters' opinions in the design of your final product.

- ✔ **VCs:** You can talk with a VC even if you aren't raising money yet. Try to get a warm introduction at a party or networking event. Make friends early, and when you do need capital, you'll find the VC much easier to talk to.

- ✔ **Acquirers:** These are companies that could purchase your company in the future. If you have talked with them about their strategic goals, then you will be able to keep those goals in mind as you grow you company. Aligning goals is easier when you know about them early on.

Find out how to allay fears that VCs may have when key business partners are also family at www.dummies.com/extras/businessanalysis.

In this part...

- ✔ Complete the necessary ground work to ensure that your company is ready for venture capital before you approach venture firms.

- ✔ Position your company for venture capital by finding the right balance between developing your product and developing your company, creating a business plan and marketing strategy, and predicting future revenue growth.

- ✔ Add high-value team members (paid or unpaid) to your company and develop relationships with others outside your company to ensure you have the customer base and knowledge base that VCs look for.

- ✔ Begin to think about exit strategies — how you will ultimately sell your company: going public, acquisition, or some other means — which is how you are going to get rich from all the hard work you've performed as you built your company.

Chapter 6

Positioning Your Company for Funding

*I*nvestors are a special kind of customer. They are not buying your product. What investors are really shopping for are great investment opportunities. This distinction is lost for many entrepreneurs who fail to attract investor attention by spending their time pitching the wrong thing. When your company has the right team, has a compelling business model, is making good progress, and has all the other characteristics that venture capitalists look for, they'll be more likely to invest.

Because a company is much more complicated than a single product, selling your company to investors is going to be more complicated than selling your product to customers. In addition, no company is perfect. Flaws and undeveloped aspects are commonplace in early-stage companies. The key is that you have a well-conceived plan about what exactly you hope to accomplish in the next few years and how you are going to accomplish those goals.

In this chapter, we explain how to plan and structure your business model, product, and promotion strategy. Some preparation is imperative and some is optional. You'll be more comfortable approaching investors when you know you've done your homework.

Viewing Your Company as a Whole Package

Venture capitalists are oddball customers that buy equity in your company instead of products. Just like a consumer making a large purchase, a VC is going to shop around, research the purchase, and kick the tires quite a bit before signing the contract. VCs are doing a lot of comparison shopping. They see a lot of companies and have many choices to consider when investing.

To attract and keep the attention of VCs, you need to understand what you're selling. In the VC's eyes, you're selling much more than your product. Just as you wouldn't focus solely on your state-of-the-art engine if you were selling a car (you'd also show off the comfortable seats, intelligent dashboard controls, and the showy paint job), you need to present your company as a whole package when you're "selling" it to VCs.

VCs are going to buy equity in your company not simply because you have a superior product but because they think that the whole company package is worth their time, and the company is poised to make a lot of money in the future. So show off your whiz-bang product, but don't forget to put the spotlight on the other things that investors care about, too. The more you are able to see the world through their eyes, the more you will understand what they care about.

Avoiding product development tunnel-vision

Early-stage companies are quite naturally focused on research and development (R&D). During the research and product development stage, you can easily succumb to tunnel-vision and forget about company development. Product development is necessary, but so is business development, promotional development, customer research, and financial planning.

Occasionally, the whole company will need to go "heads down" and work solely on product development. If your product is software, for example, all members of your company may engage in a 30-day stint of hardcore software developing, coding, testing, and debugging. If your product is something more tangible, you may be highly involved in formula or materials testing, prototyping, or building. It's normal for companies to work 100 percent on product development for very short periods of time.

The danger is endlessly focusing all of your time and resources on product development at the expense of other important areas. To avoid getting sucked into the product development vortex, plan for these strategic periods of product development and intersperse them with customer field research, marketing, and other business development activities. Don't lose sight of why you went into business in the first place.

Intersecting product development and business development

Your company needs to do a lot of business development while you are in the midst of the product development stage. Many of your business development activities will be focused on learning how to create and sell the best product to your customers.

Often, you will find yourself handling major tasks, like product development and business development, in your business simultaneously. This is totally normal in a start-up. For example, suppose you own a business called Live Again, which helps people manage their finances after a serious accident or illness. Your company plans to use insurance companies to distribute its software product and needs to create a relationship with its distribution partners early, before the product is completely developed so that it can be sure that the product will suit the needs of the insurance company's customers. In this case, a business development activity (finding distribution channels) intersects with a product development activity (product design).

If the insurance company insists that Live Again's product must be compatible with the insurance company database management software, you'd be happy to add that feature to your product development plans. If you had finished the product before trying to partner with the insurance company, you would have had to add a major feature to the already developed product, a change that may have been too expensive to implement at that time, costing your company an opportunity to reach thousands of customers.

Knowing when your company is fleshed out enough for investors

When you are raising money from investors, you have to plan your major activities three years in advance. This is important because you have to communicate your plans to investors. Although investors are often smart people, they can't read your mind. You have to spell out your thoughts. Looking at the big three-year plan and visualizing all the development that needs to take place over that time can be overwhelming. Time passes quickly, and if you have a good plan in place, you'll be ready to seek capital quickly.

When your company is in early, developing stages, you need to find a balance between the things you must complete before talking to investors and the things that you can save until later.

Using risk profiles to measure company stage

In the course of its growth, your company will hurdle some major milestones, like launching a beta website and securing your first paying customers. By achieving these milestones, you change the company's risk profile and value. The more you can reduce risk by making these accomplishments early on, the more value you add to your company, and the more attractive you become to investors. How many and what kinds of milestones need to be overcome before you become attractive to investors is unique for every situation. Your main goal is to demonstrate sufficient traction and execution ability to compete with other companies for venture capital investment.

Therefore, when determining whether your company is mature enough to approach VCs, you need to think about those milestones. Risk profiles are different for each company. To determine your risk profile, look in Chapter 10, which is devoted entirely to risk.

For the most part, investors — whether angel investors or VCs — are fair and understand risk. Generally, they'll be comfortable with a certain level of risk, but the risk level changes the conditions under which they'll consider investing in your company. Many VCs won't even look at your deal until you have a revenue run rate of $1 million per year or more. At this point, their risk is reduced because the company has demonstrated its ability to produce and sell its product or service. Seed stage investors will take on more early-stage risk, and their business model takes this additional risk into account. By overcoming risk milestones, you are increasing the value of your company and the number of investors who may be interested in your deal. The trick is to approach potential investors when your company is in the investors' favored risk zone.

Matching investor type with company maturity

Who you talk to during fundraising depends on the development stage your company is in, because different types of investors invest during different stages. Venture capital investing is highly specialized, so some firms specialize in seed stage investing ($500,000 to $1,500,000), and others only look at later stage deals at $5,000,000 or more. Furthermore, many VCs specialize by industry. You don't want to talk to a VC in the healthcare space about a new solar technology. For that reason, knowing who to talk to can save you a lot of time and increase your confidence that you're focusing on the right fundraising strategy.

A typical progression of funding rounds begins with bootstrapping rather than seeking outside funding and ends with multiple VC rounds. Here's an outline of what you might expect at each stage:

- ✔ **Stage 1: Bootstrapped company:** This is the pre-investment stage. Entrepreneur(s) work to develop a concept and may provide funding out of their own savings.

- ✔ **Stage 2: Friends and family round:** First fundraising comes from people the entrepreneur knows because it's too risky for professional investors. Entrepreneur needs to raise enough money to get to an angel/seed round.

- ✔ **Stage 3: Angel capital/seed round:** In this stage, you're building traction. The company has proven itself with early development and needs to raise enough money to attract institutional VC investors in 12 to 18 months.

- ✔ **Stage 4: Venture capital A round**: Early-stage companies are raising money to possibly finish last touches of technology or product development and go-to-market strategy to prove market acceptance.

- ✔ **Stage 5: Venture capital B round and beyond:** The venture-backed company will look to its Series A funders for B and C rounds. These rounds typically focus on capturing more market share and preparing for exit.

After a Series B round, a company may continue to raise money in additional rounds labeled C, D, E, and so forth. However, companies commonly experience a merger or acquisition before they get too deep into the alphabet. If you know that your strategy will require multiple rounds, it's a good idea to target venture capital firms that can grow with you rather than a seed stage fund that can only provide a few million dollars for early stages.

A'round and B'round we go

Here's a little note about recent history: VCs used to invest in concept-stage and pre-revenue stage companies, companies that had no revenue or product. Investing that early is no longer common because venture funds have grown larger and larger. Also, because putting together a $1 million investment takes as much work as putting together a $10 million investment, it makes more sense for VCs to move on to bigger deals. There are so many high-quality later-stage companies in the market that VCs no longer need to take the risk on seed stage investments, and this gap is being filled by angel investing groups.

Overcoming company weaknesses

No company is perfect. If you wait to talk to investors until your company is completely polished in all aspects, you could miss the optimum fundraising window. Investors *want* a little bit of risk still left in the company because it enables them to buy a good chunk of equity while the company is relatively cheap and can grow fast.

That's where thinking strategically about risks comes in. Plan your company's development around the risks that you'll leave unsolved and the risks that you choose to overcome early in development. Some planning choices are easy because they follow a reasonable progression; you can't submit a patent until you've designed the product, for example. Other planning decisions have to be made when you have less obvious path.

Answer the following questions to get yourself thinking about the company attributes that you need to address early:

- ✔ **Product development:** If your product has a long development time, can you sell a component of the larger product as a smaller product now?

- ✔ **Marketing:** Will customers actually pay for your product? Are you sure your customers have money available to buy your product? If so, how badly do they need it?

- ✔ **Sales:** What are your sales channels? Do you know the best way to reach your customer?

- ✔ **Team:** Do you have all the people that you need to grow this company greatly in the next 18 months? If not, is this opportunity compelling enough for you to recruit the right individuals?

Notice that this list doesn't include the question, "Is my whiz-bang product ready to go?" Why? Because a finished product is not necessarily the biggest goal for your company. Your company first needs to be sure that a customer exists for the product. Until someone is interested in buying your product and/or actually pays money for your product, you can't be sure that your company has a product worth creating.

Looking at Business Plan Basics

A business plan is a document that describes the details of any business. This document includes plans for the business over the course of many years. Generally, the document can be 10 pages or 50 pages or more and includes product plans, revenue plans, income and spending pro formas, team needs over time, marketing plans, promotional plans, and strategic relationship details. There is no standard length to the plan because every company is different. We have seen good plans that are just a few pages long and others that required one hundred or more pages. Regardless of the length, you should address all the items listed previously within your plan.

As a living document that you update regularly, the business plan will change greatly from one version to the next. Because nothing in the business plan is set in stone (unforeseen issues will undoubtedly prevent some plans from coming to fruition), it's a great tool to help the company plan many years in advance. The next sections give you the details.

Some people claim that, because things change so quickly in a venture company, there's no need to have a plan. We couldn't disagree more. There's an old saying that "a failure to plan is planning to fail."

Knowing who the business plan is for

The business plan used to be the way companies communicated with potential investors. A company would submit a full business plan to investors for review. The investors would then choose which companies to interview, based on the information in the many business plans that they were reading. With time, customs change. Now, *pitch decks,* or presentations typically in PowerPoint or PDF format (head to Chapter 15 for details), are used instead of business plans for communicating with investors, and business plans have a different purpose.

Business plans are now internal documents. They're roadmaps for company management to follow or change as new information becomes available. When things are changing rapidly, your plan is what keeps everyone pointed in the same direction. When the time comes to pivot, the plan ensures that everyone is on the same page and knows what you're pivoting from and where you are now heading.

Creating the plan: A primer

Many of the details in the business plan will be the result of *thought experiments,* the process of imagining a future scenario and playing it out (on paper) to its logical end. For example, you may think through what your company would look like if it sold directly to customers over the Internet, or if it entered into a distribution partnership. Each strategy poses unique challenges and costs, and a thought experiment lets you flesh these out in order to understand the best outcome for the company. The result of this analysis is what ends up in your plan. The exercise of thinking out (and writing out) all the details is invaluable.

 Some people are starting to use software technology to create dynamic and visual business plans. Instead of a static paper document consisting of white pages, words, and a few graphs and charts, new business plans are more like web pages where a front page links to multiple pages, each of which dives deeper into each main aspect of the business. No matter the format that you choose for your business plan, make sure that everyone on the team and the board has access to the most updated version of the plan for reference and updates.

Including vital components in your plan

When you create (or update) your business plan, you need to plan three to five moves ahead, just as you would in a chess game. Investors want to see that you have anticipated future challenges and that you are preparing for them. Companies that don't think things through often run out of cash or reach insurmountable roadblocks that could have been avoided. Following are the most important areas to focus on.

Key future hires

You can think about hiring key employees years before you actually need them. Thinking about human resources in advance is an important piece of planning. True, in your first year as a business, when you're likely focusing primarily on building and testing your product, you probably don't want to spend valuable money on a sales manager, for example, who would be expensive and not particularly useful when the product is not yet available for sale. Still, you can begin to discuss the qualities you may want in a sales manager, and you can begin looking for the right person.

When you develop your pro forma, you may develop key ratios, such as adding a sales person for every $1 million in sales. You can do the same for other key positions as well. Here are a few of the key roles that you may consider filling in your first few years of operation (but don't think that everyone on the founding team needs to have a C-level job title – sometimes this just looks ridiculous!):

- ✔ **CEO (Chief Executive Officer):** Responsible for leading the company, creating a funding strategy, and working with the board. Companies with a technical founder should be aware of their need for a CEO to replace the founder.

- ✔ **COO (Chief Operations Officer):** Responsible for overseeing the day-to-day operations of the company. This position can vary widely depending on what the company does. It could focus on manufacturing, quality management, measuring performance, or leading a technical team of software developers.

- ✔ **CFO (Chief Financial Officer):** The CFO is one of the last positions to come on board primarily because non-revenue companies that have never raised money don't need them. A company with minimal financial complexity should consider working with *fractional CFOs*, who may work for as many as five or six different companies. They provide high-level thinking and strategy while a bookkeeping service can handle the day to day accounting.

- ✔ **CTO (Chief Technical Officer):** The CTO is the position often given to the technical founder when a full-time CEO comes on board. This person drives the technical direction of the company and leads the engineers and/or designers in their process.

- ✔ **CMO (Chief Marketing Officer):** The CMO is a key position to develop the company's brand, messaging, and product development. Many tech-based companies need the CMO to force them to get out and talk to customers to find out what they need versus what the engineers want to develop.

If you bump into someone who has the right background, start developing the relationship now, even though you may not actually be able to fill the position for several months. If you can get a commitment from a great candidate based on your ability to raise your funding round, you can then include the new hire in some of your discussions with investors. After all, it's great to be able to say, "We have the following people on-deck, ready to join once you invest." If the VC knows the people and respects them, then that can help close your deal.

Identifying exit possibilities

Exit opportunities may occur through serendipity, but the smart route is to plan your exit from the earliest stages of your business. Your exit partner is your real "customer," and substantial thought should go into what your potential acquirers may be looking for a few years down the road. Your company will be designed to be attractive to several larger firms in your industry or parallel industries that want to break into your area. At specific times in any company development, selling the company is easier than other times. Identify and plan your company strategy around these potential exit points.

Your company will be attractive to acquirers when you have just completed major accomplishments. Companies are less attractive when they are undergoing major changes, such as hiring a lot of people, pushing out a new product or product line, or breaking into a new part of the country. However, as soon as a company succeeds in one of these major breakthrough changes, they could be attractive to an acquirer again.

The living document: Diverting from the plan

Early companies develop very quickly. With development comes the realization that some past choices were good and some were unsuccessful. To ensure that you capture key information in your business plan, plan on updating it at these times:

- ✔ **With every major decision that creates change in the business:** As you make changes to your business, play them out in the business plan.

- ✔ **At regular intervals:** Schedule times throughout the year when you sit down with management and determine whether you need to change the business plan. Regularly scheduled updates to the business plan allow a company to identify whether it's on- or off-track and whether the track itself needs to be re-envisioned.

A business plan is not meant to keep the business from changing direction. It's meant to remind you about the brilliant thoughts and intentions that you had in the past while you were highly focused on strategy from the last planning session. Strategy without execution is useless, and using the plan to drive your execution is a great way to get things done. Bottom line: You can always divert from the plan.

Highlighting Your Product as a Company Keystone

"Building a better mousetrap" is a popular idiom that refers to coming up with a product that is an improvement on all other currently available technology. Many venture companies have *better mousetrap* products and succeed in part because of their products. Therefore, as you position your company to attract the attention of venture capitalists, you want to highlight your product while at the same time remembering that the product cannot stand alone and support the company. Even as you make your product shine, you need to keep the focus on the company. The following sections have the details.

Thinking strategically about your product

Investors like to see a strategy that results in the biggest and fastest growth. To achieve rapid growth, you may have to be creative in how you work with your product. You may choose to manufacture and sell your product directly, but you may not. Following are some strategies that companies use; some larger companies use more than one of these strategies at the same time:

- ✔ **Business to customer (B2C):** The company sells its unique service or product directly to the end user who is an individual. Ben & Jerry's Ice cream makes a product with unique qualities — a more flavorful ice cream — and sells it directly to customers through its flagship store and other stores all over the world.

  In many cases, building up a company around a product doesn't make sense. The cost to set up manufacturing and distribution systems in addition to all the other overhead may make your product less competitive in the market. Also, a company with just one product may have limited growth potential unless the market for the product is huge. Before you go this route, make sure that you have a plan for a pipeline of products or that your product is uniquely positioned to be highly desirable for acquisition by a competitor.

- ✔ **Business to business (B2B):** The company sells its product or service to other businesses for use in business. SalesForce and Aloha are both software systems designed to enable businesses to manage large teams of customer-facing employees and to compete and track sales transactions.

- ✔ **Reseller:** These companies purchase products from other companies that they may modify (or not) and then repackage and sell to customers or other businesses. Republic Wireless is a cell phone company that resells minutes on the Sprint telephone system, for example. It profits by modifying its phones to use wi-fi when possible to make calls, thereby using less of Sprint's airtime.

- ✔ **Platform:** The business may have technology or a system that allows it to make or modify a variety of products. Google and Apple can be considered platform companies because they sell many products that relate to a common technology. Some companies begin as single-product companies and develop into platform companies.

- ✔ **Brand:** The company doesn't have a unique product but instead adds branding to basic products and then sells them at a premium. Ed Hardy, for example, places 1920s stylized tattoo designs on ordinary products to create branded clothing, perfume, and kitchenware.

Developing your product

Product development is the process by which your product goes from an idea to a product that customers can purchase. Product development includes obvious aspects, such as designing, including the behind-the-scenes thought that goes into an ingenious design; testing, which also involves customer testing to make sure that the product works as expected; prototyping; manufacturing; packaging; launching the product; and the development of the sales channels that will make the product a hit.

In the following sections, we look at a couple of key areas that you don't want to forget as you develop your product.

Vetting your product

Inventors are experts of idea creation. A single inventor can churn out a new product every year, and even more if he or she gets outside funding. Many inventors are great at designing the product to serve a unique purpose, and to that end, they perform product testing to ensure that what they've created truly solves the problem that they set out to solve.

It's important for inventors to undergo a reality check before setting out on the next invention.

- What problem does it solve?
- How many people or businesses will buy this invention?
- Does the customer actually have money available to buy the product?
- Is the customer bothered enough to change her habits and start buying a new product?

Many inventors never go through this reality check and wonder why their products languish on shelves. It's not enough to design, create, manufacture, patent, and label a product. Truly successful product development includes a great deal of analysis on the potential customer.

An example of an uninspiring customer might be an underprivileged teen in the inner city. Yes, that individual has a great deal of problems in her life, and many may be solved with new inventions or products, but she doesn't have the available cash to purchase the product. Another bad customer is a medical office. Sure, it may have a large budget, but doctors are notoriously difficult to sell to. They tend to adhere to their habits and are unwilling to change their behaviors quickly.

Getting customer input during product development

Investors want to understand how strong the need is for the new product, and one of the questions they'll ask is how big is the pain that your product will relieve. How big is the problem you are trying to solve? Investors are most interested in products that can demonstrate that they save customers so much pain, money, or time that buying the product is a no-brainer.

In other words, you must be able to demonstrate that your product solves a problem in a way that people want. That's where customer input comes in. During product development, you want to elicit customer input. Your customers can tell you things like the current solution is too expensive or too time consuming. They can let you know when an otherwise little detail (color, flavor, sound) is unacceptable.

Connecting with your customers throughout the product development cycle saves you time and money in the long run. You may think your customers are clueless, but if you aren't talking to them upfront (and listening), you aren't going to sell to them at the end.

The founders of Field Square initially thought that their customers needed an app to record patient data during medical house calls made by nurses. After six months of talking to nurses, plumbers, used car salesman, and others, they realized that the value of their product was actually in documenting the miles driven and hour-by-hour whereabouts of a company's field workers. They were able to build out the mobile positioning features of their iPad App product while still in development and therefore create appeal to a much larger customer base.

Your product will change between its initial prototype and when it's first sold. Your product may change again in the first and second years of sales. Little changes in product design are much easier than big changes, which can set your product development phase back significantly. By being open to changes along the way, you can make changes to your product as you learn more about what the customer wants. Although large changes are inevitable in some companies, keeping an open mind and ear about what your customer wants reduces the likelihood that you'll be saddled with large changes.

Generating excitement via prototypes and beta versions

Many entrepreneurs feel like they cannot move forward with fundraising or developing the company until they have a finished product. But you can approach investors before you have a finished product. Moreover you absolutely *should be* selling to your customers before you have a finished product.

How can you sell to customers before you have anything to sell them? Sell them on the idea. Get customers to sign up for product updates on your website. Your goal is to get a few thousand people connected with you ahead of your product launch because purchases on your opening day will look a lot better if 2,000 people are already excited about it.

Comparing companies

Company A has 2,000 customers on its mailing list, and 300 of them regularly comment in blog posts and participate in forum posts on the company website. Company A has a patented technology and a tested prototype, but the product won't be available for six months. Customers are competing on the website for a chance to test the first functional prototype.

Company B has a patented technology, too. It has already tested its prototype and is also six months away from a product launch. Company B's website gets about 500 hits per month. The company doesn't have an online forum or any way for future customers to make contact, except through a *Contact Us* form.

Which company do you think is more exciting to investors?

If you guessed Company A, you're right. It will be more interesting to investors because it's created a great deal of customer excitement around the new product. Everything else being equal, Company A can be sure that it has access to customers' thoughts and feelings on the product. By connecting with the customer early in the product development phase, Company A will great feedback on product features and will also raise awareness about the company and the product.

If you have a product worth buying, it's worth buying for a reason. Find your customers and sell them on the idea. If you have something as mundane as a new cog for a furnace, you can sell furnace manufacturers on the new lower cost cog. ("Coming soon, save on furnace cogs!") Let your customer know about this great opportunity to save on cogs. (Only six more months until savings!")

The level of product development needed to excite investors will be proportional to both the complexity of the product technology and the number of customers that you have hooked on your idea already. The product alone doesn't thrill investors. The fact that you've got potential customers discussing your future product in an online forum does.

Creating a product platform

One other strategy is to grow your product into a platform. As a platform, your product may spawn many similar products or variations on a product. Platform companies have many products that are all based on a similar technology or process. These kinds of companies are attractive to investors because they can change as trends and market demands change. In addition, because they are not tied to a single product, platform companies are less likely to be hurt by a competitor.

We recently worked with a company that had repurposed a human drug for use in dogs. This product alone made the company interesting, but even more interesting was the potential to turn this product into a platform for repurposing many human drugs for the pet market. After the company announced this new strategy, investors jumped on board, even though they had been ambivalent with the earlier single-product strategy.

Paying Attention to Your Promotion Strategy

Promotion strategy is a catchall term describing how you get the word out about your company and your products. Promotion includes the following:

- Who you will sell to
- What your competitive advantages are
- How your product is priced relative to the competition
- What connections you have in the industry
- How you can scale up quickly without overspending on marketing

 If you think you have a great product that will practically sell itself, beware. This attitude is a red flag to VCs, who know how tough it is to break into markets and compete among all the noise of competitors and substitute products. Equally scary to a VC is working with a company that underspends on marketing because it's satisfied to move along with a gradual growth rate. Don't be mislead: A larger marketing budget isn't always better. Be smart about marketing, and treat it like you would any other necessary part of the business.

 If your strategy is totally product focused rather than promotion focused, keep in mind that some venture capital deals are closed not because of some great new product or idea, but because of new promotion strategies. Think of companies like Groupon or Priceline.com, whose entire premise is based on revolutionizing promotion. Even if you are breaking into a mature market with a new product, you need to have a killer promotional strategy to win venture capital investment.

 We watched one company in action recently. This company developed a creative marketing strategy around being invited to pitch at a trade show. It was a financial technology trade show where the culture is rather subdued and primarily male. To stand out, the company made T-shirts with a clever and provocative slogan and paid a few marketing women to spend time around the bar in the convention center. The marketing team members were encouraged to strike up conversations about the company and make sure that everyone knew when the company was pitching on stage. More people attended that pitch than any other pitch at the trade show. No doubt that this company knows how to get attention.

Devising a Marketing Strategy

Although many people conflate marketing and sales, a VC is going to want to understand how your marketing strategy in distinct from your sales strategy. So what is the difference?

Marketing is huge. It's everything you do, everything you say, and everything you are as a company. Marketing is the way you answer the phone, the way you respond to e-mail inquiries, the colors on the walls of your office, and the feeling people get when they work with you. Marketing is the experience customers have with buying, installing, and using your product or service.

Your sales strategy, in contrast, is focused on the customer. Who is your customer? How do you talk with them? What do they want, when do they want it?

Marketing 101: Understanding what goes into a marketing plan

The *five Ps* of marketing are *p*roduct, *p*romotion, *p*rice, *p*lace, and *p*eople. If your marketing plan depends on the product selling itself, you have touched on only 20 percent of the power of what a great marketing plan has to offer.

Picking a strategy

When devising your marketing strategy, think about how your product differs from the competition. You will likely be able to identify one thing that is most impressive about your offerings. Here are some ideas to get you started:

- **Product-based strategy:** Is your product truly a unique solution to an important problem? If so, you may be able to use a product-based strategy.

- **Price-based strategy:** Your product may be great, but can you produce it for less than the competition? If so, then you should have a price-based marketing strategy.

✓ **People-based strategy:** Is your brand all about friendly or knowledgeable sales staff? Then you should have a people-based strategy.

✓ **Place-based strategy:** Is your brand all about mobile or web-based sales? Then you should have a place-based strategy.

✓ **Promotion-based strategy:** Is your brand all about pushing ads out to users based on known psychographics or big data mining that reveals their buying habits? If so, you should have a promotion-based strategy.

Ultimately, you want your marketing strategy to combine elements of all five of the five Ps of marketing. Use your strategy focus as a theme that you keep in mind as you flesh out the five Ps.

Telling a compelling story

Venture-backed companies depend on incredible marketing plans to allow them to scale rapidly in order to sell at the multiples that venture capitalists and their limited partners (LPs) require. To gain investor interest, you should be prepared to tell a compelling story about your brand and how you intend to leverage that through various channels. If you can't prove that you will scale at huge multiples every year, then venture capital may not be for you.

So how do you tell a compelling marketing story? There are only five ways to increase profit; your story should focus on these:

✓ Story 1 – The number of leads that you can generate

✓ Story 2 – The number of these leads you can convert to customers

✓ Story 3 – The number of transactions you can generate

✓ Story 4 – The $ value per transaction

✓ Story 5 – Your total profit margin per sale

A debate is raging in the venture capital world about the value of numbers 4 and 5. The strategy some companies use is to get as many "customers" as possible, even if the customers do not generate even a dollar of direct revenue. These customers may have strategic value to an acquiring company or value as "eyeballs" on display ads. Although companies have been successful in generating millions of non-paying customers followed by astronomical exits, most companies need to focus on generating more immediate revenue. One way to do that quickly and cost effectively is to develop effective distribution channels for your product.

Including strategic partners in your distribution channels

If your company is a typical start-up or early-stage company, then you're big on ideas and short on resources. You need to leverage your marketing strategy by including strategic partners as a part of your distribution channel. If your sales strategy includes having you and your two sales staff knocking on doors, then your ability to scale up is limited. But if you can enlist others as a part of your distribution channel, you can grow more quickly by leveraging the pre-existing infrastructure and client relationships that distributors already have in place.

When you think of your distribution channels, you need not be limited to traditional retail or B2B channels. Creative venture companies are always finding new ways to reach their customers. Here are a few to think about:

- **Affiliate marketing:** In this approach, you create a network of affiliates who make the sale for you while taking a cut of typically 10 to 20 percent on each sale. Thousands of bloggers and other content-laden websites that draw traffic are able to convert their visitors to customers, thus monetizing their sites while increasing your sales and profits.

- **GPS-based marketing:** In this approach, you reach customers based on their location. Imagine an app that causes your cell phone to vibrate whenever you pass a sushi restaurant or bookstore. This type of thinking turns traditional distribution channel thinking on its head by creating customers in non-traditional ways. Peter remembers visiting Italy and Greece many years ago where hawkers in the streets would grab passers-by and tell them about how wonderful the restaurant was "right around the corner." These individuals made their money by driving customers to the restaurants. Now GPS-based technologies can do this on a greater scale and with greater efficiency.

Think about how you can use technology and the existing relationships that other businesses have in order to leverage your sales process. Your powerful distribution channel may outweigh your patent portfolio when it comes to the eventual valuation and exit strategy for your company.

Acquiring new customers

Your marketing strategy should have three main goals:

- Finding new customers
- Reducing the cost of acquiring new customers
- Increasing the lifetime value of a customer (keeping the customer happy)

Although some companies such as Instagram have been successful by focusing on acquiring new customers — even though each customer does not directly pay anything to use the service — most companies need to both acquire new customers and generate revenues from them, over a single transaction or a subscription model that lasts for years.

Although start-ups can use distribution channels to increase their sales at relatively low overhead costs, VCs are also attracted to companies that are on the leading edge of trends that can monetize increased sales quickly and be sold at high multiples to brick and mortar retailers who can leverage smart technologies to reduce their cost of acquiring customers and increase lifetime customer value. If you can demonstrate to a VC that you have a way to generate customers at a substantial discount to the lifetime value of a customer and that you can do so in large numbers, then you may have a venture-class company.

Generating customers for less

Creative venture companies are finding new ways to generate customers at lower and lower costs, even among incredibly competitive landscapes. Companies using social media have been very successful in reaching millions of people without spending anything on traditional advertising and marketing media. Venture capital investors are interested in companies that can routinely upset accepted costs of acquiring new customers through new media and other creative approaches that leverage millions of customers at relatively low costs.

One example of using social media to reach customers involves Nabisco. Nabisco's Twitter team was on-call during the 2013 Super Bowl, ready to respond to anything unusual that happened during this highly viewed event. When the power went out at the stadium, the Nabisco team tweeted, "Power out. No problem. You can still dunk in the dark." By leveraging the Twitter platform, Nabisco created a virtually no-cost ad that was, according to *Advertising Age* magazine, "Arguably the best ad of the game." The *Wall Street Journal* wrote an article entitled "How Oreo 'Culture-Jacked' the Super Bowl." This type of attention is impressive in a venue that typically demands $4 million for a 30-second ad.

Upselling to increase customers' lifetime value

Increasing the lifetime value of a customer can be an equally compelling strategy to draw VC investment. Upselling is a common strategy. While the classic phrase "you want fries with that?" is a simple way to increase revenues per sale, other companies have even more ingenious methods of increasing sales.

Amazon.com is well known for using business intelligence to anticipate customers' needs. (*Business intelligence* just means collecting and analyzing business data to make smarter business decisions.) Amazon increases its revenue per customer by offering free shipping for orders over $25. It also offers additional items that were purchased by people who bought what the customer is buying.

Predicting Future Revenue with a Pro Forma

The pro forma financial statements are your way of communicating your plan in financial terms. *Pro forma* is a Latin term meaning "for the sake of form." In the case of your pro forma financial statements, you are giving form to your ideas by providing detailed projections for your revenues and expenses, as well as your assets and liabilities. Think of the pro forma as the thing, rather than the product, that you're selling to the VC.

The VC uses the pro forma to answer questions she may have about how fast you can grow your business, how profitable you will be, and ultimately how big of an exit you can expect based on your projections. Because these are the things that the VC cares about, you need to spend a fair amount of effort to make the pro forma aggressive yet believable and informative, as you explain the "how" of your plans as well as their outcomes. In fact, the pro forma may be the first page your VC flips to in your pitch deck so she can see whether the rest of the plan is worth reading.

Some business owners drag their feet when creating a pro forma. Because the prediction isn't going to be exactly right, they aren't comfortable going forward. The pro forma is your crystal ball. It lets you take a stab at predicting the future. Even though you cannot be certain that the reality will follow your pro forma, a well-conceived pro forma provides a pretty good vision of what is to come. Most financial predictions include five years of future financials.

Gathering the right financial statements

You need three major financial statements to create for your pro formas:

- **Income statement:** Also called the *profit and loss statement* (P&L), the income statement shows your revenues and expenses and the resulting profit. You typically break out multiple types of revenue and different types of expenses so that the reader gets a good understanding of where the money is coming from and going to. The basic formula is

    revenue – expenses = profit (or loss)

- **Balance sheet:** The balance sheet shows your assets and liabilities and the owners' equity. Your assets may include real estate, inventory, office equipment, and so on. (Be sure to work with a CPA to determine the value of some of the trickier assets, such as the value of a patent.) The basic formula for the balance sheet is

    assets – liabilities = owners' equity

✔ **Statement of Cash Flows:** The statement of cash flows is like your income statement except that it shows how your cash position changes as your business grows. Although it seems reasonable that, if your sales are increasing, then your cash would also increase, the opposite is more often the case. Because you have to pay your suppliers, increase your inventory, and carry increased accounts receivable from your customers, you are likely to run into a cash flow crunch if you grow too quickly without sufficient capital resources. The statement of cash flows helps you demonstrate to the VC how you'll use her cash to increase your net profit.

Testing and updating your pro forma

Smart business owners are constantly trying new things and seeing what the results are. If you increase your advertising by 1 percent, for example, what is the effect on sales?

Venture companies are typically growing exponentially over a very short period of time, and the rules are constantly changing. The more you fine-tune your financials, the closer to reality your projections will be and the more control you will have over your business. Constantly testing and updating your pro forma is one way to keep control when it seems like you are running at maximum speed.

Ratios are a key to a well-designed pro forma. You should understand key ratios in your industry. For example, in the restaurant business, you should know that the food cost for a meal should be 30 percent of the retail price. You may also want to know that advertising typically accounts for 3 to 6 percent of gross revenues. As a company grows, however, the ratios change. Your costs will decrease as your volumes increases, for example, and you'll develop economies of scale in personnel, product cost, marketing, distribution, shipping, and other areas of your company. As a venture company, make sure your pro forma shows these changes.

You may have a genius idea that makes your business different from others in your industry. In this case, have solid justification for why your ratios are significantly different than the norm; otherwise, your projections will likely keep you from getting the venture capital funding you need.

Building a model to shape your business

An entrepreneur should create pro forma financial statements for two reasons. First, skilled entrepreneurs can create models for what their businesses will look like and can make decisions about their companies based on those models. For example, assume that you know what producing your product costs, but you don't know how much profit you'll make. By creating the pro forma income statement, you can test out the effects of different price levels and different sales volumes on your bottom line. If you know the cost of your product and the cost to acquire a customer, you can make a pretty good guess about what your total sales volume will be, based on your available marketing resources and the competitive state of your market, which will drive your pricing decisions.

Second, a pro forma financial statement lets you communicate your business plan in a concrete and detailed fashion to your investors. Investors like to see how detailed you are and what research you have put into your assumptions; they make judgments based on what your pro forma reveals, intentionally or not.

VCs have experience with hundreds of companies and can spot irregular assumptions in a split second. They know how much bringing a product to market costs, for example, and if you have substantially underestimated this cost, the VC sees this as a red flag showing your lack of experience.

If you don't have extensive experience in your market, consider hiring an accountant to review and validate your pro formas so that the version you present to the VC matches the VC's expectations.

Creating multiple pro formas for multiple outcomes

You may be throwing your hands up and saying, "There's no way I can predict the future!" Well, you're right. One way of solving this problem is to create multiple pro formas with multiple outcomes, each based on differing assumptions about your costs, resources, sales volumes, and more. (This is the beauty of creating models — you can model many different future worlds!)

One common approach is to create three scenarios: a "safe" scenario that is pretty sure to be reached, even if things don't go so well; a "likely" scenario, which is your primary projection, the one that you believe is likely, but not assured; and a "best case" scenario, in which everything goes right, sales take off, and costs are under control. These three scenarios cover the likely range of outcomes that you may expect. Plus the exercise of just thinking through what each scenario looks like in detail is highly useful. Here are two other important benefits of creating multiple pro formas:

✔ **You can begin to see which factors are in your control and which are not.** By understanding which variables cause your best case scenario to occur, you are in the best position to be successful. You can then present the most credible arguments to your VCs in support of your projections.

✔ **It prepares you for a variety of risks.** Because VCs are always thinking about risks, your ability to demonstrate how you would respond to a variety of negative situations shows that you have thought through the risks and made plans to address them. By creating multiple scenarios, you also can identify the actions common to all your successful scenarios and focus on those while avoiding the risky ones.

Validating your numbers

Anyone can create a great looking pro forma with huge sales growth and giant profits. VCs see these all the time, and yet they often don't invest in companies with these rosy projections. Why? Because they don't believe the numbers.

Validation is the process of demonstrating the rationale behind the numbers you have presented in your pro forma. You want to show the research that underlies your assumptions. Consider these examples:

✔ If you did market research using Search Engine Marketing, you may have collected data about the conversion rates that your advertising campaigns command. The conversion rates tell you how many people who visited your page "converted" to customers by buying your product. If you know that each click to get someone to your site costs $1.00 and that you have a 10 percent conversion rate, you know getting a new customer cost you $10.00. You can use this research to show that your marketing budget will drive your sales at a rate of $10 per sale.

✔ If you know that your customer service reps can handle 100 calls per day and that you have 1 call per 1,000 units sold, then you know that you need to hire new customer service reps for every 100,000 units you sell.

✔ If your cost of goods sold drops as your volume increases, then you may want to make a spreadsheet with all of the components that go into your product and show what the cost of the product is at various volumes. Then as your volumes increase, you can add a formula into your spreadsheet that inserts the lower cost of goods sold.

You can go to a lot of places to validate your numbers and assumptions, but your industry probably has various associations that collect data from companies like yours. You can use those numbers to validate your assumptions. Of course, because you're running a venture-class company and not just a lifestyle company, you may have a business model that breaks the mold and doesn't abide by industry standards. If so, that's great, but you need to do your own original research to validate your new model when industry data is no longer relevant.

Integrating all the data without going crazy

How do you integrate all this data without creating a master spreadsheet so big and complex that nobody could ever understand it? Validating your data means adding a lot of detail. But adding lots of detail creates complexity, which can make your spreadsheet unwieldy. Here's what we recommend: Make the main tab on the spreadsheet a high level summary that gathers data from the detail tabs related to staffing, cost of goods sold, marketing costs, and so on. Anyone looking at the main tab can see your projected income statement and can dive into the details if they have questions about your assumptions. In some cases, you can produce a document explaining the rationale behind the numbers and formulas on the spreadsheets, a strategy that's useful when you can't be present when the VC reviews your pro forma.

Identifying your variables and assumptions

Variables are one way that you can make your pro forma into a great analytical tool. By clearly identifying the major variables and assumptions on your spreadsheets, you can make changes to the assumptions and create what-if scenarios. Clearly identifying the variables also enables VCs to challenge your assumptions and enter their own variables. Most VCs have analysts on their teams who do this kind of work all day, and they'll rework your projections to fit their own models of what they think will really happen.

Chapter 7

Cultivating Relationships

∙ ∙

In This Chapter

▶ Leveraging your limited resources with strategic partnerships

▶ Timing your VC approach

▶ Attracting employees, consultants, and advisory boards

▶ Starting your exit strategy now

∙ ∙

*Y*our company is more than the employees and the management team. You are building a series of nested circles made of intellectual and social currency. In the innermost circle are the founders, the management team, and the employees — people who work on your company's mission every day and for whom the company is everything. Just outside the immediate company team circle is the support group of advisors and mentors — the consultants, investors, and strategic partners who make their living off your company's needs but who truly care about the company and want to see it and you do well. Your customers are in the third circle. Although they're often very removed from the operations and inner workings of your company, your company's relationship with them is the most important relationship it has. The customer base means everything in terms of traction, revenue, and future goals.

The relationships you develop within each circle have a direct impact on your success both as a company and in securing venture capital. Relationships open doors, create opportunities, and make your life easier in real ways. This chapter outlines the people in your company's world and explains how they can help your company connect with funding.

Setting the Company's Course: Founders and Those Who Make the Company

Within your company's inner circle are the founders, the management team, the advisors, and the mentors who make the daily decisions and move the business ahead.

When companies start they often have just one or two people involved. The shared interests, personalities, and goals of those people create the basis of a company culture. Every single person that is added to the company should add to and reinforce the desired culture. Even though your company may not seem like much in the beginning, deciding who you bring on board is of critical importance. In fact, it's one of the things that VCs look at very closely.

VCs will tell you that team is the most important factor that they consider in making investment decisions. The reason for this is that ideas are cheap and execution is dear. VCs invest in companies that can take an idea and grow it big. The team that can do this is a rare find.

Your company value increases every time you add a high worth member to the team. One way to grow your team wisely is by adding people recommended by your VC. VCs will identify whether you have any holes in your management team, and they can make introductions to great talent who can join your team. The experienced leaders in your community have many options available to them as far as employment or start-up projects go. Their choosing to join your team says a lot about you and the promise of your company to succeed.

Adding high-value members to your team

You are putting this team together to execute on a plan and grow your company. Create a team growth strategy that will allow your company to be successful. Although the biggest indication of a great team is the ability to execute, these factors are noticed as indicators of potential greatness:

- **Experience:** How many combined years of relevant experience in your specific niche does your company have?

- **Ability to work together:** Has this team been working together just recently, or have the members teamed up on other successful projects in the past? What are the dynamics among the team? Are roles well defined? How have disagreements been handled?

- **Education:** How many PhDs or MBAs do you have on the team?

- **VC experience:** Have team members worked in venture-backed companies in the past? Do they know how to work with a board? Do they understand how to work with a VC to everyone's benefit?

- **Financial success:** Have the principals had successful exits in the past? How big were the exits? Did investors do well? What role did the principals play in the exit?

- **Ability to scale:** Does your team know how to create, lead, and manage the hierarchy that comes with being big? (Novice entrepreneurs may incorrectly assume that running a company worth $1 billion is the same as running a small company — just bigger.)

✔ **Full team:** Does your team have any big holes? Do you have a chief financial officer (CFO), chief operations officer (COO), chief technical officer (CTO), chief marketing officer (CMO), and so on?

Although you don't need to have the full roster at this time, having identified candidates or having candidates ready to join once your funding comes in is helpful.

✔ **Passion, hunger, and enthusiasm:** How excited are the team members about the company? Have they committed all of their time to this company yet?

✔ **Honesty and integrity:** What will happen when the company runs into some inevitable challenges? Will team members work together with the VC promptly when challenges arise?

VCs want to know if they can trust the entrepreneurs. Trustworthiness goes beyond just trusting that the entrepreneur won't take off for Mexico with the VC's money; it's the foundation upon which a working relationship is based.

As you build your team, be sure to think about these things and search far and wide to find the best people. If your team is comprised of two programmers with a total of three years experience, and you describe yourself as a great team, VCs are going to assume you don't know what you are talking about.

Addressing founders' personal needs

As you add founding members and additional team members to your team, you'll struggle with compensation issues. All participants have their own thresholds for how long they can go without compensation. Some people simply can't work for start-ups if they have kids in college or other financial constraints, while others are more than happy to work for 100 percent equity. In most cases, you'll work out some sort of combination: a relatively low salary that helps pay a mortgage in the short term with stock or stock options that serves the person's long term interests.

Here are some things to think about regarding compensation for your early team:

✔ **When you pay your employees with stock, they are essentially becoming investors in your company.** You are beholden to them as stockholders, and you cannot rescind their ownership. To protect yourself, create a transparent vesting plan in which stock is not immediately given to employees but awarded later for those employees who stay with the company for longer periods of time. Typical vesting may be from one to three years, with vesting occurring gradually over a period of time.

Another issue for you to think about when you issue stock as compensation is how much stock should be used for employee incentives. The standard practice is to set about 20 percent of the stock aside for this purpose in an employee pool.

✓ **Discuss tax consequences with your tax advisor.** Giving stock requires that you put a value on the shares, and there will be tax consequences for the receipt of stock, even if it ultimately becomes worthless and even though it may have involved no cash compensation. You don't want to make this employee benefit backfire when the employee ends up having to pay thousands of dollars of taxes without having received the cash to pay for it.

✓ **Consider creating an "on deck" team of people who are ready to join you as soon as your funding comes in.** Doing so is a good way to get people involved while they continue to hold down a day job elsewhere that pays their bills until they're ready to fully commit.

You can start recruiting these people now, even though you don't have the funds to keep them on the payroll. If you have their firm commitment to join the company under certain circumstances, you can add them to your team slide in your pitch deck as if they were employees — be sure to disclose this to the VC, of course (head to Chapter 15 for information on creating your pitch deck). These pre-employees can also attend investor meetings and pitches with you to represent the company and answer any questions the investors may have.

Advisory boards

Early-stage companies don't have a lot of resources to add a full team of employees. At the same time, young companies are making dozens of critical decisions every day that will shape the future of the business. How can you take advantage of the substantial collective wisdom of a team when you can't afford more than a handful of employees? The answer is that you need an advisory board.

VCs like advisory boards. They look great on your team slide when you're making your VC pitch. Having a strong advisory board with recognizable names in your community tells the VC that others believe in you and that you have the wisdom to seek the advice of others, suggesting that you'll be more coachable in your relationship with the VC.

Distinguishing between advisory boards and boards of directors

An advisory board and a board of directors are two distinct entities. Here's what you need to know:

- **Board of directors:** Although your board of directors often plays an advisory role, board members have primary duties to the management of the company and are responsible for major decisions that are made. The boards for start-ups are typically small and include your CEO, your VC or representative from a group of angel investors, and one outside board member that the other members mutually agree upon. The board has a fiduciary responsibility to the company and is liable for many of the actions of the firm.

- **Advisory board:** The advisory board does not have official decision-making power for the company. Advisory board members provide advice and connections to the right people and can scout for new talent when the time comes to hire. They also can help provide strategic relationships with investors or large corporate clients. Piece together the right advisors to create a strong outer circle to surround your team with knowledge.

The advisory board should provide expertise in areas where you have skills gaps. Many early companies are strong in technical knowledge, for example, but weak in financial, legal, and marketing experience. Other types of needed advisory board expertise may include expertise in technical issues, connections, the industry, operations, international issues, manufacturing, supply chain, and more.

Compensating advisory board members

Compensation for advisory boards is highly variable. Many people are willing to provide a few hours once a month for a group strategy meeting for free as a way of giving back to the entrepreneurial community. They may be hoping for a fulltime position once the company gets its financing in place, or they may be fully employed elsewhere.

Others are paid a stipend commensurate with the amount of effort they put into the company. A typical amount is $1,000 a month, but it can be much higher or lower as the circumstances warrant. Some companies may pay their advisors with equity in the company — a great option for companies that need to conserve cash and for advisors whose interests are now even more tightly aligned with the company. Be sure to talk to your tax advisor, though, because the tax consequences can be substantial for both you and your advisors, depending on how you value the company and issue the stock.

A typical compensation package for industry advisors is between 0.1 to 0.25 percent equity share, all travel-related expenses, and a cash compensation of $80 to $100 per hour if the advisors do work beyond attending board meetings. If you have a great advisory board, you should find that this compensation is well worth their involvement.

Determining how frequently the advisory board should meet

The frequency and structure of meetings can vary depending on what issues the company is facing. Some advisory boards meet together once a month; other companies prefer to meet with their advisors one-on-one as needed to focus on an issue within a specific discipline. Good arguments can be made for either arrangement. Your company should work out what works best for you.

Sometimes an advisory board that meets together creates a synergy that you don't get in one-on-one meetings. Meeting together also lets board members interact and share their impressions, which may enable them to provide better or more impactful information. Having a united team deliver a strong or difficult message to the management team often has a greater impact than having the message come from an individual member or all the members individually.

Connecting with Outside Firms and People

Business is not just about your management team, board, and employees. You will hire work out to outside firms throughout the life of your business.

When you're building a venture company, which outside firms and specialists you hire is vitally important. You need people or firms who are not only experts in their fields but who have reputations that give your company clout just by mere association. Although going with the little guy is okay for many businesses, it's not okay for venture businesses. Your choice of professionals is yet another way of validating your company to a VC.

The caveat here is that VCs want to see that your company can run lean. If you can get a stellar job out of a highly affordable firm, thereby saving yourself thousands of dollars, by all means go with the affordable firm. Balance your association with fancy consultants with your need to preserve capital in your bank account.

Finding top-notch consultants

Your choice of consultants says a lot about your company and where you are hoping to go with it. There are small consulting groups and individuals who can do quality work for your company. Alternatively, large firms bring along a brand and clout because they don't accept just any client. If you work with these consultants, you'll pay the premium, and you'll get your money's worth.

When you choose consultants, look for specialists rather than generalists. You wouldn't want a general practitioner doing brain surgery any more than you would want a legal generalist doing your patent or securities work.

Key consultants are lawyers and CPAs (certified public accountants). A good CPA or lawyer can make warm introductions to venture capitalists when they see that the time is right. In this way alone, the top consultants are worth more than just their niche service. Here are some things to think about:

✔ Even though you may know a great small business attorney who charges reasonable rates, visiting a name-brand attorney in your market may make sense. Such a visit lets you understand the differences in what the two attorneys have to offer.

✔ Although a CPA at a small firm may be able to file your taxes for you and do an audit, if your goal is to grow big, you need a name brand CPA who can help you through the merger and acquisition (M&A) or initial public offering (IPO) process. Big VCs will also want audits done by reputable firms that they know.

Other consultants you may work with include marketing, human resources, branding, graphics, web development, recruiting, and more. Choose these professionals carefully because they all impact your brand as seen by customers, suppliers, the community, and your VC.

It may not be obvious at first, but your consulting firm can be a direct connection to a VC. Venture capitalists tend to have relationships with certain firms and will gladly talk to a founder when they've been introduced through their friendly law or accounting firm. If you are thinking about working with a firm, ask which VCs they have relationships with.

Locating reputable finders

Finders are fundraising consultants: They help companies find capital for a fee. Some finders are legitimate consultants, and some are shady characters.

Legitimate firms perform actual work: They help you create a pitch deck, business plan, and other backup materials that you'll need in your capital raising process. They may help you structure your investment deal and negotiate terms with investors. Good finders have relationships with VCs. They know what the VC wants because they've sat down together many times to talk about it. If the VC trusts the finder, he may pay the finder to perform due diligence on your company (a scenario limited to situations involving small VC firms or VCs who need to contract out due diligence in busy times). Reputable firms also have fixed rates or hourly fees. They should also have a good standing with the Better Business Bureau and a positive reputation in the community.

Can your other consultants act as finders? Sure. Your CPA, lawyer, and business banker can make introductions to investors for you. However, they should offer to do this for free as an added perk of working with them. After all, if you have working capital, you will be a better client!

Stay clear of finders who simply make phone calls to investors for you and who offer access to their well-crafted contact list but only after charging you a pretty penny — often a 1 to 10 percent cut of the investment raised. Heed these points:

✔ In recent years, the Securities and Exchange Commission (SEC) has pretty much closed up all the loopholes that allowed people to charge a fee in return for these finder services (that is, just making calls and charging for access to contacts). Even though the finder is the one breaking the law, you may find that your relationships with potential funding sources are ruined rather than enhanced by an introduction made by an unscrupulous source.

✔ If you take your capital search online, you'll be approached by many entities preying on companies looking for funding. In some cases, these services may be valuable, but in others, you may be asked to pay a retainer of thousands of dollars, or you may be charged exorbitant fees for a list of "investors."

The SEC requires that anyone who performs and charges for finder services be registered as a broker-dealer. Follow up with any consultants who seem to be performing finder activities to determine whether they are in-fact broker-dealers.

VCs make their money by actively soliciting deal flow. Although introductions can be helpful, most VCs are more than happy to look at your pitch deck and eventually meet with you if your company meets their profile. You shouldn't need to hire a finder to make those introductions.

Entering into strategic partnerships

Forming strategic partnerships is one of the best ways for a small company to do big things. Let's face it: You are under-resourced. You have a small team and little capital, and you've got to make that capital go far. By forming strategic partnerships, you can leverage your team and idea with much larger organizations.

What constitutes a strategic partnership? A broad range of partnerships exist, from informal arrangements to highly complex ones. In broad terms, strategic partnerships are divided into three categories.

- **Equity partnerships** exist when your company owns and/or is owned by another company in part to take advantage of the synergies of working together.

- **Non-equity partnerships** are simpler and far more common. In these partnerships, no formal exchange of ownership occurs, but other formal or informal agreements are made.

- **Joint ventures** are created when an independent third company is formed for competitive advantage.

Entering into equity or joint venture partnerships may create advantage, but it may also limit your options in several ways. VCs may be hesitant to invest in complex ownership situations where things could go wrong. Also be cognizant of the fact that a relationship with one company may close doors to having a relationship with another company. Competing companies generally don't work with the same partners. Be sure to work with your attorney through strategic partnerships of any kind.

In general, strategic partnerships should help you and another company do business more efficiently or less expensively. You can form as many partnerships as you need, with the understanding that, as you grow, you'll bring those services back in-house as you are able to afford them. Consider strategic partnerships for things like

- Manufacturing
- Design and development services
- Wholesale and distribution
- Retail distribution
- Sales affiliate relationships
- Work space (shared lab space or shared kitchen space, for example)
- Drop shipping and warehousing

You can share costs and increase efficiency by partnering with other groups — commercial partners, governmental agencies, non-government organizations (NGOs) — throughout the lifecycle of the product. Government agencies and NGOs can support the development of a product, where international partnerships can be useful for overseas manufacturing, sales, and distribution. Commercial partners can help every step of the way.

Genentech and the City of Hope

The story of Genentech demonstrates the value of strategic partnerships. When founders Robert Swanson and Herbert Boyer approached VC firm Kleinman, Perkins, Caufield & Byers for several million dollars in venture capital, they were soundly rejected. No one had ever heard of genetic engineering. And several million dollars was a big bet on an unproven area of science.

Thomas Perkins, a partner in the VC firm the entrepreneurs approached, recommended that the pair create a strategic partnership with a larger company, City of Hope National Medical Center, to do the early research needed to prove the company's concept. Swanson and Boyer raised just a few hundred thousand dollars and outsourced the development to the City of Hope labs, enabling them to achieve success with relatively little money. Now, of course, genetic engineering is a multibillion dollar industry.

The lessons learned from Genetech: Even though it may cost more on a unit basis to work through a partnership, the leverage you gain can mean the difference between being able to be in business or not.

Strong strategic partnerships validate your company in the eyes of the VC. When he sees that you have made a major distribution deal or that your product is being stocked on the shelves in Whole Foods, for example, he knows that you are able to think big and to execute on your goals. Your strategic partnerships add measurable value to your company and will enable you to raise money under more favorable terms.

Building Relationships with Customers

Every company has different types of customers. In some industries, you have personal relationships with your customers, and in others (like web-based companies where customers perform all transactions online), you may never meet or talk to your customers. Regardless of which type of customer your business is cultivating, you need to know who your customers are and why they are doing business with you.

You may be wondering why customer relationships matter at this point in the funding process. Perhaps you don't have any customers yet because you're still developing your product. Here's why your early customer relationships are of key importance:

- ✔ **A portion of any VC's due diligence on your company relates to your customers.** VCs are very interested in what the market thinks of your product and your company. Will it really save customers tons of money? Will it really allow customers to do business more effectively in some way? A good VC is going to do some research to make sure that you can gain the traction that you've claimed is possible.

- ✔ **Customers are critical in helping you ensure that you're not developing your product in a bubble.** Some entrepreneurs keep their heads down for months or years, just working on their product, with the expectation that they'll get customer feedback when they're done. This strategy is never a good one. Fast-moving companies need to get feedback early and often so that they can reduce the number of development iterations they need to a minimum, saving time and money and getting to a market leadership position more quickly.

Pre-selling your product

You can often get customers to pay for your product before it's even finished. Why are we talking about sales in a chapter on relationships? Because you need to make relationships with your customers even if you don't have product to sell them yet. One way to do this is to create a crowdfunding campaign on one of the major crowdfunding platforms. Another option is an extended product rollout, in which you sell a smaller product but enable customers to upgrade after you've completed the development for your product suite. Crowdfunding tends to make more sense for tangible products, and the extended product rollout makes more sense for software.

Crowdfunding

People will support young companies that are cool or have a product that seems very innovative. When using crowdfunding to gain popularity with customers, the first customers are called *backers*. They buy your product online, knowing full well that you haven't finished designing or manufacturing it yet. They know you won't be able to ship your product immediately, and they are willing to wait.

Backers are supportive and flexible only to a point. When you go beyond that point — by not staying in communication with them, for example — they'll begin to rebel in the comments they post on your website. One frustrated backer can start a firestorm of backlash and anger in the comments. This scenario isn't just annoying; it can be damaging to your reputation.

Assuming that you're able to stay on schedule and keep communication open with your backers, crowdfunding can be a huge boon to your company. If your product is low cost, you are effectively pre-selling the product and using the

funds to complete product development. And if you get a lot of backers —
enough to raise a hundred thousand dollars, for example — well, that's great
validation.

Extended product rollout

You can get customers to pay you for an unfinished product if you plan it
right. Plan an MVP (minimum viable product) development strategy where
your whole product is broken down into smaller products. Think of the
Microsoft Office Suite: The Suite itself is the whole product, and Word and
PowerPoint are the subproducts.

Break your product down into viable subproducts, and then choose one of
the subproducts to develop and finish first as your MVP. If you can attract
customers to adopt that product, you'll have revenues and a customer base
to work with for the additional products that you're developing. This strategy
lets you generate revenues more quickly than you would by waiting for the
whole product to be done before offering it to customers.

Turning customers into early investors

If you have large, early customers who'll be doing thousands or hundreds of
thousands of dollars of business with you, you can often find an opportunity
to turn these customers into investors. The trick is to demonstrate the value
that your product will provide to your customers and then to show how their
investment in your company will enable you to provide the solution that
much faster. If you can demonstrate that they will get a return on investment
within a year or less, this strategy may make sense.

If you go this route, the proposition — what the customer gets out of it — has
to be clear. For example, your customer gets a return on investment because
he'll save money by buying your product because it's better, cheaper, or
longer lasting than competitors' existing products. Alternatively, your product
may enable your customer to make more money through increased revenues
if he can sell faster. And don't forget: This deal comes with the added benefit
of the customer becoming an equity holder in your rapidly growing company.

 Working with businesses as your customer is a lot easier than working with
individuals. Businesses make purchasing decisions based on two things only:
saving money or making money. Individuals buy for all kinds of reasons that
are hard to predict.

Offering free trials and beta tests

Qik was a video-share company that had $150 million exit (purchased by
Skype) without a business model to speak of and small revenues if any.

Although these exits do happen, they are the exception rather than the rule. Most companies must have a demonstrated growing revenue stream, whether that revenue comes directly from the users of the product, advertising, or selling customer data.

Some argue that users are the next best thing to revenue. Getting people to use your product can certainly be a good first step in getting them to pay for it.

Beta testers

Having non-paying customers during your beta testing period is fine because these customers are essentially volunteer consultants helping your company by providing valuable product feedback.

One key piece of data that you will want to collect at the end of your beta period is the percentage of free customers who convert to paying customers after your product launches to the public. If you can show that a high percentage of your beta customers convert, then you are in a great position and are ready to start marketing to new customers. If you have a high attrition rate, however, then you probably have some more work to do before you go on to your full launch.

One of the best things about beta testers is that they are generally experts and very technical. They will push the limits of your product in ways that the general public may not do. They are unpaid troubleshooters who will give you a new view of your product after they spend some time with it. They may even suggest methods of fixing bugs.

Be careful about how many people have access to the beta version of your product. Limit it to an exclusive few, even if the "exclusive few" numbers into the hundreds. If you roll out a product to the public and call it a beta version, you've just undercut your own market.

Setting up free trials

Companies allow customers to use their product for a short time or to use a version that doesn't include all the features. This strategy makes sense for a few reasons: First, it allows you to collect e-mail addresses for the people who are interested in your product and industry, enabling you to build a targeted e-mail campaign for future advertising. Second, free trials allow you to determine who really needs your product versus who downloaded it just because it's a free trial. You can get this information by comparing the list of people who download versus the list of people who actually opened and are using the product a few days later.

Use free trials to calculate conversion rates, market interest peaks (do more people download the trial in September after school starts, for example) and other valuable data about your customers.

Using payment as proof, not just revenue

Revenue is always a good thing, but when you are in the process of seeking venture capital, getting paid for your product or service returns dividends far greater than the cash value of your revenues.

The revenue you earn from early customers serves as proof that real people are willing to pay real cash for your product. Especially in the early stages, the value of this validation is huge. By giving you money, people are saying that you are providing value and that they're willing to risk being a customer of a start-up that's not yet recognized in the industry.

As you develop your revenue stream, do these two things:

- ✔ **Use metrics to show what percentage of customers you approach are buying your product.** Demonstrate conversion rates so that a VC can understand how easy or hard your product will be to sell as you scale up.

- ✔ **Always increase momentum.** Nothing smells like death more than a company that builds up to a few thousand dollars a month in revenue and then plateaus. The VC will wonder whether this revenue stream is as good as it gets.

Creating Relationships with VCs through Networking

Networking is the number one way to get integrated into the VC and funding communities. By being a part of the community, you quickly come to understand who the important players are and can keep tabs on the other companies raising money to see who is successful. This information helps you learn what works in your community. Refer to Chapter 5 for more about becoming visible to venture capitalists.

When to start networking

Creating relationships takes time. Therefore, when networking, you want to start early. Raising capital is all about relationships and less about your killer pitch deck (though that's important too; see Chapter 15). If you start networking when you need funding immediately, you've missed the boat.

Why earlier is better

To understand why you need to approach VCs early, imagine that you're ready to raise some capital, so you knock on the door of a VC who's never heard of you or your company. If your company matches the profile of what the VC is looking for, he will likely talk to you and perhaps see your pitch. He may or may not be excited about your company and may give you some advice. Great, right? Not really because you don't have time to do anything about the advice. Remember, you need capital *now*.

Instead, imagine that you make an appointment to see the VC six months before you think you'll need to raise funds. When you pitch, the pressure is off for an immediate investment. You let the VC know about your plans, what your goals are for the next six months, and that, when those goals are achieved, you'll be ready for institutional investment. After hearing you out, the VC gives you advice about additional goals or recommends changes to your existing goals. If you're looking for people to fill out your team, the VC may have recommendations for who in your community would be a good fit. Because you approached him early, you can work on making the changes that would make you even more attractive.

Start networking at least 6 to 12 months before you start your search for VC funding. Find out what the top networking groups for VCs are in your area, and scour the community calendars for events that involve VC participation. Attend every pitch event you can and watch other pitches to learn what the audience likes and doesn't like. Listen carefully to the questions the VCs ask and take notes.

You should approach a VC before you need money, but not so far in advance that your company looks like a distant future dream. When you approach a VC early, you need to make clear that you're raising money not now, but soon — after you meet certain milestones and your company looks a little different.

Fitting in the face time

On the surface, networking can seem equivalent to a party in its value — fun, but not a way to grow your venture. But making time for networking meetings is actually imperative. You must get out and meet people when you plan to raise capital. It's not just for fun.

Some communities host so many events that, even if you were to go to something every night of the week, you'd still be hitting only half of what's going on. Rather than spend a minimal amount of time at all, it's better to go deep with a few groups to become known as a part of the community. Get known, get referred to others, and build a network over time.

Strategizing for efficient networking

Attending a group for the first time is like looking through an unfocused camera lens. After several meetings, you'll develop some "anchor" relationships, and the image becomes clearer. After you know who the key players are, then you'll know who you need to meet. Good networking is methodical and practiced.

Here's a good strategy for networking in an unfamiliar group. You can work this method all night:

1. **Find someone with whom you can build rapport quickly.**

2. **Ask that person to point out some big targets and for advice on who you should to talk to.**

3. **Then ask him for an introduction.**

Networking events can be fueled by excitement, loudness, and wine, which isn't conducive to remembering everything that was discussed. To ensure that the people you've met in networking events don't forget you, follow up:

- ✔ Add your new contacts to LinkedIn, send each new contact an e-mail reminding him or her about the things you discussed, and so on.

  Use your social network connections on LinkedIn, Facebook, Twitter, and others to leverage the relationships you create in the face-to-face environment over time by sending periodic "touches" via social media.

- ✔ If you promised something to your new contact, whether it's a meeting or something non-business like a bike tune up, be sure to follow through.

"Always give more than you get." This is a great tenet of social interaction and a theme in many of the books and blog posts published by the partners at Foundry Group, a VC firm, in Boulder. Try to find ways to help the people you meet at networking events. Being a good start-up citizen will help you get your needs fulfilled as well.

Becoming a leader in your field

Leadership and networking are tightly connected, but you wouldn't guess it by observing the behavior of many entrepreneurs, who think they should wait until they have their IPO before they start writing or speaking to groups.

When you're seeking venture capital, you want to establish yourself as someone with deep and useful ideas who is insightful about things that are happening in your community. So learn how to tell a great story and get out there. Begin with a blog and follow up by getting involved in discussions on Meetup, LinkedIn, Twitter and Facebook groups. If you truly don't have anything to say, then share articles you find interesting on TechCrunch (http://www.techcrunch.com), Forbes (http://www.forbes.com), Inc. (http://www.inc.com), or other publications.

When sharing articles and news with your online followers, be sure that what you share is reflective of your personal brand and company brand. If you have a strong political bent, but your company has customers on both sides of the aisle, you may want to avoid sharing political articles or materials.

Making sure the initial meeting goes well

Here's a caveat: After they've seen you once, some VCs and angel investing groups feel they don't need to see you again. Because you may have just one chance to impress the VC, you need to do it right. Therefore, your first meetings must be carefully arranged. Here are some tips:

- ✔ Even if you're six months ahead of schedule, you still need to have a compelling story. Be sure you put your full attention into the pitch; don't just wing it.

- ✔ Make sure the purpose of your meeting is understood to be simply a fact-finding mission where you would like to begin developing a relationship and get advice.

- ✔ Spend most of your time asking questions and taking notes, not going on and on about your great company.

- ✔ Ask in-depth questions about what the VC is looking for and how he works. He'll appreciate that you are taking the time to get to know him. Be careful not to ask rudimentary questions that you can find on the VC's website, however. Know that stuff inside and out.

- ✔ Research companies in the VC's portfolio and understand how they are doing. Be clear about how your company is similar and different from the companies that the VC has already invested in.

- ✔ Between meetings, be sure to follow your VC's blog, tweets, publications, newsletters, or other communications and keep up to date on the issues that he's thinking and writing about.

Planting seeds for funding

By approaching the VC early and sharing your plans, including your desire to seek funding after you meet milestones, you can establish a relationship, such that, when you walk into the VC's office six months later, he already knows who you are. Since your initial meeting, you may have sent periodic updates just to keep him abreast of your progress. By doing so, you've given him (and his team) a chance to get to like you.

In the meanwhile, you've planted a seed in the VC's head about your project, and he'll have been taking note of trends in your area when talking to people or reading journals. He's now more up to date on your specific project and has more insights about its feasibility. Even better, you can now demonstrate your ability to execute. You can point out how you had set a number of ambitious goals six months ago and show that you have not only succeeded in executing those, but you have also accomplished some additional goals as well. Maybe you have even implemented some of the suggestions that the VC made last time and hired the right people or developed new partnerships.

Building a Relationship with Your Acquirer

You have spent time developing relationships with business partners, employees, suppliers, clients, VCs, distributors, and more, but the most important strategic relationship is with your acquirer — the company that will eventually buy you.

Disabuse yourself of the notion that M&As are all about finance and numbers. They're actually all about relationships. If you're hoping that someone will buy your company for $50 million, $100 million, $500 million or more, then you need to start developing those relationships early.

For many of the same reasons that you want to build relationships with VCs early in the process, you also want to begin meeting with your potential acquirers at the same time. You want to build your strategy around meeting the acquirers' needs and providing some kind of strategic advantage for them.

These days it's common for companies to shut down their R&D departments and to perform research by acquisition. In other words, they buy companies that have the capabilities they want rather than developing that capability in-house. This strategy reduces acquiring companies' risk of failure, because your company will have already developed the product and market for the exact thing they're looking for. This is called *buying innovation*. Companies can either innovate internally or buy other companies that have created new technology. Many larger companies choose to buy the company out to acquire the technology. They often take the employees on as their employees. It's a positive arrangement for both parties.

How do you know that you have the thing your potential acquirer is looking for? You ask. Create a short list of companies that you think will need what you've got and get to know them. Find out their goals and what they want to accomplish.

As you approach potential acquirers, watch out for two things:

✔ **Don't share too much of your project with the company.** Potential acquirers may well find your story so compelling that they undertake the project themselves. With their greater resources, they may be able to complete the project more quickly than you can; even if they like you, they may decide that expedience is their priority.

✔ **Don't put too much stock into what people tell you they want.** Henry Ford said, "If I had asked people what they wanted, they would have said a faster horse." The point: You need to innovate and demonstrate value, not just incrementally improve on the existing model. And according to Steve Jobs, "You can't just ask customers what they want and then try to give that to them. By the time you get it built, they'll want something new." In other words, innovators need to move quickly and be ahead of the market.

Not all exits are acquisitions, of course, so if your strategy is for an IPO, you want to begin making relationships with investment bankers who will potentially be taking you through the IPO process sometime down the road.

Chapter 8

Providing an Exit Strategy

● ●

In This Chapter

▶ Beginning with the end in mind

▶ Realizing 50 percent of the company's value at the exit

▶ Choosing between acquisition or IPO

● ●

*T*he second habit Steven Covey outlines in *Seven Habits of Highly Successful People* is to begin with the end in mind. This may be the second habit of highly successful people, but it should be the first habit of highly successful venture firms. And for VC firms — and the entrepreneurs trying to attract them — the "end" is the exit.

Exits are important to investors because, without an exit, they don't make money. Sure, you've got a plan that will generate a lot of profit, but that profit doesn't get to the investor. Unless you have a revenue-sharing or dividend agreement, the money that your company makes as it grows stays with the company. The VC is working hard to help you, making connections, attending board meetings, and risking his portfolio and reputation on your success, but he doesn't make a penny until the exit.

This chapter is all about the end — the time when you no longer own your start-up anymore. A founder's exit is a mixed blessing because you often walk away with a decent payout, and you are no longer responsible for your employees' paychecks and the success of the company. However, it can be a hard time for a founder who doesn't know what to do next. All successful venture-backed companies have an exit. This chapter tells you how to plan your exit well in advance.

Understanding the Value of a Good Exit

A typical VC fund may have a 10- to 12-year lifecycle: The first 1 or 2 years are spent raising the fund, followed by 5 to 7 years of investing, followed by 3 to 5 years of harvesting. During harvesting, exit strategies are executed.

Seeing how value increases near the end

Up to half of the ultimate value of the company is realized in the 6- to12-month period leading up to the exit. The graph in Figure 8-1 shows how value is added to a company over time. The value is relatively low at the early, "idea" stage, but as various benchmarks are reached and risk is reduced, the value of the company continues to grow. The interesting thing to see is how the value doubles at the end.

Why does value increase so much at the exit? While you're growing your company, you're building value, and the company is (hopefully) churning out a certain amount of cash flow. You can calculate the present value of future cash flows to calculate value all throughout this process.

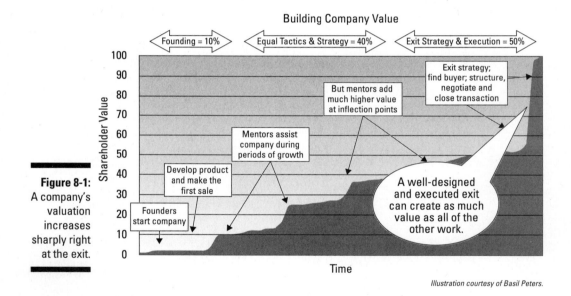

Figure 8-1: A company's valuation increases sharply right at the exit.

Illustration courtesy of Basil Peters.

At a well-planned exit, you're talking to potential acquirers who will be able to significantly increase those cash flows or realize some other factor that exponentially increases value. By understanding what these people are looking for and building your company around that, you will get the most from your company and garner the greatest interest from VCs.

Basing valuation on your exit

When VCs perform due diligence on your company, they compile a variety of valuation models. Most of these models involve predictions about the kind of an exit you'll have and what value your company will likely have at that event. Valuation models are often based on the present value of future cash flows. Developing a convincing story about a big exit potential for your business can translate into a higher valuation because your exit is the future cash flow that VCs care most about.

VCs are very good at doing this projected valuation work; however, by their own admission, the process is somewhat imperfect. If you were to show three separate VCs the same company and ask them to come up with an exit valuation, you'd likely see three very different numbers.

VCs come up with today's value through a process by which they take into account and apply a discount for the time value of money, risks, and other factors. You can influence the numbers that the VC comes up with by helping with the research and understanding a wider range of exit possibilities than would be immediately apparent. As an expert in your field, you may apply your knowledge and creativity to understand who may find the most value in your company and to develop a story around that. (See Chapter 11 for more details on the valuation process and ways you can influence it.)

Checking Out Your Exit Options

A lot of confusion exists about what constitutes an exit, also called a *liquidity event*. At the exit, the investors convert their investment in your company back into cash (hence the use of the word *liquidity*). The liquidity event can happen in a number of ways (outlined in the following sections), but the important thing for investors is that they get to put cash in the bank.

An exit does not mean that *you* have to leave the company. In fact, in many cases, the exit terms may require that you stay for a minimum of one to three years after the acquisition in order to ensure continuity and value for the buyer. Some founders spend the rest of their careers with their companies, even though the company is now owned by someone else. Other founders — think of them as serial entrepreneurs — move on to start something else after every exit.

When it comes to exits, you have options. Different companies pursue different liquidity options. Typically, your agreement with your VC specifies what the exit for your company will ideally look like. You don't want to enter into a relationship thinking that you'll buy back the shares while the VC, unbeknownst to you, is thinking that you'll have a huge initial public offering (IPO).

The type of exit you choose early on doesn't necessarily mean that you are bound to follow that strategy blindly. Your actual exit strategy will be driven by short-term trends in the economy, the markets, and in private corporations. If it's a hot time for IPOs, then an IPO may be a good option. If corporations are sitting on piles of cash, then a merger or acquisition may be your best strategy. Ultimately, the exit is up to the acquirer. If they don't like the terms or the type of exit, the transaction won't close.

Mergers and acquisitions

The most common way for venture-backed companies to exit is through mergers and acquisitions (M&As). Mergers and acquisitions, despite often being clumped together, are two different things:

- ✔ **Mergers:** Typically a *merger* is the joining of two similarly sized companies into a new single entity. Several corporate names reflect these mergers: JPMorganChase, GlaxoSmithKline, ConocoPhillips, AOL Time Warner, and ExxonMobil, for example.

- ✔ **Acquisitions:** An *acquisition* typically occurs when a larger company acquires a smaller company. The acquired company may continue to exist as a company on its own with its same name but new ownership, or it may be folded into the parent company and its operations. In some cases, a smaller company will acquire control over a larger company, such as when Qwest acquired US West. This situation can occur through a leveraged buyout arrangement, though it is relatively rare.

For venture backed companies, M&As typically need to be cash transactions. In some cases, the transactions involve both cash and stock, an option that can work as long as there is not a significant lockup period, when the stock can't be sold on the open market.

To identify companies that may want to acquire you, look for those that have a strategic advantage to gain from purchasing your company. Although a company may have many motivations to acquire you, focus on finding companies that can benefit in some of the following ways:

- ✔ **Vertical integration:** Vertical integration is a strategy some acquirers use to control the *full value chain* — that is, the full process that goes into making the product valuable to a customer. An example of vertical integration would be an oil drilling and exploration company buying a refinery company to refine the oil they pump from the earth, a trucking company to deliver gas to retail outlets, and a company that has a lot of retail locations. Vertical integration makes sense for companies that already have expertise in your field because it may allow them to develop unique products or processes that they would not otherwise have access to.

- ✔ **Diversification:** Diversification refers to buying companies outside of the company's main line of business, and it offers almost the opposite value of vertical integration. Companies may want to diversify to offset potential market risks. An oil and gas company, for example, may want to diversify into solar energy to complement market volatility in oil and gas.

✔ **Rapid growth:** Companies that want to grow quickly can often do so by acquisition. In this case, the acquiring company would be most interested in your customer list and will value your company based on your total sales and the likelihood of repeat customers.

If you are looking at companies who would acquire you for rapid growth, your strategy should include customer retention data and growth rates for your company to show how you can help your potential acquirer grow quickly.

✔ **Geographic growth:** If your company has plans to develop a regional or national presence, you may position yourself to be an attractive acquisition by companies that have strong, established bases within certain regions. For service-based industries, this strategy means acquiring a company that has people on the ground immediately rather than following the long pipeline of hiring, training, and building business within the territory on their own. Manufacturing- or product-based industries may look to acquire warehouses and shipping centers in new regions.

✔ **Economies of scale:** Some companies want to get bigger so that they can benefit from economies of scale. A business may find that it can reduce costs by 20 percent or more by having a larger operation that can spread costs across many more units. Similar to rapid growth in that the acquiring company wants to get bigger, there is an important difference: Rapid growth focuses on benefits of increasing revenues' economies-of-scale focuses on the benefits of reducing expenses.

✔ **Intellectual property:** Many companies are now using acquisition as their R&D strategy. Rather than spending millions on internal research and development, these companies seek businesses that have successfully developed products or technologies that the company seeks. In these cases, your focus is on overcoming your technology risks; market development is not as important — a distinction that helps you decide how to allocate your resources.

IPOs

In some cases, becoming publicly owned and traded on the stock market is better for a company than undergoing a private acquisition. In these cases, the company has an initial public offering (IPO), when it sells stock publicly for the first time.

Qualifying for an IPO

To be qualified to have an IPO, your company needs to achieve several benchmarks that differ, depending on the exchange you want to be listed on. When you seek an IPO, the general assumption is that your company has grown to the point where its ongoing earnings are relatively predictable. Examples of earnings benchmarks required to be listed on public exchanges include the following:

- ✔ **NYSE:** $10 million in pre-tax earnings over the past ten years with $2 million minimum profit in each of the past two years

- ✔ **NASDAQ Global Select Market:** $11 million in pre-tax earnings over the past three years and $2.2 million minimum in each of the past two years

- ✔ **NASDAQ Global Market:** $1 million or more in pre-tax earnings in the most recent year or two of the past three years

- ✔ **NASDAQ Capital Market:** $750,000 or more in pre-tax earnings in the most recent year or two of the past three years

- ✔ **AMEX (American Stock Exchange):** $750,000 or more in pre-tax earnings in the most recent year or two of the past three years

Some other measures that the exchanges require may include some combination of net tangible assets, market value of publicly held stock, number of shares that are held by the public, number of public board lot holders, trading price of listed securities, and total shareholder equity.

Benefits of an IPO

For some companies, an IPO is the best strategy and offers a variety of benefits:

- ✔ It opens up your company to a huge audience of potential investors who are interested in investing in public companies because the shares are much more easily sold and can be traded on public markets. Investors trading in the public market can invest $50,000 on one day, for example, and pull the money back out the next day, next week, next month or whenever. That flexibility is attractive to a lot of investors.

- ✔ Capital raised on public markets is typically raised at lower costs than for private equity. Being public also opens up opportunities for non-equity financing at relatively lower interest rates than private companies may pay. Earnings multiples are higher than for private companies, often by as much as 35 percent.

- ✔ A lot of publicity and prestige comes with being a public company, which can accelerate your growth. Customers may have higher awareness and confidence in the stability of a public company.

- ✔ Access to public markets provides a strategic advantage if you are pursuing an acquisition strategy to rapidly grow a market. As a publicly traded company, you can use liquid, easily valued stock for acquisitions rather than having to use cash. You may also use stock for executive compensation to attract the best and brightest in your field.

Deciding whether to pursue an IPO

Going public is not for the faint of heart. First, there's the expense. The process itself is expensive, costing millions of dollars:

> ✔ You need to pay 7 to 10 percent of every dollar raised to the underwriters who sell your stock. If you value your stock too low, you can leave millions of dollars on the table, and if you value your stock too high, your offering can be a flop with nobody buying your stock.
>
> ✔ You need to add staff for investor relations, internal legal counsel, compliance, and more.
>
> ✔ You'll be working with (and paying) an underwriter to prepare the marketing materials and plans for your road show in which you pitch your company to investors.

And after all of these expenses, you're not guaranteed that your IPO will be a success and you may not raise the money you need.

Second, to prepare for a public offering, your company will need to be scrubbed clean and formally audited by one of the major CPA firms. Prior to going public, you need to update your processes to be in compliance with all of the regulations that the Securities Exchange Commission (SEC) has, a task that can take a year or more and cost hundreds of thousands of dollars.

Last, as a public company, your financial information and much of your strategy will become public and available to your competitors. In short, you need to have a really good reason to pursue the IPO strategy over other options. Companies that pursue an IPO too early can collapse under all the regulatory requirements.

Stock buybacks

In a *stock buyback,* the company buys stock back from the angel or VC investors. In this exit, the VCs get their money back directly from the company instead of from new investors in an IPO or from another company in an M&A. When a stock buyback is your exit strategy, VCs usually look for the purchasing company themselves. Entrepreneurs who think they can buy the stock back in the future are typically inexperienced and unrealistic in their expectations. Although stock buybacks can and do happen in the real world, it's not usually a strategy that VCs find attractive.

Publicly traded companies may have many reasons to pursue a share repurchase: defending against a hostile takeover, reducing dividend payout expenses, increasing earnings per share, and "investing" excess cash. In most of these cases, unless a leveraged buyout is involved, stock buybacks are partial repurchases of shares. Even big public companies cannot afford to buy back all of the outstanding shares. Your smaller nonpublic company is not likely to have the resources to make a complete buyout, and VCs are not going to be interested in a piecemeal buyout.

Options for angels but not VCs: Royalties and revenue shares

Royalties are small amounts of money that are returned to investors regularly. The amount of the royalty is generally based on how well the company is doing at any given time. The frequency of the royalty payment is defined in the term sheet and is set at closing. Royalties are typically earned on licensing of intellectual property (IP) of some kind. They represent ongoing, passive income and can be attractive to some investors.

Except in unusual circumstances, VCs are not interested in royalty revenues because they typically don't have the opportunity to scale like other investments. The investors may get their money back, but this exit strategy doesn't offer the homerun ability that VCs need. Angel investors are more likely to get involved in a revenue share deal.

Revenue sharing can be used to buy out investors as the company grows. (It's similar to increasing payments on a loan over time and then eventually paying off loan and the interest.) Although revenue sharing may be attractive to friends and family investors and some angel investors, you'll never get a VC to enter into this kind of deal. However, if you can demonstrate that your company will generate huge amounts of free cash flow such that you can return the investors' money in a year or two and then keep that cash flowing until a pre-agreed upon cap is reached, this may be an exit worth pursuing with angels.

Remember: The SEC has certain restrictions on the types of investments that exempt VC funds can make, and one is that the investments typically need to be equity based, so royalties and revenue shares may not be an option for most VCs, even if they wanted to do them.

VCs need to have "homeruns" with one or two out of the ten investments they make. If you have a stock buyback agreement with your investors, you are not likely to offer 50X ("50 times") return, but this is what every VC is looking for on every deal. If the potential return absolutely cannot go higher than 2X or even 10X, the deal will just not be interesting to them.

Designing Your Exit Strategy

With the exit being absolutely critical to the outcome of a venture deal, it's surprising that entrepreneurs spend so little time thinking about it. From the very beginning, a company should be designed to be attractive to potential acquirers, and that attractiveness should be part of the company's DNA. The following sections outline some things to consider as you design your exit. As you do so, you need to think about three different customers, each of which want different things:

✔ **The people who are buying your product:** These are your real customers. These people may be happy about an exit for your company if it means that they can get their products faster, cheaper, or more easily in more locations.

✔ **The investor:** This is the customer to your investment deal. The investor is happy when you have an exit because this is when she gets her money back.

✔ **The acquiring company:** This is the final customer who will buy your company down the road. The acquirer is your ultimate "customer" because the acquiring company is buying your company. It's looking to acquire your company for some strategic reason, such as growth or competitive advantage.

Knowing your industry

Exits are different in every industry. You must know yours. If you want to impress your VC, make sure you have intimate knowledge of current history of exits in your industry. VCs follow exits very closely and are usually up to date, but they may have fallen behind if your deal is somewhat outside of their normal area of expertise. You can help by researching exits in your area and gathering the following information:

✔ The name of both the acquiring firm and the acquired firm

✔ Total revenues of the acquired firm

✔ EBITDA (earnings before interest, taxes, depreciation, and amortization) of the acquired firm

✔ Acquisition price and date

This information enables you to provide multiples of earnings and revenue that will be helpful in crafting a valuation story. Any additional information, such as the reasons for the acquisition and any strategic advantages that were understood by either side, would also be helpful.

Gather as many of these acquisition stories as you can because doing so lets you connect the dots and spot trends. Industry trends are important to understand. Showing that the multiples are increasing or decreasing in recent years, for example, can be useful (unless the multiples are decreasing, of course). Look outside your industry, too. What other industries are similar to or dependent on yours for their products or services? Where might you find an unforeseen strategic advantage? Be sure to look in every nook and cranny for opportunity.

Thinking about timing

Coming into the market too early or too late can cause you to leave money on the table and to miss your best deal. For that reason, timing is an important factor in your exit strategy.

Time is money

The longer your investment takes to pay out for the VC, the lower his return. Developing an exit strategy that happens sooner rather than later can end up looking good for the VC. The VC calculates her deal based on *internal rate of return* (IRR) which is a combination of how long her investment dollars are at work and how much profit she makes on a particular deal. The faster the VC can get her money back, the higher the IRR is.

Having said that, keep in mind that VCs need to swing for the fences, and the big homeruns often take time. If you're looking for a $100 million plus exit, your deal is likely to take more than three to five years. Your strategy's timetable should take into account where the biggest potential for exit is and when that will occur.

Time lets you take advantage of trends

The goal in terms of timing is to spot trends and ride them to gain the greatest exit advantage for your company. You can identify many opportunities by keeping your ear to the ground and your eyes on the distant (five year) horizon — remember you're on a five year strategy cycle. Even though you may be putting in 100 hour work weeks, take the time to keep current on the journals, blogs, trade shows, and conferences in your field so that you can spot trends early. Early-stage companies do well to heed Wayne Gretzky's advice to skate to where the puck is going and not where it's been.

Developing strategies early

Many entrepreneurs say that they can't possibly come up with an exit strategy because the exit is five years away, and too much can happen between then and now. True, things will change, but the solution isn't to refuse to plan for the future.

Nobody, not even the most cynical VC, expects entrepreneurs to carry out their business plans exactly as written. VCs expect that changes and modifications will occur. This is one reason why VCs put so much stock in their assessment of the management team. VCs want a team that can pivot quickly when needed and push forward when possible. VCs will tolerate a shift in plans, but they're typically unimpressed with early-stage companies that have vague and unwritten plans.

By planning early for your exit, you can focus on what acquirers want in a company and then easily build that value in from the start. This approach is far more effective than going in one direction for four and a half years and then having to pivot in the last six months, scrambling to implement what your acquisition targets may want.

If you know at an early stage which companies are likely to be acquiring you (information you may be able to glean during your extensive networking efforts; refer to Chapter 7), you can begin networking in the circles where those companies are active. Look for events they sponsor and conferences they speak at. By becoming familiar with the decision makers early on, you enhance your chances for serious consideration when the time for your exit comes around.

Understanding the Role of Advisors in Your Exit

Even the most seasoned entrepreneur will have direct experience with only a few exits. This lack of experience can put you at a disadvantage when you are negotiating with professionals who work full time in M&A. To balance the relationship, you'll need a team of advisors to take you through the process. Your VC can help make introductions to the people they've worked with in the past who would be right for you.

Listing the types of advisors

M&A is complex and requires a lot of preparation. Before you put yourself out there, you need to get your ducks in a row. Getting ready for an exit is similar to getting ready to raise venture capital: You want to be ready for what's coming so that you don't lose momentum in the process. In addition to updating your online due diligence database (see Chapter 13), you also need to make sure your legal and accounting issues are clear.

Certified public accountant (CPA)

The best way to handle your accounting is to do it right — and early — the first time rather than wait until you're on the doorstep of an exit and need to restate five years of financials. Your CPA can work with your internal accounting staff to set up policies and procedures for proper GAAP (generally accepted accounting principles).These are the standards your acquiring company will look for to ensure that your financial statements represent reality.

Your VC may require audited financial statements every year to demonstrate to her limited partners (LPs) that she's conducting proper oversight of their investments and to facilitate a problem free exit. Auditing financials represents a significant cost, though it's relatively low for start-ups that have fewer transactions.

Attorneys

Yes, *attorneys* is plural. You need these attorneys to walk you through the exit process:

- **A corporate attorney:** This attorney will want to work through your articles of incorporation and bylaws to make sure everything is clean. She'll organize any contracts you may have and ensure that your closets are free of any legal skeletons that would disrupt a deal.

- **A securities attorney:** This attorney will oversee the process of the securities transaction, transfer of stock, board responsibilities, and other technical aspects of the transaction.

- **An M&A attorney:** This attorney will perform due diligence on both sides, advise on company structure post sale, and deal with legal ramifications for all parties after the closing.

For information on finding attorneys to help with your venture capital deal, go to http://www.dummies.com/extras/venturecapital.

Investment bankers

Investment bankers are effectively the salespeople for your exit. They help you with valuation and developing a marketing plan. In addition, they can extend your reach and get more offers on the table (a real benefit unless you already have a direct connection to an acquirer). In return for their services, investment bankers receive a commission ranging from 3 to 10 percent of the total IPO or acquisition price. Although the amount may sound pricey, hiring an investment banker who can bring you the best buyer available at the best price will be the best investment you can make.

When negotiating, you want to have as many offers at once as you can so that you're creating excitement and buzz about your deal. Bidders who know that they are competitively bidding for your company are likely to offer 25 to 50 percent more than bidders making unsolicited offers.

Recognizing why the CEO shouldn't lead the exit

You may think that the CEO should lead the exit process, but nothing could be farther from the truth. Here's why:

✔ Leading the exit is a fulltime job, and no time is more vital for the CEO to be at the helm than during the exit when the performance of the company will be under more scrutiny. An active and engaged CEO can ensure that sales targets are met and that the company is running smoothly. A CEO distracted by all the details of an acquisition may lose track of what's going on, and the penalty for that could be a drop of 10 to 25 percent in the company's value.

✔ Unless they were investment bankers during past lives, CEOs don't have hands-on experience with more than a handful of exit transactions, and they won't be as attuned to what's going on as someone who has 10,000 hours of M&A experience.

✔ If the acquisition is successful, the CEO will become an employee of the acquiring company. This potential relationship puts the CEO at a disadvantage in the negotiating process. Negotiation is not always pretty, especially when both parties are driving for the best deal. The relationship between the CEO and her future bosses could be damaged in the process.

Creating an Exit Story

Crafting an exit is a lot like crafting your venture capital pitch (Chapter 15) and valuation story (Chapter 11). You want to have as much data as you can gather and weave it together into a plausible story that leads to an inevitable conclusion.

Amassing your data

There is no better way to prepare for a big business decision than to collect and analyze data to help you understand the nuances. Try to gather quantitative data, including numbers about sales, but also qualitative data, like the reasons that sales were successful. Sometimes the deal closes due to a strategy that isn't directly about numbers.

Developing a list of possible acquirers

The place to start is to think of every company who would have any reason to own your company. Look through lists of companies in your industry and select those that have the following characteristics:

✔ Are large enough to be able to afford an acquisition

✔ Have a strategic reason to acquire your company

✔ Have shown a pattern of acquisition in the past

✔ Are in the press for reasons that may be positive or negative but that indicate an opportunity

Researching acquisitions in your industry

When researching acquisitions in your industry, start with your list of preferred companies and, if they're public, research their activities over the past few years. Move beyond your target list and gather all information you can about transactions in your industry during the past three to five years. Bring in information from complementary industries as well, if it enhances your case. Here are some sources for gathering this information:

- ✔ 10-K reports filed by public companies (the SEC requires that these reports be submitted annually).

- ✔ Business transaction databases from companies like ValuSource (http://www.valusource.com), Thompson ONE (http://www.thomsononeim.com), and Bloomberg (http://www.bloomberg.com). These pull in private transactions from SEC, IRS reports, and other services.

  Most of these organizations charge fees to use their information, so check them all out to find the one that fits your needs and budget.

- ✔ Google search for top companies in your field.

Describing relationships with potential acquirers

Exits are based on relationships, so begin making relationships with investment bankers as well as with M&A people in your target companies. Your VC can help you with a target list, and you can use resources like LinkedIn to begin connecting into the community. (For most entrepreneurs, this environment will be totally unfamiliar, so get started early; Chapter 7 offers advice on networking and building relationships with potential acquirers.)

When you can describe specific relationships that you have with potential acquirers, your VCs will be more likely to buy into your exit strategy story, and you'll show yourself to be someone who has her eye on the prize — things that will reflect well in your discussions with VCs.

Identifying strategic reasons why they would acquire you

The final component for your exit strategy story is a list of reasons why the target companies would want to acquire you. If you can weave together a pattern from their past acquisitions and current initiatives, along with trends that you see in the industry, you can build a credible story that will not only convince a VC of your awesome exit potential, but also demonstrate that you're leading your company where it needs to go to make your exit story come true.

Developing the story

After you collect all your information, you're ready to develop your story outline. Companies that have done the homework are able to describe their processes in a way that seems totally natural and easy to execute. Companies whose stories are vague and unclear leave VCs feeling like getting the deal done is going to be like slogging through molasses.

Your story should go something like this:

> We see a lot of consolidation trends in our industry in the past few years. This is because of the opportunities that have opened up due to developments in emerging markets and our unique ability to serve them. We have identified Company A, Company B, Company C, and Company D as the top acquirers in our industry recently. Altogether, these companies have acquired 18 companies in the past five years with an average acquisition price of 8X EBITDA. We are projecting $5 million EBITDA for our company in five years, so we feel we could reasonably expect $40 million for our exit.

> We are especially excited about the prospects from Company B which is the only company among the active acquirers that does not have representation in Brazil or India, two countries that we have a strong presence in. We have met with Mike Smith from Company B on several occasions at industry conferences and have developed a good relationship that we feel will be useful when it's time to carry out our exit strategy.

If you deliver a story like that, even with some risks to overcome between now and exit, a VC will appreciate your thinking and may increase your valuation when negotiating because of the line-of-sight connection to the possible exit.

Spreading the word

As soon as you begin the exit process, let your employees know what is going on. They'll know soon anyway, but it's better that they hear the news from you. The following months will be stressful, and you need everyone's cooperation now more than ever.

Your employees may still have some uncertainty, especially if the acquiring company's objective is to cut costs rather than to grow the top line, in which case, you'll likely have to lay off part of your staff after the merger — an eventuality that your staff may suspect from the start. Be sure you understand what you're looking for in an acquisition and that you communicate honestly with your team what is happening.

Avoiding Mistakes That Can Blow an Exit

You can blow an exit in lots of ways, and it's easy to miss some key things. Depending on how you measure success, something like 50 percent of acquisitions end up as failures. By avoiding a few mistakes, you increase the chances that your exit will be a success:

✔ **Failing to focus on what happens after the sale:** It's easy to understand why so many companies fall into this trap. They're focused on the acquisition, which is what they've been working for so long. Everything they've done has been about the exit. The thing to remember is that the exit is not the end. You still have to continue working on the company, and most exit deals require the management team to stay on for a year or more to ease the transition.

✔ **Having an earn out clause with metrics out of your control:** With an *earn out clause,* you get paid only if certain benchmarks are hit. More work has to be done after an acquisition than before the exit. Not only do you have to run your company, but now you have to learn how to deal with a new management team, new policies, and integrating with the other company. This period can be stressful, especially if the acquisition includes an earn out clause. If you have this kind of agreement, make sure that you think through what resources will be at your disposal after the exit and whether achieving the benchmarks is actually within your control.

✔ **Letting the CEO lead the exit:** If the CEO leads the exit, who is leading the company? The CEO should be involved to the extent that she helps select the team that will actually work on the acquisition and shows up for key pitches and interviews, but she should spend the rest of her time running the company.

✔ **Losing momentum:** A company that's focused on the exit can lose momentum, and revenues may start to decline. Be sure that everyone understands that the exit is the time for the company to fire on all cylinders and meet all projections. If you fail to hit projections, your company's value will drop precipitously over night.

✔ **Company cultures not mixing:** A mismatch of cultures is one of the primary causes of merger failure. It's easy to have dinner with the acquiring team a few times, but to ensure that you can actually work together, you need to pay special attention to the acquiring company and its culture.

A lot of aspects of culture don't make themselves immediately apparent, so your own self-awareness is important. Ask yourself what the main features of your culture are and which of them you're willing to abandon. This exercise helps you determine the fundamental parts of the company's DNA. Also ask what will cause you to start losing employees or to fail to get cooperation from the acquiring company's sales and support team and others you need to depend on for your success.

✔ **Feeling genuine reluctance about the exit:** You should be passionate about your business, but it's not your baby. VCs can smell exit reluctance a mile away, so before you take the VC route, make sure that you're going to be ready to sell the company a few years down the road. (This is one of the main reasons that VCs like to work with CEOs who've previously worked with VCs. After you've' been through the process, you know what the expectations are and have experienced the rewards that playing in the big leagues can bring.)

You can't have it both ways — being hesitant about the exit while pursuing it at the same time. The more you're on board with the exit — showing your excitement and doing the homework necessary to demonstrate your excitement to the VC — the more likely you'll be to raise that venture capital investment you're looking for.

Part III
Getting Your Ducks in a Row: Deal Design and Due Diligence

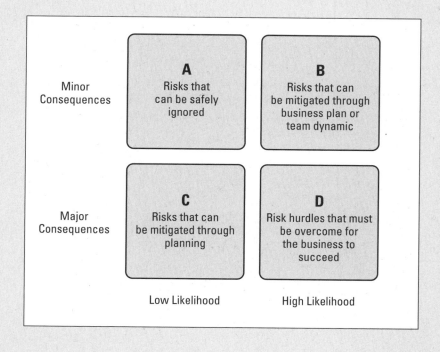

	Low Likelihood	High Likelihood
Minor Consequences	**A** Risks that can be safely ignored	**B** Risks that can be mitigated through business plan or team dynamic
Major Consequences	**C** Risks that can be mitigated through planning	**D** Risk hurdles that must be overcome for the business to succeed

Having an attorney is vital during deal structure and negotiation. Find what to look for when hiring an attorney at www.dummies.com/extras/venturecapital.

In this part...

- ✔ Recognize the key stages of the funding lifecycle, from boot-strapping to venture capital.

- ✔ Put together a term sheet, anticipate necessary restructuring, and avoid early pitfalls as you get ready to approach VCs.

- ✔ Identify and mitigate the kinds of risk that, if left unaddressed, could destroy your business or undermine your venture deal.

- ✔ Discover a variety of techniques that help you determine the value of your company. Learn what to do when the VC calculates a different value.

- ✔ Negotiate the specific terms in your contract with a VC and know which points to challenge and which to accept for a successful outcome.

- ✔ Understand the elements involved in due diligence and the timeframe in which it happens. Prepare business and legal documents that facilitate the VC firm's investigation of your company prior to investment.

Chapter 9

Structuring Pre-VC Deals

- -

In This Chapter

▶ Understanding term sheet terms

▶ Planning early fundraising

▶ Choosing between equity and convertible debt

▶ Making the transition between early rounds and VC rounds

- -

*W*hen growing your business, expect to raise money in stages. It's not common to start a company and raise venture capital immediately. Instead, founders use their own money (called *bootstrapping*), raise money through friends and family, or take angel capital to develop a company to the point where a venture capital firm will be interested in the deal.

Early fundraising is a minefield because the decisions you make can potentially muck up your deal such that VCs won't touch it with a ten foot pole. You can unwittingly strike a deal with some angel investors for a couple hundred thousand dollars that totally ruins your fundraising accounting for future deals. The worst part is that such mistakes aren't the result of someone setting out to ruin the company; they're the result of the founder and investor not realizing the potential ramifications of the contract.

This chapter helps you plan deal structures in rounds leading up to a VC round. If you haven't raised any money yet, use this chapter to figure out how to raise early money wisely so that your deal doesn't become too messy for VCs. If you have raised early money, use the tips we include here to clean up your deal so that VCs won't be turned off. Head to Chapter 12 for all the details you need when negotiating your term sheet.

Recognizing the Red Flags

VCs are looking to see that your company can grow very large and can make a lot of money in a short period of time. They are also looking to see that you are not going to be a huge risk in their portfolios. Risk can stem from problems with your technology or from instabilities in the market. Risk can also stem from the agreements that you made with individuals that invested in your deal early on. Although you can't always control what happens in the market with competition and buyer behavior, you *can* control the terms of your early investment rounds.

Tons of variables exist in the pre-VC rounds, and many of the choices you make when structuring these early deals can have an impact on your future ability to raise money with a VC. Just a few of the red flags for VCs include

✔ Having large numbers of investors (VCs prefer fewer investors who have invested larger amounts)

✔ Investors who negotiated stranglehold terms

✔ Including non-accredited investors in your capitalization table

Tallying Your Investors in a Cap Table

From the moment you take on your first investor, you need to be very careful to account for the money that investors have given you and the company shares that they own. The standard way to do this is with a capitalization table. This table is just a list of who owns what. In its simplest form, a capitalization table is a spreadsheet that includes the investment, shares, and percent ownership for each individual — including founders — invested in your company. As you take on more investors and undergo more rounds of funding, your capitalization table will get much more complicated.

The capitalization table, or *cap table* for short, has to be regularly updated with information as things change. When you hire a new key employee, you will probably give him or her some stock and add that to the cap table. When you raise another round of capital, you will update the company's valuation and add all the new investors to the cap table.

Downloadable cap table templates are available online. Venture Hacks has a good one that you can download for a $9 donation; alternatively, you can watch the site's how-to video for free. Go to `http://venturehacks.com/articles/cap-table`.

Fundamentals of the Funding Lifecycle

The *funding lifecycle* refers to the recurring iterations of funding that companies go through as they grow. Money comes from different sources at different times during the development of the company. The "normal" path for a company through the funding lifecycle is not set in stone. The path changes with trends and the economy, and is variable because of other factors like geography.

The basic pathway follows this order:

Bootstrapping→Friends and family→Angel capital→Venture capital

Some companies skip a step in the funding lifecycle, but rarely (or never) do companies go backward (that is, a company that has gotten to venture capital funding generally would not go back to friends and family).

The concept stage — bootstrapping

In the concept stage, companies don't have a product or customers, and they've not made significant gains toward product development or R&D. In this stage, companies often have to come up with cash through bootstrapping, in which the founders use their own money to get the company off the ground. (The term suggests that you're pulling yourself up by your bootstraps).

Bootstrapping is always a good thing for a company. The founders have equity in their company, and they are responsible for its early growth. If the initial founders don't have enough of their own money, they often seek an additional founder who can bring capital to the company. A bootstrapped company is attractive to investors for three major reasons:

- ✔ **Commitment:** The founders are putting not only their blood, sweat, and tears into the company; they're also putting their money in, too.

- ✔ **Belief:** The founders truly believe in their product or technology.

- ✔ **Leadership:** The founders are especially leading the way for investors by putting their own money behind their company.

Baron Munchhausen's bootstraps

A German nobleman, Hieronymus Carl Friedrich von Münchhausen, who lived in the second half of the 1700s, was known as a teller of tall tales. His stories were transcribed into many volumes by writers who created a character called Baron Munchhausen. The name Munchhausen has been linked with a medical disorder, Munchhausen's Syndrome, where sufferers tend to have dramatic and false medical needs on a regular basis. Although none of this has anything to do with fundraising, the term *bootstrapping* comes from a Baron Munchhausen story where he pulls himself out of the sea by his own bootstraps. Just as the Baron defied physics while bootstrapping, founders seem to possess a little magic while bootstrapping too.

The early start-up stage — friends and family

You can raise money from friends and family when your company becomes established enough to prove to them that you're serious about your business endeavors. Depending on who you know, you can raise quite a bit of money this way.

Taking money from people you know can really help you grow the company. However, you have to be careful that you only take money from people who can stand to lose it. Also, you want to treat friends and family investors like any other investors. Because these investments seem informal, they may not be as well structured as formal investments. To protect both you and your family from misunderstandings, regardless of whether things go well for your company, do the following:

- **Issue stock or promissory notes with very clear terms.** Family members tend to come down with sudden amnesia about the original terms when they want to cause a ruckus at the Christmas dinner table.

- **Have a clear buyout plan for friends and family.** That way, if later-stage investments require cleaning up your capitalization table, you'll have a pre-arranged and agreed-upon mechanism for doing so. This is especially important if some of your friends and family are non-accredited investors with a net worth under $1 million or income under $200,000 per year.

- **Be clear about the future.** Friends and family need to understand that they will be minority investors in your company as soon as you start working with angels or VCs.

Your capitalization table is a list of all the people who have invested in your company, how many shares each person owns, and the terms of the investment. Friends and family rounds can complicate your capitalization table (read, there are people involved in the deal that could be a liability in the future). Refer to the earlier section "Tallying Your Investors in a Cap Table" for information on how to compile a capitalization table.

The traction start-up stage — angel capital

At the traction start-up stage, companies have proven traction, either by finishing their product development to at least a minimum viable product

(MVP) stage, or they may even be selling their product. Companies at this stage have likely attracted five to ten people to the team, including those on an advisory board. When your company is selling a product or is about to sell a product, you can raise money with angel investors. Angels are high-wealth individuals who invest in the companies owned by people they don't know personally.

Angel investments are great for raising between $200,000 and $2 million and can help companies get through 6 to 18 months of development, after which the company will be poised to attract VCs for subsequent rounds of financing.

You have to be careful working with angel investors. They're not trained investors, and they may be naïve in their negotiations. Some angels may negotiate odd or restrictive terms in the deal. Work with a good securities attorney to ensure that your angel term sheet doesn't kill the deal in later rounds. Refer to Chapter 4 for details on angel investors.

The growth stage — venture capital

By the time a company is ready for venture capital, it is fairly established, may have a product available to consumers, and is ready to have unusually fast growth over the next five years. If your company has made revenues of $1,000,000 a year from selling an excellent product in a high growth market with a rock star team, then you may be ready to consider venture capital. VCs are all different and have different criteria, but most VC deals involve investing sums between $2 to $20 million or more.

Putting Together the Term Sheet

The process of entering into a seed round with angel investors and entering into an A round with VCs is similar in some ways. Both rounds require a discussion of investment terms. Terms are just standard factors that you and the investor must consider and agree upon in the course of the investment. They can be broken into three main categories: those that describe the amount and type of investment, those that describe the investors' rights, and those that describe board representation, warranties, and other assorted agreements.

A term sheet lays out the terms of the agreement that investors and founders need to discuss. When the terms have been agreed upon, the term sheet is used to create a legally binding contract.

The terms of the deal are often more important than the price and valuation you put on your company. Terms can define control, including the ability of investors to fire the CEO if they want to. They can also control when and where your company is sold, so don't take the terms lightly even if you get a great price for your company.

Start with a term sheet template rather than building one from scratch. Several commonly accepted templates are available, and the best ones are from the National Venture Capital Association (NVCA). You can find a great term sheet template at www.nvca.org; click on the Resources tab.

Including general terms

Although all terms in a term sheet can be negotiated, some are more easily agreed upon. In this section, we cover the general housekeeping terms and terms that are generally settled in early conversations before the term sheet is written. (Of course, if your investor insists on a specific set of terms in one part of the term sheet, she may be more flexible about another part of the term sheet.)

Type of investment

Are you offering equity or convertible debt? Briefly, *convertible debt* is a loan at a reasonable interest rate, typically 6 to 8 percent, with an option to convert to preferred stock at the next financing round. Convertible debt typically has a discount such as 20 percent, enabling debt holders to convert with a 20 percent discount on the stock price. If the price is $1 per share, investors can buy in at $0.80 per share. If you choose convertible debt, define in your term sheet the convertible debt details like valuation caps, percent discounts, time to conversion, or events that cause conversion. Later in this chapter, in the section "The entrepreneur's friend: The attraction of convertible debt," we discuss convertible debt in detail.

If you choose equity, which means that you are selling a percentage of your company to investors, then in this section of the contract, indicate whether the stock is common (like stock given to founders) or preferred (like stock given to VCs). Stock is offered in series. Each series has certain characteristics, like special rights for voting on big decisions and which investors receive cash first when the company liquidates.

Repurchase and redemption rights

Repurchase and redemption rights refer to the rights of shareholders to demand that the company buy back the investor's shares. Typically redemption requires a majority vote of shareholders and may have a time-based trigger where a vote for redemption may come up after seven years. Although redemption rights are almost never exercised, they can help an investor eliminate a company from his or her portfolio when the company is doing very poorly. This capability is important for an investor because occasionally companies can survive for long periods of time on small revenues but will never grow to make a profit for the investor. Redemption rights help an investor end the relationship.

Although redemption rights sound bad for the entrepreneur, a healthy company has nothing to worry about. Plus, investors generally won't do the deal without these rights in the contract, even though they are very rarely exercised (when an investor would want to redeem shares, there is typically not enough cash in the company to do so; after all, redemption rights are useful to the investor only when the company is about to go defunct anyway.)

Conditions to closing

Conditions to closing is a legal backside-covering section that lists all the things that have to happen before the deal can close. Most of these conditions fall into the category of complying with laws: Securities law has been followed, closing certificates have been delivered, certificates of incorporation have been filed, a certain number of shares have been sold, and the board has a specified number of people on it.

Fees and who pays them

You can accrue different kinds of fees when you close a deal: bills from a lawyer, bills from a broker, and bills from other service providers for work done to complete the deal. This section of the term sheet defines who is responsible for paying them.

Employee pool

The company should reserve some percentage of stock in an employee pool. Reserving up to 20 percent of your total stock for the employee pool is common. This unowned stock is offered as an incentive to new employees. Start-ups rarely are able to pay their employees a competitive salary, so stock is a way to make the position more attractive.

Voting rights

This section determines whether the series of stock issues allows for voting rights. These voting rights are general. Some stock or debt does not have voting rights, and this term defines whether all types of stock vote on the same terms, or whether special provisions exist. Voting rights for critical decisions is defined in the upcoming section "Protective provisions."

Commonly negotiated terms

During the course of your discussions with investors, you will have to come to an agreement on some important topics, such as how much money you'll raise right now, how much the company is worth, who's in charge of major decision making, and who gets paid first when the company is sold. In ten years, after your company is bought by an industry giant, these are the terms that you'll either be thankful for or wish you had done differently.

Amount of investment

This section of the term sheet is straightforward. Two main values are listed here: the amount of capital being raised and the percentage of the company that the investor will own after the investment has occurred. If a regularly scheduled return is expected, generally in the form of a dividend, that would be discussed in this section. (*Dividends* are a distribution of profits to all shareholders based on a set percentage per share. Some companies have dividends for shareholders, and some do not.)

Determining how much of the company to sell to the investor in exchange for his or her investment is a hard thing to do. You have to determine how much your company is worth before the investment occurs. This is called *pre-money valuation.* Because this valuation is often a giant concern for entrepreneurs going into a deal, we discuss valuation in detail in Chapter 11.

Liquidation preferences

Liquidation preferences describe who gets paid first when the company is sold. Liquidation can occur when the company is dying and any assets are sold to cut losses. Terms to consider in this section include investor preference, participation, and multiples:

- **Preference:** Describes the order in which the stockholders get paid back when the company sells. People holding preferred stock typically get their invested money back before everyone else.

- **Participation:** Describes whether the stockholder is eligible to get paid back in a certain way.

- **Multiples:** Describes how much of the initial investment the stockholder is eligible to get back in the preferred payout. Sometimes its only 1X ("1 times), but it can be higher. Although it can happen, seeing a multiple over 2X in today's market is rare.

If your pre-VC rounds have large multiples, VCs won't be interested in investing unless you have had a huge growth in value since the last round. Otherwise, their risk increases because the earlier investors have too much power in liquidation preference, as Figure 9-1 shows.

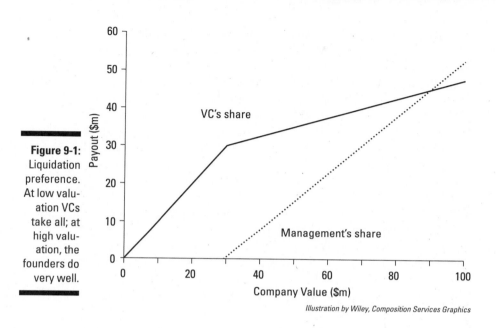

Figure 9-1:
Liquidation
preference.
At low valu-
ation VCs
take all; at
high valu-
ation, the
founders do
very well.

Illustration by Wiley, Composition Services Graphics

Board of directors

The board of directors has the right to make big decisions about the fate of the company. The board approves budgets and acts as the boss for the CEO. This part of the term sheet defines who gets representation on the board.

This line item can be more important than the pre-money value of the company but is sometimes overlooked, even though what's determined here has important implications. If the board is made up entirely of people elected by the investors, then the investors control the company. If the investors don't get representation on the board, they have no control over the company.

A common board for a small start-up consists of three to five people and includes representation from the investors, the founders, and industry experts.

Protective provisions

Protective provisions allow shareholders to block certain actions in the company, akin to veto power. These provisions require a vote by a subset of shareholders before the company can go forward with a large decision. Here are some standard provisions addressing the major issues of company structure and ownership:

- ✔ Selling the company assets, merging, or being acquired
- ✔ Change the number of shares in the company
- ✔ Redeeming or repurchasing stock shares
- ✔ Changing the number of board members
- ✔ Taking on any new significant debt
- ✔ Changing the dividends for any class of stock

When any of these events are proposed, the people holding the protected stocks get to vote to determine whether the event will actually occur.

Although most protective provisions are reasonable, we have seen past protective provisions that have blocked any new deals from happening with a company. In one case, the investor required that she approve all checks over $1,000, which put an operational stranglehold on the company and was a red flag to investors.

Anti-dilution clauses

Companies that intend to raise multiple rounds of funding have to reassure early investors that future investment rounds won't dilute their investment. This dilution most often happens in *down rounds* (the stock is at a lower price than in the previous round) or *flat rounds* (the stock is at the same price as the previous round). A lower share price can happen because the company's value decreased. Following are two main ways that a company's shares would be lower in the current round than in previous rounds:

- ✔ The company's value was artificially high due to a misunderstanding of company valuation, investor speculation, or a bubble in the economy.
- ✔ The company has lost value due to poor performance or poor management.

Two kinds of anti-dilution provisions may show up in your term sheet: weighted average and ratchet-based. These provisions have to do with how the down round is calculated.

Ratchet-based anti-dilution

With *full ratchet* anti-dilution, an investor who purchased shares in a Series A round receives additional shares if a subsequent round comes in at a lower price. A few problems exist with full-ratchet anti-dilution, most notably that, if the company is experiencing a down-round, investors will be hesitant to come in if all of the previous investors are receiving additional shares. The Series B investors are effectively being diluted before they even invest.

Weighted-average anti-dilution math

Here's a formula you can use to calculate a weighted-average anti-dilution (this formula comes directly from the NVCA.org Term Sheet template)

$$CP_2 = CP_1 \times (A + B) / (A + C)$$

where

✏ CP_2 is the Series A conversion price in effect immediately after new issue

✏ CP_1 is the Series A conversion price in effect immediately prior to new issue

✏ A is the number of shares of common stock deemed to be outstanding immediately prior to new issue, including all shares of outstanding common stock, all shares of outstanding preferred stock on an as-converted basis, and all outstanding options on an as-exercised basis; it doesn't include any convertible securities converting into this round of financing). The "broadest" base would include shares reserved in the option pool.

✏ B is the aggregate consideration received by the corporation with respect to the new issue divided by CP_1

✏ C is the number of shares of stock issued in the subject transaction

The second challenge is that if the company is not doing well, the Series B may be much smaller. So even if the company raises only $100,000 in a Series B that follows a $2 million Series A round, then _all_ of that Series A stock will double, even though it is disproportionately large relative to the new stock issuance. Weighted-average anti-dilution is one way around this problem.

If an investor purchased shares at $1 each in the Series A round, but the company doesn't perform well and the price for Series B comes in at $.50, or half the amount, the investor in the Series A round is entitled to double the number of shares in order to keep their proportionate investment percentage. Note that in most cases actual shares are not issued, but the conversion price from Preferred to Common stock is changed. This means that, when a liquidation event occurs, the preferred stock will convert to common stock at 2X the original rate, effectively doubling the number of shares purchased.

Weighted average anti-dilution

Weighted-average dictates that if the Series B is smaller than the Series A, then Series A shares will increase only in proportion to the size of the Series B raise.

Although you can go through the math if you like (it involves a rather ugly formula; see the nearby sidebar entitled "Weighted-average anti-dilution math"), the important part is that, with weighted average anti-dilution, your shares will only go down in value in proportion to the amount of new capital raised

Pay-to-play

If your company is successful in going through multiple rounds of financing, you may see a pay-to-play term in the term sheet. Pay-to-play refers to situations where first round investors need to continue making investments in future rounds in order to maintain their current percent of ownership. Various scenarios can happen in which investors can pay for only a portion of their pro rata round or where they may want to be able to assign that right to others. In many cases, if the investor doesn't participate in the next round, her stock will convert from preferred to common stock.

Anti-dilution clauses (refer to the preceding section) protect investors if the company issues another round of equity at a lower price, but only if those investors participate in future rounds. In other words, the investor has to keep putting cash in your company each round if she wants to keep the same percentage of ownership.

Even when investors aren't able to pay-to-play in future rounds, they will make money on your company if the value of your company continues to increase. Therefore, investors who own a lower percentage of the company in subsequent rounds will still be happy if the value of their shares continues to increase. Anyone would rather own 1 percent of a $100 million company than 50 percent of a $1 million company.

Drag-along agreement

The drag-along agreement comes into play when a majority of preferred stockholders want to sell or liquidate the company either through an initial public offering (IPO), merger, or acquisition. When the majority want to do the deal but the founders, who may now be minority stockholders, do not, the majority has the right to "drag" the minority along into the deal whether the minority wants to do it or not. This investor-friendly term prevents the founders from turning the company into a low-growth company (or lifestyle company) with no hope for a liquidity event for the investors.

No-shop agreement

Usually you see a no-shop agreement only with VCs, although some angel groups require them as well. The agreement says that if you sign the term sheet, you agree not to continue to look (or shop) for financing with other investors until either your deal is declined, your deal is funded, or a set period of time elapses.

The reason for this agreement is that, at a certain point, the investor will be investing time and money through legal and due diligence work; she wants to make sure that when she's ready to invest you won't have given the deal to another investor. In some cases, you can still shop with other VCs, but you have to pay a specified fee to get out of the deal. We recommend avoiding no-shop agreements that take more than 45 to 60 days so that you're not tied up with one VC who may just be keeping her options open at your expense. This begs the bad joke, "How is a VC like a cell phone contract?"

Comparing Equity and Convertible Debt

If you are pursuing venture capital, the VC that invests in your company is going to want equity in your company in return for the investment. By owning a piece of your company, the VC can make big bucks when you go public or are acquired.

Banks have no interest in investing in venture companies because they can't take equity in your company; they can only charge interest on loans that they may make to you. Because interest rates are far below the risk in early-stage investing and no upside exists, most banks won't touch early-stage companies.

What if you could find an arrangement that offered a little bit of both equity and debt? Then convertible debt may interest you.

Convertible debt is a traditional note payable with interest rates typically around 6 to 8 percent. Because that return is not enough to justify the risk of investing in your company, the investor also wants the note to be convertible into stock at some future time, at which point the investor wants to be able to buy the stock at a substantial discount to what other investors are paying for that round — typically about 20 percent off.

The entrepreneur's friend: The attraction of convertible debt

Convertible debt is a good way to fund a bridge. *Bridge financing* refers to the tactic in which a little bit of money is accepted now to help the company get to a lot of money in the future. Bridges should occur only when a very high expectation of the future inflow of cash exists.

Convertible debt ensures a company has cash on hand as it approaches a Series A round. If you have a commitment for a future close date or are just waiting for a fairly certain funding incident, convertible debt can fill the bill nicely.

Entrepreneurs like convertible debt because it's fast, cheap, and allows them to grow without giving up equity until a later date when it may be worth a lot more and can be sold at a premium price. Convertible debt is fast and cheap because all the provisions and terms don't have to be negotiated and no preferred stock is issued. (Attorney's fees can get quite steep with preferred stock and equity.) Convertible debt requires just a quick, few-page contract.

Entrepreneurs also like convertible debt because it puts off the question of valuation. Valuing an early-stage company is hard, and convertible debt is one way of delaying that difficult task. Plus, the ultimate value of the company comes later, when a VC invests and sets the price for the round. If the VC invests at $1 per share, then the convertible debt holders can buy stock up to the value of their initial investment for $.80 per share.

Investors who buy convertible debt get the stock cheaper because they committed to the deal a few months prior. When they committed, the deal looked different, more risks existed, and the company wasn't as developed.

The investor's barely tolerated cousin

Investors dislike convertible debt (usually, but not always) because it offers no upside other than the interest and discount price, at least until the note converts to equity.

The investor has more risk with a convertible note and loses upside potential. The investor has more risk because the note might never convert, or many years may pass before a conversion occurs. If, during this time, the company's value doubles, the investor doesn't see a penny of that increase in value because he has to pay the high stock price at the time of conversion. This is the reason why convertible debt is almost never an option for institutional VC investors, although it seems to work for friends and family who are willing to lend you money just to help you to succeed.

Investors can demand provisions in the note to protect themselves from bad situations.

Setting caps: Provisions to protect investors

One such provision involves setting a cap on the stock share price. Say that you set a cap at $1 per share. If VC investors come in after 18 months and give it a $2 valuation, then the investor doesn't pay any more than the $1 price. In this way, the early investor can benefit from the increase in value by buying stock cheaper than the new Series A investors.

Some people feel that, by the time you have negotiated a cap, you have effectively set the value, and no good reason exists to not just do an equity round anyway.

Caps can sour the deal for VCs. VCs understand that early-stage investors have taken a risk and should be rewarded for that, but VCs don't like to see others coming in at the Series A round for half of what they're paying. If a VC thinks that others are getting too good of a deal, they may back out or demand that the cap on previous investors stock price be raised closer to the Series A price before they will invest.

Setting a time-based conversion trigger

Conversion triggers are not always limited to happening at the next priced investment round. Investors can set a time based trigger so that the stock converts on the earlier of a Series A investment or 12 months. Of course, this conversion requires a valuation without having a VC on board to set the price, so this solution can be tricky.

Imagine that you issue a convertible note for $100,000 and pay 8 percent interest with a 20 percent discount. If the note converts in a year, the investor has made a 28 percent return on his investment. That's about normal for an early-stage investor. But if the note goes for two years, then the return on investment is only 18 percent (half of the 20 percent discount — you're spreading it out over two years instead of one — plus 8 percent per year).

Restructuring as You Move from Early Rounds to VC Rounds

You can plan all of your company's funding rounds before you raise a single cent. Even the best-laid plans might cause you to restructure a few things as your company develops. It's only natural. You'll have to restructure the office floor plan to put everyone's desks in the office as you hire employees, and it stands to reason that you'll have to restructure other things, too, namely the board and the capitalization table.

The board is one of the main things that will be restructured every time you raise a new round of capital. The board may grow, shrink, or simply change in composition. Your capitalization table, or the list of people who own stock in your company, will also likely change over time. The next sections have the details.

Later investors may force early investors to sell their shares or to take a different deal. If the early investors refuse, the company will fail to raise money. Early investors almost always allow the capitalization table to be restructured so that they can get something back for their investment. Their maxim: Don't tip the boat if you are in it!

Tidying your capitalization table

A capitalization table is a spreadsheet that lists all of the people and entities that have invested in the company. For each shareholder, it lists how many shares are owned, the preferences, the series provisions, and the voting rights. (Refer to the earlier section "Tallying Your Investors in a Cap Table" for more on the capitalization table.)

Companies are required to get quite a bit of traction before VCs will invest. Therefore, chances are a company will have raised capital at least once before it raises a VC round. Many companies will have done a few early rounds with friends and family, crowdfunding, or angel investors.

Cleaning your cap table by creating LLCs: An example

Freestyle Space is a company that helps owners of event space book their ballrooms, bars, and clubhouses. They are doing business in two states and would like to expand nationwide. Over the last two years they picked up a lot of momentum and a lot of investors. Initially, they closed a friends and family round where they raised $100,000 from 6 family members. Then they raised $1,500,000 through an angel round that included 23 individuals.

Freestyle has 29 investors in its cap table, which is not unusual at all. However, the 6 family members investors are all physicians and don't know anything about event-space management or advertising, which is Freestyle's main revenue stream. The angel investors are mixed in expertise; 3 of them are in advertising, but 1

has specific industry experience and has been helping as an advisor.

For Freestyle Space, forming LLCs for these investors makes sense: One LLC would be created that includes the family members from the friends and family round, and another LLC would include the angels from the angel round. For the angel LLC, the industry expert angel can represent the whole team of angels in stock votes and act as the go-between. The family LLC can elect a representative who might attend shareholder meetings.

By creating LLCs, the cap table would show two previous investors instead of 29. Important shareholder meetings would be easier to schedule with the 2 LLC representatives than with the whole group of 29.

If you have a mix of investors, each with different goals, your company will quickly find itself in trouble. At some critical point — maybe your company is in crisis or it's considering a big exit — you'll need to bring your investors all together to make a big decision. At such a time, you need your investors to work together like a well-oiled machine.

Putting early investors in an LLC

You can simplify your capitalization table by grouping investors into an entity called a *limited liability corporation* (LLC). If you have a group of investors who invested at the same time with the same term sheet, putting those individuals into an LLC can be reasonably easy. The individuals are then legally considered a single entity. They vote as one if they have voting rights, and they are represented by a single body in the room in meetings.

Buying out early investors

Sometimes a VC chooses to buy out early investors to clean up the capitalization table. As you can imagine, this solution may disappoint the early investors: They get compensated but are ultimately kicked out of a growing company. On the other hand, many early-stage investors are happy to just get their money back! If your company can't receive venture capital because of an early investor in the cap table, that early investor either has to give in or he will ruin the company's chances of getting funded. After all, any percentage of a defunct company is zero dollars.

Renegotiating terms with early investors

Two things can happen when you have structured a deal poorly in the first rounds. One possibility is that VCs will flee from your deal permanently. The other possibility is that you may be able to go back to your first round investors and renegotiate a new deal that will be more attractive to next round investors. Doing so is often in everyone's best interests (although structuring a reasonable deal the first time around and avoiding the pain and headache of renegotiating is always the best option).

Because many deals need to be renegotiated with previous investors to move forward with the next round of investment, you may want to warn your early investors of this potential renegotiation, especially when those investors are friends or family. If they don't understand the process, they may think that you've become too big for your britches now that your company is doing well. And they'll have a point; after all, you'll be taking sides with the big VCs rather than Aunt Jenny.

Shifting deal structure as the company grows

We once saw a deal where the Technology Transfer Office (TTO) that was instrumental in patenting the company's technology owned 51 percent of the company. TTOs are generally associated with universities, and they help professors commercialize their technologies by securing patents and connecting professors with business-savvy people. By the time the deal was placed in front of angel investors, it didn't look very good.

The TTO had control of the company and had a board seat that stopped new investors from getting much power over the company if they invested. TTOs, which are known for being experts in securing patents and forming new companies, aren't generally very strong in business development. So it was important that the control of the company shift to someone who was strong in early-stage business development.

The lead angel in the investment group understood the company well. He had just purchased a similar company and performed a great service by growing it quickly over the initial year he was involved. The lead angel renegotiated the terms with the TTO so that the seed round investors owned a majority share. He also negotiated for a board seat, which unseated the TTO's board representation.

If the company takes VC funding in the future, the tides will turn again. The lead angel from the seed round will be asked to step down from the board and the VC firm will control the majority share.

Unseating board members

Board seats are very valuable. Small companies have only three or five board seats, which illustrates how important each seat is. Boards are generally made of up a mixture of people who represent investors, founders, and outside industry experts. Boards tend to change around the time when the company closes an investment round. Investments are times of change in a lot of ways.

If you have given a board seat to an angel investor, you probably have to remove that member when you take venture capital. When you begin seeking venture capital, have a conversation with your board so all members understand that the angels will be replaced with representative from the VC firm. There is no way around this. VCs will take a board seat.

Overcoming Pitfalls of Early Deal Structure

If you ask VCs or private equity consultants (people who help companies get ready for VCs), they'll tell you that they see so many companies that have great opportunities but that they can't raise a new round of funding for because of poorly structured past deals. This unfortunate situation is very common and can permanently ruin a company's chance for VC funding.

The best way to prevent this kind of critical growth failure is to plan your fundraising from the beginning. Know whether your company plans to use VC funding as part of a growth plan and make sure that your early raises have that goal in mind.

Creating a capitalization plan: Your funding roadmap

If you were going to take a road trip, you'd get out a map and figure out what your options were to reach your destination. You'd map out cities that you would pass through on your way to your goal. If your goal was to reach your destination as quickly as possible, your route would be as close to a straight line as possible.

That seems very reasonable, but we see entrepreneurs every day who plan their trip to the first waypoint without having any understanding of where they are going and what the interim steps they should take. That oversight can lead to a road trip where your ultimate destination is west, but you head out eastbound only to spend a lot of time backtracking in order to go in the right direction. You'll also spend a lot of money and time cleaning up things that could have been easy if you had done them properly from the start. Even worse, you may find yourself in a situation where nobody will fund you, even though you've made progress with your company development.

So how do you create a capitalization plan? The key components are time, burn rate, and milestones.

Figuring out your timing

The timing between investment rounds is critical to your success. The guidelines differ for every industry. In a life science company, a company might go years between investment rounds, whereas a web app company might raise a round only a few months after the last. The general guideline is that funding rounds are separated by 12 to18 months.

Timing is important because you need to accomplish two major objectives between each round. One, you need to achieve your milestones. Two, you need to raise your next round. The tricky thing is that you can't raise your next round without having achieved your milestones, but if you spend all of your efforts achieving your milestones, you won't be able to raise your next round, and you could be stuck.

The amount of time raising capital takes is a factor, too. Depending on the economy, the size of your round, your own ability to raise money, and the network surrounding your company, fundraising could be a full time job that lasts a while. Plan on 6 to 12 months to raise a round of funding. We have seen a few companies do it in weeks, but they had prepared the deal down to the last detail before they told anyone they were fundraising. We've seen companies take more than a year to raise money as well.

Knowing your burn rate

Investors always ask you about your *burn rate,* that is, how fast you're burning through their cash. In a mature company, you don't talk about burn rate because you have revenues and expenses, and hopefully your revenues are greater than your expenses. In a pre-revenue company, however, it's all expenses, and the rate at which you burn though cash says a lot about how you're running the company.

Investors appreciate your understanding of burn rate. It's helpful to have an analysis of ways to speed up or slow down the spending. In their eyes, a too-slow burn rate is just as bad as a too-fast burn rate. Too slow means that you are not thinking like a venture company with super fast growth. Too fast means that you are out of control and spending the investors' money recklessly.

Burn rate is also tied to your milestone achievements. You need to match the amount of money you spend each month with the amount of achievement you need to make towards your milestones. Your main objective is to make sure you have enough cash to get your goals achieved and raise the next round before you run out of money. You probably don't run your car out of gas between fill-ups, and you shouldn't run your company out of liquid capital either. Plan to have a refill of financing before your tank is three-fourths empty!

Tackling milestones

Milestones may be the most important part of your finance strategy. You need to think about milestones in a way that involves clusters of value. Just accomplishing a random collection of tasks does not add value in the way that a milestone strategy will.

We see a lot of companies who are fixated on solving the next big challenge in front of them. Software companies focus on finishing the beta and getting the working version done and live on the Internet. That's great, but if your funding round gets you to a live version of software with no customers, you may be stuck.

Think about your milestones in terms of risk. Each milestone you achieve is a reduction of risk for your investor and an increase in value for your company. Early risks tend to be technology risks. You need to prove that your software, patent, invention, or whatever can do what you say it will do. Later risks tend to be market risks. Can you establish viable channels for your product? Will people buy it at the price-points you have set? Can you leverage a small marketing budget into measurable results that will be repeatable with a bigger budget? If you can't answer "yes" to these questions, you have significant market risk that will scare investors away. We discuss the concept of tying milestones to risk more in the next chapter.

Your milestone strategy should combine multiple risks so that investors are confident in investing in your next round. Don't just raise enough money to satisfy your technology risks, but be sure to add another $100,000 to $200,000 to test market your product and be able to consistently demonstrate an increasing conversion rate on customers who see your product.

Calculating how much you should raise

First time entrepreneurs are often diligent and work out a detailed plan of expenses and burn rate needed to launch their company. They then set out to raise that amount of money. This approach is flawed!

Your company increases in value with every milestone that you hit. If you raise 100 percent of what you need at the beginning, you'll be lucky to end up owning 1 percent of the equity by the time your liquidity event comes along.

To raise the money you need while maximizing your own equity stake, you need to develop a phased capital raising strategy. Most companies have four or more phases, starting with friends and family, then angel funding, then a Series A, followed by Series B. Some companies even get up to Series D or E offerings.

If you raise too much money, then you have given up too much equity at a cheap, early-stage price. Just a little bit too much is okay, since that's like an insurance policy that you have enough runway to make it to your next round. If you raise too little money, then you won't be able to achieve your milestones, which means that you may never raise another round and you may end up closing down your company.

Deciding how much to pay yourself

You're CEO – right? So your salary should be $1 million? Not if you want to raise venture capital! The rule of thumb is that even if you're a CEO, your salary should be the minimum amount needed to get by. Just rent and groceries — no fabulous trips to Tahiti on your yacht, at least not yet!

The VC wants to have your rewards aligned with theirs. That means that both of you need to be focused on the exit. Big salaries are for people who work in big companies and don't have the windfall of a big exit hanging in the future like a carrot in front of a horse. At an early-stage company, everyone should be working for some combination of equity and salary, and the salary should be as little as possible.

Avoiding a bridge to nowhere

Here, we use the concept of a bridge to help people talk about investment rounds. The company is *here* now, and with financing, it will be able to get to *there* via the bridge of capital. The bridge to nowhere refers to a poorly defined financing round. The company is *here* now and wants to raise $500,000 to get through its next milestones. If completing those milestones doesn't happen on schedule or if completing the milestones does not represent a significant reduction in risk, then there may not be a pool of available investors for the next round. You need to be creating a strategy for each funding round that will make your company increasingly attractive for future rounds.

Financing a company with a bridge to nowhere leaves the company with more investors or debt, and no more milestones achieved. This situation is often caused by over-optimism on the part of the entrepreneur who failed to plan for the possibility that their original plans would take longer to execute than they thought. These cases can be prevented by consulting with fundraising experts and listening to their advice so that you understand what investors are looking for at each phase of investment and what the norms are for milestones to be accomplished in each round.

One advantage of working with VCs and building a strong relationship is that the VC who invested in your Series A round will likely be the VC who invests in your Series B round. In many cases, the VC will invest simply to have the option to continue investing if your team is able to execute. Most venture capital funds keep 50 percent of their fund in reserve to fund Series B investments. If you work with one of these companies and you are able to perform on your plan, then you are most likely to raise your Series B round and avoid a bridge to nowhere.

Chapter 10

Leading the Risk Conversation

Risk is an inherent element in early-stage companies. The word *risk* itself suggests danger, possible failure, and a whole package of bad feelings. In the world of venture capital, *risk* means something a little bit different: risks are the milestones that your business must accomplish before your company can reach its goals. These potentially beneficial steps along the way are referred to as risks because they've not yet been accomplished. If the company doesn't achieve them or doesn't achieve them in a reasonable time frame, it stands to fail at accomplishing its final goals.

In a meeting with founders to, we were discussing risk and its relationship to valuation. One of the entrepreneurs slapped his hands down on the table and said, "Why do you keep calling it 'risk'? These are opportunities." And so they are. The milestones that investors see as risks are exactly the opportunities that entrepreneurs see as potentially great moments in the history of their companies. If the opportunity is not seized, the company will not succeed as planned. That is the risk. If this book has one theme, it's that early-stage investing has two sides. If both sides don't understand each other, you've got a problem.

In this chapter we explain how to approach the risk/opportunity discussion and delve more deeply into the fundamentals of investor perception. Thinking like an investor enables you to have more effective discussions surrounding your deal and your company.

Getting into the Mindset of Venture Investors: Horses and Wolves

Ask yourself this: If entrepreneurs and investors are like horses and wolves, which is the horse and which is the wolf? This analogy, the brainchild of Adam Rentschler, CEO and founder of Valid Evaluation, helps clarify the communication and perception challenges that exist between entrepreneurs and investors.

Interestingly, when answering the question, entrepreneurs typically say that the investors are wolves, because they are "vulture capitalists" trying to take away control and ownership of their business. Investors, on the other hand, typically say that entrepreneurs are the wolves, because they're trying to take the investors' money with wild valuations and without exercising proper care toward preserving their investment.

Clearly, when it comes to investing in early-stage companies, a lot of fear exists on both sides, and both sides perceive the other to be the aggressor that must be approached carefully.

Horses or wolves? The eyes have it

So which really is the horse, and which really is the wolf? Investors are the horses, and entrepreneurs are the wolves. Surprised? The answer is in the eyes.

Horses (investors): Playing it safe in a risky world

Horses' eyes are on the sides of their heads — perfect for prey animals that must always be on the lookout for wolves or other predators that may attack. With their eyes in this location, horses have a wide field of vision and can scan the horizon for potential hazards.

Now think of investors. If you were to visit the websites of a half-dozen wealth advisors and pay attention to how they position themselves to be attractive to investors, you'd find, almost without fail, the words "preservation of capital." Investors are interested in investing and making a profit in order to grow their portfolio, but they also want to maintain their wealth and preserve their capital. Their attitude is fundamentally conservative.

Why are investors so concerned about risk? Probably the biggest reason is that, for a typical venture fund, something like 60 percent of investments will return no money at all back to the fund. Venture investing is really that risky.

Venture capital funds need to provide high returns to their investors, so they must take risks, but they are also constantly evaluating those risks in order to preserve the capital of their limited partners.

Wolves (entrepreneurs): Keeping their eyes on the prize

Now think of wolves' eyes. They're positioned close together and focused forward. The wolf needs to focus on its prey, undistracted by peripheral vision. Entrepreneurs are focused on building a successful business to the exclusion of all else. This single-mindedness can sometimes create a blindness to risk and excessive confidence in success which is all that some entrepreneurs can see on the horizon. This kind of personality can be a good thing; entrepreneurs who have it are the ones who can achieve success in the tough business of running a venture-class company — but it's an inherently different attitude than the one investors have.

Learning to speak "horse"

As an entrepreneur, you should always keep your eye on the ball while at the same time learning to speak "horse" — the language of risk — to your investors. When entrepreneurs show sensitivity to risk and an understanding of all the factors that can go wrong in pursuit of their goals, they'll gain the confidence of the investor. By speaking openly and transparently about risks, you're speaking investors' language, reinforcing that you both share a similar outlook, and giving them confidence that agreement in future decision-making is possible.

So should you reveal all of the risks to potential investors? Won't an excessive focus on risks cause investors to shy away from the deal? Although a pitch that focuses 100 percent on risk won't be a compelling story for any investor, a pitch that avoids discussion of risk is also a turn-off. The best pitch is one that balances the opportunity (the company's competitive advantage in gaining market share in a large and rapidly growing market) with the risks (the challenges and milestones that must be overcome in order to achieve success).

Venture capitalists see hundreds of deals, all of which have significant risks. They see many companies in the same industry, all of which face similar risks. They've seen many companies fail and a few succeed. In short, VCs have the background and expertise necessary to be able to connect the dots between risks and rewards. They have an extraordinary ability to hone in on what could go wrong and what needs to be done in order for things to go right. Despite this expertise, many investments that VCs make still end up in failure; therefore, they want to have a clear understanding of what can go wrong and what you plan to do about that.

The best way to create a compelling risk story for the venture capitalists you present to is to put yourself in their shoes. VCs have a duty to their limited partners (LPs) to invest carefully and to research every investment to uncover problems that may kill the company in the future.

Every investment that a VC makes needs to be able to return between 10 and 50 times (abbreviated 10X–50X) the original investment. (Remember, up to half of the investments made will end up as failures or "the walking dead" — companies that return minimal cash flow but don't have any real opportunity for exit.) Your job is to provide a great risk story: one that's open about risk while simultaneously giving the VC a justification that he can provide to his LPs about why your company is a great investment.

Understanding Risk

As we note earlier, you need to include risks in your communication with investors. How you go about doing that is important. First, you must understand the types of risks that investors will closely scrutinize during the due diligence process. The more you've thought about them, the more easily you'll be able to respond to questions when the time comes. The following sections have the details.

As you address your company's risks, you can begin to weight them in your mind. Which risks are going to be easy to overcome and which are actually pretty daunting? Which risks would be smaller problems if you had more money — or more time? Which risks are completely out of your hands and in the hands of fate instead? Think about these questions as you draw together your company's risk profile.

Identifying business risks to success

The following sections outline the most common risks that VCs look at during due diligence. Keep in mind, however, that thousands of other risks may be important to your business. You may have environmental risks, for example, which you would want to address. The main thing is to think comprehensively about what could go wrong and to develop a strategy around each issue that your company faces or is likely to face.

Each milestone is a separate project and has its own risk profile. An early-stage technology company, for example, has lots of technology risk early on, but then these shift to market risks after the product is complete and sales begin. (The market risk is always there, even from the beginning, of course, but it isn't really experienced until the company starts selling its products.)

A forward thinking company thinks about market risk even during technology development, ensuring that product development take into account actual conversations with customers and a true understanding of what they want. A perfectly designed app that isn't of interest to anyone is a technology success and market failure.

Sales and marketing risk

Sales and marketing are perhaps the biggest risks for many early-stage companies. Many tech companies, for example, spend a lot of time focusing on their technology and not enough time on how they are going to sell it. When new products are introduced, gauging their reception can be difficult: How well will customers accept them? How much are they willing to pay? What will the sales cycle be? What competitive pressures exist? What will the sales costs be? VCs like to see that you have talked to a lot of potential customers, that you have thoughtful and appropriate sales channels identified, that key relationships have been established, and that you have test marketed your product (if appropriate) to demonstrate market demand.

Other risks in this category include

✔ **Competition risk:** Think holistically about your competition. If you're the sole manufacturer of lavender-colored bikes, your saying that you have no competition because nobody else has lavender colored bikes isn't going to go over very well. Your actual competitive environment is always much larger and there are many more competitors than you may think. Your biggest competitor is almost always apathy. People are often happy to just continue doing whatever they were doing before your product came along.

VCs expect you to be an expert in your market area. Have a good rundown on all of the other companies with similar products and services in your area. If they have succeeded or failed, you should have a good understanding of why. If the VC knows about competitive threats that you don't, that's a bad thing!

✔ **Reputation risk:** Investors are worried not only about your reputation, but also about their own. Reputation risk can impact early-stage companies that don't have well-developed communications policies. If your company is involved in e-commerce and decides to get into distributing pornographic materials, for example, this decision would severely impact your ability to get funding from certain investors.

In addition, in the Internet age, there is a lot more transparency and a long-tail of memory when significant quality or ethical issues arise with your company. Be aware that your reputation is a big part of your brand and is represented in everything that your company does, including not only your business decisions but also how your company engages in social media sites, like Twitter or Facebook.

✔ **Social risk:** Social risk refers to trends that may impact demand for your product. Trends that cause huge demand for your product can be great, but how long will they last? Is your product just another Pet Rock or something that people will want for a long time? Fashion industries are particularly impacted by social trends, as are green technologies, games, apps, media and entertainment, and anything that depends on widespread popularity.

Technology risk

Technology risk is at its highest for early-stage companies where a high degree of uncertainty exists about whether the product will work or not. If you have developed a prototype, you must still ask whether it will work when manufactured in quantity, or whether it can be scaled up in size for commercial and industrial applications.

Later stage companies also face technology risk in the form of data security issues, continuity concerns, Internet hacking risks, and other technology risks that impact large volumes of data, customer credit card records, HIPAA medical information, or even simply the ability to provide service if your e-commerce site crashes.

Manufacturing risk

Regardless of whether you make things in your own factory or outsource your manufacturing elsewhere, you have risks related with the production, storage, and delivery of physical goods. These risks range from labor practices in foreign operations to safety issues, perishability of products, breakdowns in supply chains, labor strikes, materials availability, quality management, freight and logistics interruptions, currency fluctuations, and more.

Management risk

Several types of management risk exist. The first risk is departures of key personnel. When your company has 100 or more people, losing people may not be a big problem, but when you're a start-up with a team of four, the departure of key personnel can be critical. VCs will want to know

✔ That you have developed a vesting program that provides incentives for key personnel to stay with the company.

✔ That you have *key man insurance,* which ensures that funds are available to buy out the equity of a key management team member who is killed or incapacitated so that you can recruit a replacement team member.

Other management risks include key personnel taking business ideas to competitors, health issues, conflicts of interest, or personality clashes.

An entrepreneurial company with an idea is worthless if the executive team can't demonstrate that it can execute the plan and build the idea into a company that creates cash flow. This is why VCs are so concerned with the team. They want to know whether the team is experienced in execution and can pull together to solve big problems, or whether they will resort to finger pointing and blame.

Financing risk

Risks related to financing include the following:

- **Funding risk:** If your plan includes multiple rounds of funding, then the overall risk of your company is higher than if you could reach your exit with just one round. Going through three, four, or five rounds before an exit isn't uncommon. Each time you have a new round, you're expected to achieve key milestones. If you fail to reach those milestones for whatever reason, your ability to raise the next round is in jeopardy.

- **Exit risk:** Exit risk is important because if you can't execute on your exit plan, then the VC won't be able to return capital to his LPs. Understand the macro trends in your industry so that you can anticipate what might make acquisitions more or less attractive a few years down the road. What will make you uniquely suited for an acquisition when the time is right?

- **Economic risk:** Economic risk refers to a macro trend that is possibly equally impactful for all businesses in your industry. What if the value of the dollar drops or goes up? Currency risks may be significant for your company if it does a lot of international business. Economic risks are things outside of your control that may have a huge impact on your business and other businesses in your industry.

Legislative, regulatory, and political risk

Some companies have huge legislative and regulatory risks. Think about anything that has to do with healthcare. The FDA approval process can take decades and cost hundreds of millions of dollars without any guarantee of success. Some regulatory processes are expensive, time consuming, and seemingly capricious in their application. If your company faces these risks, your ability to raise venture capital will be impacted.

Political risk can be important for companies that depend on a certain party or local government official being in office. Changes in tax policy, employment law, or compliance with new securities regulations could all have an impact on your company.

Litigation risk

Litigation risk refers to how likely it is that your company will be the target of a litigation. This type of risk increases as your company grows bigger. Smaller companies may not be perceived as being worthwhile as a litigation target. But as your company grows and becomes either a threat to others or is perceived as having sufficient assets to justify a legal battle, then litigation risk increases.

Your industry also impacts litigation risk. A company that makes socks faces substantially less risk than a company that makes infant car seats. Food products can also have significant litigation risk, as does anything in the medical or transportation fields.

International risk

International risk applies to all companies in some way or another, but it is especially important to those companies that have a direct link with international business, including imports and exports. Currency risk is an example of international risk. If your currency drops by 20 percent and you are buying on a fixed contract, then your cost of goods just went up by 20 percent. If this amount represents your entire net profit margin, your company is at risk. Other international risks include wars, protectionist barriers, tariffs, international regulatory risks, problems with international distributors, shippers, and more.

Betting on the jockey, not the horse

Because so much risk is involved in early-stage investment and many companies pivot in response to risks and opportunities, by the time the exit occurs, a company may bear little resemblance to the company that was originally pitched to the VC.

VCs often say that they look for five things in a company: team, team, team, large or rapidly growing market, and an innovative product or service that creates an unfair advantage in that market. The fact that the first three factors are the same (team, team and team) reinforces the idea that execution risk is the most difficult of all risks to assess.

In the case of Pinterest, the company didn't follow its original plan, shared with VCs, but the team was smart enough to spot an opportunity and to pivot into a new model, resulting in amazing success.

Your company may have started with a bunch of friends or people in a Startup Weekend group or class at business school. Although such serendipitous meetings can be great, in most cases though, the best way to build a team is to network widely in your community and put together a team intentionally, finding people you think will give your company the best chance of responding to risks and opportunities. VCs appreciate your having the best jockey in town.

Seeing how risk changes over time

A company's risk profile changes over time. The farther along a company gets in achieving its strategic plan and hitting its milestones, the less risk the company has. Although risk generally goes down as a company grows, new risks come with being larger and operating at a later stage. Early risks tend to focus on technology, and later risks tend to focus on marketing. You need to understand how to address new risks as they come along and incorporate them into your overall risk profile and management strategy.

Don't be fooled, though. The reduction of risk isn't a straight line, nor does it always go down. Some companies have catastrophic events that occur and increase risk for a period of time. When this happens, you need to involve your VC in working out a new strategy to deal with the problems. Your objective is to overcome any adverse incidents and get your milestone back on track as soon as possible.

Tying Risk to Valuation

Several valuation methods use risk as the primary driver for early-stage valuation — an approach that makes sense because early-stage valuation is driven primarily by uncertainty and risk. Later-stage valuations can be done relatively easily using revenue, profit, and asset methodologies, but early-stage valuations have more to do with whether the investor thinks you can actually do what you say you're going to do and whether the market will accept it.

Understanding how risk impacts value helps you make your best presentation and lets you negotiate the valuation for your company more effectively. Having a clear and transparent methodology that makes all risks clear also helps to dispel any vague concerns that the investors may have about your company.

It is always better to be able to have conversations in which the risks are clear and you can discuss the pros and cons openly rather than trying to counter concerns that investors may have with little more than a hunch.

The important thing to remember about the valuation methods that quantify risk is that the inputs are essentially all subjective. Although you may come out with a number, that number is only as good as the inputs you have started with. The benefit of using these or other risk based valuation methods is that the risks and your attitudes toward them are transparent. You and the VC may not agree on the impacts of all of the risks, but at least they're on the table and can be discussed rationally. See Chapter 11 for more examples of risk valuation methods.

Using the risk factor valuation method

In the risk factor valuation method, you list all the major risks for a company and assign a value to them. To find this value, start with the average valuation for venture businesses in your area. Nationwide last year, the average valuation was about $2.5 million, skewed mostly by values on the coasts. The numbers in the Midwest may be more like $1.5 to $2 million. Do some research to learn what your local basis is. For this example, assume a $2 million average valuation in our area.

Take the average valuation amount and apply risk values either positively or negatively. (This task is similar to what you'd do to adjust the Blue Book value of a used car, based on the mileage, special options, overall condition, and so on). For each category, add up to three points for high value or deduct up to three points for extraordinary risk. Each point is worth $100,000. After you enter all the numbers, you can calculate your valuation.

Here's an example: Assume that you are an early-stage company called Game-ibuy.com. You have a unique e-commerce site that gamifies the shopping experience where customers can compete with each other for bargains. Your company will make money using an affiliate model where you collect 20 percent of all the transactions completed on your site. You're looking for $500,000 to finish the technical work on your site and get it ready to launch. At launch, you'll raise a Series A round for another $3 million which will fund your national launch and bring you to cash flow positive. You have a team of four, comprised of two developers, a CEO, and a CMO (Marketing) who has worked in retail but has limited online experience. All have experience in start-ups, and the CEO has had a successful venture-backed exit in the past. The CEO has started conversations with Amazon who has expressed interest in the company's technology, if they can get it to work.

For the purposes of this example, assume that your risks are those listed in the earlier section "Identifying business risks to success." Create a worksheet listing these risks in the left-hand column. Then fill in the necessary detail: Describe your company's status in that category and then apply the risk factor. Table 10-1 shows an example valuation worksheet.

Table 10-1	Risk Factor Valuation Method for Game-ibuy.com	
Risk	**Description**	**Factor**
Business stage	Early stage — typical.	0
Competition	Others in development, lots of affiliate shopping sites.	−1

Risk	Description	Factor
Economic risk	No unusual risk.	0
Exit risk	Have had conversations and interest was expressed early on. Past exit experience also helps.	+3
Funding risk	One more round.	−1
International	Domestic company.	0
Legislative/regulatory/political	Internet tax applies to all competitors equally.	0
Litigation	No special risk.	0
Management	Small team, experienced, venture backed exit.	+3
Manufacturing	Not applicable.	0
Reputation risk	No unusual risk.	0
Sales and marketing	Increasing cost to gain online market share, lots of competition with similar offerings, lack of online marketing experience.	−3
Social risk	Possible fallout from all these affiliate sites. Gamification is a huge trend that may not last.	−1
Technological risk	Application not yet complete. There are unique challenges to building the gamification components.	−2

Now do the calculation. Determine the value of all your positive and negative ratings to get your net adjustment. Subtract the net adjustment from the starting average to get your valuation prior to investment. Table 10-2 shows an the calculation based on the information in Table 10-1.

Table 10-2	Value Calculation for Game-ibuy.com
Starting average regional valuation	*$2 million*
Value of all positive ratings	+6 x $100,000 = +$600,000
Value of all negative ratings	−8 x $100,000 = −$800,000
Net adjustment to value	$600,000 − $800,000 = −$200,000
Pre-money valuation (starting average minus total adjustments)	$2,000,000 − $200,000 = $1,800,000
Pre-money value	$1,800,000

Assessing risk with the scorecard method

Many VCs use a scorecard technique of assessing risk which can also be mapped to value. Table 10-3 shows what this might look like. This valuation method breaks the risks into five main categories: technology, disruption, market, financial, and people. These are the biggest risk categories for a company, so this is the simplest way to assess risk. Table 10-3 lists and describes these risks.

Table 10-3	Scorecard Method Risk Categories
Type of Risk	**Description**
Technology	R&D risks: Likelihood that the technology will fail testing
Disruption	Major, unforeseeable change that will negate all plans
Market	Time to capture market and amount of addressable market
Financial	Likelihood that the company will run out of liquid capital
People	Chance that the right people will not be available to drive company growth

Different risk types may overlap. Technology risk, for example, overlaps with management risk. What would happen if the company lost key development personnel? It also overlaps with funding risk if the entrepreneur depends on future capital raises to complete product development.

To use the scorecard method, VCs perform a series of steps. Table 10-4 shows an example of what the scorecard method might look like for game-ibuy.com, the company described in the preceding section; refer to this table as you read the steps:

1. **The VC assigns a weight to each of the five risk factors.**

   This weighting is different for each company, but each VC may have a standard value that he uses for most companies he looks at. If the VC believes that the most important factor is the team, then he may assign 30 to 40 percent for the team, for example. If the competitive environment in the market is small, then that may only get 10 or 15 percent.

2. **The VC creates a confidence factor for each element.**

This factor has a base amount of 100 percent. If the VC is extremely confident in the team, for example, he may give a factor of 150 percent for team. If he is less confident about the market, then that may only get 70 percent. Using this model, you can go as low as 0 percent if risk of failure is certain or 200 percent in an extraordinary event where success is absolute and without risk.

3. **The VC adds all the weighted factors together to get the total weighted factor.**

4. **The VC multiplies the total weighted value by the company's initial value to arrive at the company current valuation.**

Table 10-4   **Scorecard Method of Valuation for Game-ibuy.com**

Risk Type	Description	Weight	Confidence Factor	Weighted Factor
Technology	Technology not yet done.	20%	70%	0.14
Disruption	Environment is competitive.	10%	80%	0.08
Market	Huge market.	20%	100%	0.2
Financial	Need Series A in 12 mos.	10%	100%	0.1
People	Great team.	30%	140%	0.42
Other	Other factors – supplier relationships.	10%	110%	0.11
Total Weighted Factor				1.05
Initial Valuation	Based on early-stage companies in your area			$2 million
Adjusted Valuation	Initial valuation × total weighted factor (2,000,000 ×1.05)			$2.1 million

---

Sharing risk through syndication

In venture capital, *syndication* means having a number of investors get together and share in the deal rather than making the entire investment alone. Investors syndicate on a deal for three main reasons:

✔ **They don't have enough money to fund the deal.** Perhaps their limited partnership agreement limits the size of the deal that they can invest in. Maybe they are nearing the end of their investment period and have limited funds available.

✔ **They want to share risk with other investors.** If a VC invests in just a few high risk deals, his chance of hitting the jackpot on one of them is relatively small. On the other hand, if he can syndicate with others and get in on many deals, he shares the risk and increases his chance of success.

✔ **Syndicating gives VCs an opportunity to take advantage of increased deal flow.** Having pre-screened, pre-researched deals fall into their laps is much easier than constantly looking for deals and screening for the very best ones on their own.

Syndicating with other investors also puts more eyeballs on the deal. The new investment partners who are asked to look at the deal may not be as swayed by a personal relationship that the first VC may have formed with the entrepreneur. Syndication partners add depth to the due diligence process and increase the chances of success.

Exposing Risk: Strategies That Keep You in the Game

You may want to hide your risks and sweep them under the carpet, but this tack is the worst one you can take. Venture capitalists are trained to spot risks. They'll likely see the risks that you've chosen not to mention, plus a few more that you haven't even thought of yet. When risks are unaddressed, the VC will believe that your team may be inexperienced and unprepared to deal with bad things that happen to the company as it progresses through its plan.

Preparing a risk assessment or a risk-based valuation model (discussed in the earlier section "Tying Risk to Valuation") is a good way for you to communicate that you understand the risks and have thought long and hard about their likelihood and severity.

Addressing both constants and variable risks

Your risk assessment doesn't need to be like the ones that Fortune 500 companies perform in which teams of people assess global trends to uncover political, economic, and social risks. For the most part, these things are out of your control, and they'll impact your company the same way they'll impact your competition. Getting into the weeds assessing risks at this level will only distract from your story and lead the VC to believe you are not sufficiently focused on your goals.

Other risks are ones you can control. When you discuss these risks, you want to show how your company is poised with regard to that risk. Your job when you create your strategic plan is to navigate risks and opportunities with an understanding of what you can reasonably control and what you cannot. Therefore, when you communicate risks to a VC, accompany them with a mitigation strategy — the actions you plan to take to address the stated risk. Hearing this information, the VC gains confidence in your ability to anticipate and prepare for or prevent bad things from happening.

Outlining your mitigation strategies

Mitigation strategies are the things that you can do to eliminate or reduce risk for your company. For every risk you list, you should also list your mitigation strategies.

When you're assessing risk, the overall impact is actually a calculation of the total risk, the probability of the risk occurring, and the impact of the risk minus the effects of your mitigation strategy on the likelihood or impact.

Using risk framework to prioritize risks

Almost every risk *can* be mitigated, but not all risks *will* be mitigated. The reason is that mitigation strategies have costs attached to them. The costs may be in hard dollars, such as purchasing a key man insurance policy for all of the members of your management team, or they may have resource costs, such as the time it takes to create a strategic partnership with a company or organization that would shield you from risk.

One of your tasks, then, is to determine which risks you can — and should — mitigate. The risk framework (see Figure 10-1) is one way of categorizing your risks according to their likelihood and severity. All risks fall into one of the following four categories:

- ✔ High likelihood/major consequences (must be addressed)
- ✔ Low likelihood /minor consequences (safely ignored)
- ✔ High likelihood /minor consequences (modest effort)
- ✔ Low likelihood /major consequences (modest effort such as insurance policy).

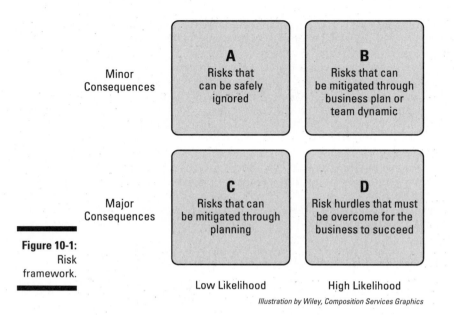

Figure 10-1:
Risk
framework.

Illustration by Wiley, Composition Services Graphics

Turning a barrier into a boon

Risks are not always bad. Some risks, for example, may create barriers for entry that effectively keep your competitors out of your space, forcing them to stay out of certain market segments or avoid certain strategies. If you can develop a mitigation strategy that circumvents the risk waylaying your competitors, then you have created opportunity for yourself.

Try to figure out what constraints your competitors believe they're operating under. If you've also considered these constraints to be risks that should be avoided, have your team brainstorm ways that you can turn them into opportunities. If you can find an opening that you're competitors haven't, you've gained a competitive advantage.

Think of how Facebook entered into a business where the *network effect* (a phenomenon in which a company can only be successful if a huge number of people join into the network) is a huge barrier. Everyone thought Myspace had that market locked up, so there were few competitors, but Facebook turned that barrier into an opportunity and created a huge network.

Outlining past risks that the company has overcome

Don't just tell the VC about the risks that you have ahead of you. Be sure to tell the stories about all the risks you have overcome on your way to where you stand today. Your past risk stories demonstrate how your team addresses risks and shows that you can accomplish significant things in a short amount of time.

If you've faced and overcome challenges in the past, share these stories with the VCs you're pitching to. VCs know that bad things happen. By sharing your past experiences, you help them see how your team approaches difficulties and works together to overcome them. Showing that you've successfully overcome challenges in the past gives them some comfort that you'll be able to do so in the future.

TIP

Ideally, you'll meet with your VC several months before you're actually ready to ask for funding (head to Chapter 5 for more on how to make these early connections). When you do, share the upcoming risks your company is facing. Then the next time you and the VC meet, you can demonstrate what you have accomplished.

REMEMBER

Milestones and risk are tightly woven together. The more milestones you achieve, the lower your risk. Every time your company achieves milestones, you are adding value. To put your valuation conversation into context and demonstrate your ability to execute, demonstrate all the milestones you have achieved in the past as well as the milestones you've got ahead of you.

VCs want entrepreneurs to have skin in the game — they've invested their own money in the business or they've worked for a long time without being paid, for example. It can also mean that you have built up a lot of momentum overcoming risk before the VC comes to the table. In any case, they want to see that you are 100 percent committed to making this venture successful.

Connecting Cash Raises to Risk and Company Success

Company growth — regardless of the type of company — follows a predictable pattern. There will be times when your teammates have their heads down and everyone is working on developing the plan and times involving a great deal of turmoil — for bad or good. Major changes to the business model and significant hires, for example, can be tumultuous for a small company. Adding a revenue stream can throw everyone's schedule out of whack as you sort out who manages which roles.

When you and your team are working nonstop to develop your product and grow your business, you may be wondering when is the best time to fit in fundraising. There are a lot of things to consider, but the simple answer is between milestones. Schedule your fundraising to occur just after you've achieved one big success and have the next big milestone on the horizon.

The key is to raise money before you run out of money. Fundraising isn't just about needing money. It's about letting investors buy future success.

As a manager of an early-stage venture company, you need to pay special attention to your *burn rate,* the rate at which you're spending the company's cash. If the burn rate exceeds the company's resources before the next round is raised, then the company may go bankrupt. You can control your spending, but you can't always control your funding rounds and their timing. When you plan your fundraising timeline, allow for extra time to raise your next round so that your coffers don't get depleted before the next infusion of capital (see Figure 10-2). If you depend on cash from sales to keep your company afloat, for example, be careful because you can't always control whether someone will buy your product or service.

VCs keep about half of their funds in reserve for follow-on investment. These funds are reserved for only the most promising companies and those that have trouble may find themselves out of business if they can't raise another round.

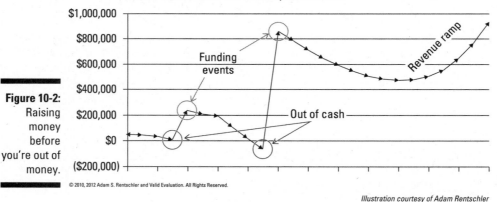

Figure 10-2:
Raising money before you're out of money.

Illustration courtesy of Adam Rentschler

Using lower risk hurdles to plan fundraise timing

Looking at your risks graphically can help you to determine what the optimum times are to raise VC money. The best time to raise money is when risks are low. The worst time is when your risks are high and you're out of cash.

Try to model your risk profile over time and start your fund raising to coincide with achievement of key milestones that add value to your company.

Figure 10-3 shows a risk stairs model, created by Adam Rentschler, which you can use to schedule your fundraising rounds. This graphic lets you communicate that your risk is lowered over time, which is just as important as showing increased revenues over time.

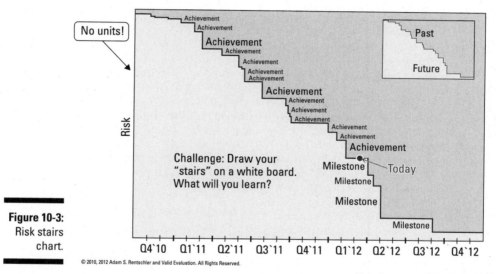

Figure 10-3:
Risk stairs
chart.

Illustration courtesy of Adam Rentschler

The model is simple to complete. Simply list the major milestones coming up for your company as well as those that you have successfully completed in the past. Assign a weight to each milestone. The milestones with larger weights appear as larger stair steps. Those with smaller weights will appear as smaller steps. The purpose of this exercise is twofold:

- ✔ To identify your key milestones and their overall impact so that you can have a transparent discussion with your investors about the risks and opportunities that you are facing.

- ✔ To help you plan for optimal fundraising timing. Because the risk stairs model shows you when your risks are lowest and therefore your company value is highest, it can help you to raise funds at the time your company will have the greatest value to investors.

Every time you raise money, you will be selling a portion of your equity and you don't have more than 100 percent to sell, so your strategy should focus on selling equity only at the best times.

Here's an example of how your risk stair steps impact your ability to raise funds: Recently a company was looking to raise $600,000 to take its security encryption software to market. The entire marketing strategy was to take this product to the U.S. government because of its remarkable encryption strength. To sell to the government, the company needed a key testing for effectiveness and certification from the National Institute for Standards and Technology. The certification had a cost of $35,000.

Did the company spend the $35,000 to prove that its software worked and that it would be a viable contender in the government markets? No, it didn't. Instead the company continued seeking $600,000 from VC and angel investors. Needless to say, the risk-to-reward ratio was far too high at that point for any rational investor to write a check, and the company didn't raise the round. Worse, its reputation was tarnished in the community. Even if the company later pursued the certification, fund raising would have been difficult, if not impossible. The company should have achieved this major, relatively low-cost milestone well before approaching investors, and its failure to do so was a major management mistake.

If the company had used a risk stairs model, it could have easily seen that there was a major risk with low mitigation costs that should have been addressed before seeking funding.

Looking beyond the next milestone

Even though the best time to plan your fundraising endeavors is between milestones, you're not raising money merely to complete the next milestone. Raising funds to just achieve the next milestone can be a huge mistake — and one many companies make.

Early-stage tech companies, for example, often look for funding to complete their website, app, or whatever they're doing. Imagine that they raise the round and successfully achieve their milestone. Now they have to go back to the trough for another $3 million for their go-to-market funding — not an easy task.

Instead, think about linking your milestones together so that one flows easily to the next. Doing so helps you ensure that funding won't be interrupted due to a gap between milestones. The software company in the preceding paragraph would be smarter to have part of its seed round include a small amount of money — maybe $25,000 — to get a jump-start on its marketing plan. If it had conducted a limited marketing campaign and demonstrated strong customer demand, it would have crossed a huge risk threshold without running out of cash and made raising the next round much easier.

Finding ways to lower risk

Think about your funding strategy in terms of risk and ask your team, "What can we do to lower risk?" Some of the things you may come up with might include securing patents; filling out the team; gaining traction through technology or product development; or establishing early sales. Setting up strategic partnerships and other relationships are another way of reducing risk by partnering with companies and organizations that can help you break through barriers by using the systems that they have already set up.

- ✔ **Patents:** Although patents can lower risk, whether you should pursue a patent isn't so cut and dried. Patents are expensive and require a large investment of time. In some cases, you're better off taking that time and money and just focusing on developing a big market and dominating it quickly. Still, VCs look for companies with unfair market advantages. One way to achieve that unfair advantage is to lock up your technology or product with a suite of patents that cover key elements that will keep your competition at bay. Having quality patents in your hand can add value to your company and make it more fundable.

- ✔ **Team:** The biggest risk VCs see in early-stage companies is with the team. Do team members have the necessary expertise? Do they know how to work together? Can they scale this company up to be really big? To minimize this risk, create a staffing plan that projects out through your next few years of milestones — what kind of people do you need now? What kind of people are you going to need in the near future? — and start recruiting them now. Your company will have a more attractive risk profile if you've already found the people you will be moving ahead with. Chapter 7 has more information on finding potential team members.

- ✔ **Traction:** *Traction* is a big word for VCs and refers to the extent to which you are able to get stuff done. The more traction you can get (demonstrated by your milestone achievements, especially in getting people to buy your product or service), the less risk your company has. Think about the kinds of milestones you need to accomplish to develop traction: completing your product, launching your website, and clinching your first paying customers, for example. If you can accomplish these quickly, your company will have less risk for investors.

✔ **Relationships:** Your ability to establish strategic relationships with other organizations is a way for you to grow your company fast and build influence based on the expertise of other organizations. Look for ways you can leverage strategic partnerships to cut costs, avoid getting distracted by work outside of your core competency, and gain access to markets and distribution channels, and more.

Even though you may pay a higher rate by going through distribution partners, for example, it is still worth is. Keep your eye on the primary objective at this point: getting going as fast as possible first. Later, after you've captured the market, you can look at improving your margins.

Chapter 11

Telling Your Valuation Story

- -

In This Chapter

▶ Identifying the various ways to determine valuation

▶ The art and science of negotiating valuation in early-stage companies

▶ The dangers of establishing an inflated valuation

- -

*W*hen you approach investors and ask them to invest in your company, you are actually asking them to buy shares in your company. Anytime you offer something for someone else to purchase, you have to give them a price. To determine the price of a share, you have to determine how much the whole company is worth and how many shares you want to break the company into.

Although valuation gets a lot of attention, it's not the most important thing in a negotiation. By the time you get to negotiation, the investors' stock preferences and other term sheet terms make the exact valuation of your company less important. (See Chapter 9 to get the details on structuring the deal and Chapter 13 about negotiating investment terms.) The one time when your company's valuation *is* really important? When you are trying to attract investors. If you blurt out the wrong valuation for your company, you can send investors running in the other direction.

Understanding the valuation of your company is easy — it's the price that the market is willing to pay. So what is the market willing to pay? Figuring that out is the hard part! Countless rules for calculating valuation exist. This chapter discusses a few ways to determine valuation and dissects the importance of being flexible.

Valuing Early-Stage Companies

Determining a valuation for an early-stage company can be a great challenge. The traditional methods used to value mature companies don't really work because a young company doesn't have the track record that a mature company has. The track record of income, assets, and established market is what drives later stage valuations.

Why traditional approaches don't work

When people want to find the value of mature companies, they take one of three traditional approaches:

- Income approach: In this approach, companies are valued using annual income or profit.
- Asset approach: With the asset approach, the value of the company's assets on the balance sheet is what matters.
- Market approach: Here, comparable transactions in the market are looked at to show what the market will bear.

Traditional valuation methods typically emphasize one (income, assets, or market) over the others, depending on the particular situation of the company in question. These approaches are not sufficient for early-stage companies. Without the track record of a mature company and the data from income, assets, or established market, early-stage companies have to get more creative and flexible about how they come up with a company value.

We're not telling you all this to make you depressed about getting a valuation done for your company. If you understand the malleable nature of valuation, you will be better able to navigate the negotiations that will eventually come up!

Traditional valuation methods are still useful to keep in mind when you are valuing an early-stage company. Think about your company a few years out when it is more mature. Traditional valuation approaches will be appropriate when your company has income, assets, and/or a well-defined market. You will have to plan for your valuation to increase over time as your company matures.

Being flexible when talking with a VC

When you talk with an investor about your valuation, you have to be flexible and willing to negotiate on the actual value based on the VC's input, but you shouldn't just leave the valuation up to her. You must have an opinion even though the value you propose will probably change. One of your biggest challenges when talking to a VC is that you don't have the experience of seeing hundreds of early-stage company valuations like a VC does. A VC's experience gives her a broader, more informed, perspective.

We all read about the big exits in the newspaper, but most of us don't stop to think that those companies have been working hard for five or ten years to get to that point and that thousands of companies tried and failed during that same time period. The $300 million dollar company was only worth $1.5 million a decade ago.

The thing to understand is that less than 1 percent of companies hit it big; when a company is still in the early stages, its value is just a tiny fraction of its potential. As tempting as it may be, you can't simply look at a mature company in your industry — say one worth $200 million — and work backward ten years to find the value. Your company may not survive long enough or have all the right luck to be worth $200 million in ten years.

When you are negotiating with a VC, remember that she may have access to information you don't. The playing field may not seem level, so you have to do everything you can to make sure you understand how the VC is valuing your company. Transparency is the key to successful negotiation. You need to be forthcoming with information that will be useful to the VC while simultaneously demanding the information, comparable transactions, supporting worksheets, and rationales that the VC is using.

Choosing the best way to discuss valuation

At some point in your search for funding, an investor will ask you for your company's valuation. In some regards, this is a trick question because any VC worth her salt is going to come up with her own valuation for your company using her own methodologies. Sometimes this value may be higher than what you came up with, and sometimes it will be lower. Unfortunately, once you've been asked, you cannot duck the valuation question. You've got to answer it.

Sometimes the VC doesn't really care what number you come up with as your valuation. She cares about how you think; she'll likely be more interested in your logic than in your result. You have a few options available when you answer the valuation question. Ultimately the valuation is going to be whatever someone is willing to pay for your stock, so one strategy is to get as many offers as you can. Then you'll have a reasonable set of data points with the various deal terms to justify your valuation.

If you are talking with an angel investor instead of a VC, you can duck the question by using convertible debt as your finance instrument. Convertible debt is a common way to avoid early-stage valuation and leave it up to the institutional investors a year down the road. *Convertible debt* is basically a note payable (a loan) with an interest rate such as 8 percent but with a clause that says that, when a round of investment occurs in the future, the convertible note holder can convert his or her investment into stock, usually at a discount from the price everyone else has to pay. A 20 percent discount is a common amount, meaning that an investor who owns a convertible note for $800,000 can buy $1 million worth of stock. Most VCs won't entertain convertible debt, so use this ploy carefully.

Just saying it

Deciding on a valuation, sticking to your guns, and just blurting it out is one communication strategy that many founders use, but we don't recommend it. When the conversation turns to valuation, all participants shift a little in their seats. If the investor asks you, "What's the valuation?" and you reply bluntly, "$4 million," you're bound to have a problem afterward. If your number is lower than the investor expected, she'll be suspicious of your generosity. If it's higher than she expected, she'll wonder how you could be so hard headed. You can't win.

Instead, consider one of the following communication tactics. Both get the point across that you don't think valuation is a hard number, but instead a negotiating point to build from.

Stating your valuation as a range

When asked the valuation question, suggest a range. You could say, for example, "We're looking at $2 to 3 million, depending on the deal structure." This answer implies that some deals may allow for higher or lower valuation. For example, a single investor would be more attractive than having to syndicate multiple investors or that smart investors with contacts in your industry would be more valuable than opportunistic investors who bring nothing to the deal but money. The problem with stating a range, of course, is that in most cases the bottom of the range is the number you are going to be stuck with.

Telling your valuation story

You can tell your valuation story. This is a way of stating a number, but instead of stating the number outright to an investor, the story includes a preamble and rationale for the number so that by the time you say it, the investor will hopefully have no choice to but agree with your irrefutable logic. Because valuation is inherently a subjective exercise, whatever you can do to provide a sound rationale for your thinking can only be helpful.

We think the valuation story is the most effective method of communicating a value, especially after seeing so many entrepreneurs blurt out a number only to hear the groaning response of investors who had another number in mind. By the time you are done reading this chapter, you should be able to put together a pretty good story.

Timing your valuation

Valuation occurs at single points in time, such as when an investment is made, when stock is issued to employees, or when some other factor "prices" the stock. You want to time these events to occur at the points where you have achieved the most important milestones and your value is highest.

Valuation is always part of a more holistic funding strategy that should be considered in relation to future and past funding rounds and never just as a one-time deal. Your valuation should be designed to take your company through the stages that it will need to go through in order to achieve a successful exit, and each valuation point at which you raise more money should build upon past success so that you can pursue further rounds of funding as needed to get to your exit.

Some companies need only one round of investment. These companies are attractive to angels and early-stage investors because the time to exit may be shorter and, therefore, less risky. With a single fundraising round, there is no risk of being diluted in future rounds. Most companies, however, need two, three, or even five or six fundraising rounds before they are ready for exit. Some VCs prefer these companies because they have the potential to become really big and to have significantly larger exits than companies that don't require a lot of investment.

As an entrepreneur, you want to time these rounds carefully so that you always raise money when you have accomplished big things and your valuation is at its highest. Just think: If you have only one round of funding and you sell 30 percent of your equity, then you still have 70 percent when it's time for your exit. If you need to go through four rounds, though, you'll be selling equity at each funding round, and your share of the company will decrease at each step. This isn't necessarily bad because having a little piece of a very big pie is usually better than having a big piece of a little pie. But it can be bad if you don't hit your milestones, and you need to raise capital when you haven't added a lot of value since the last round of funding. When this happens your valuation may drop, and you'll need to sell even more shares to raise the money you need.

Getting the first round price right

The pricing of your first round is perhaps the most important consideration of all. Why? Because selling equity in your company is not like selling a used car.

Coming to grips with uncertainty in equity

When you advertise a used car for sale, you look at comparable sales and understand what the market will bear; you get the car cleaned up and looking good; and then your goal is to get the maximum amount for the car as you can. When someone buys the car, you negotiate on the price and eventually the deal is done. The more you get for the car, the better.

When selling equity, the situation is very different. For one thing, there is much more uncertainty in investing in an early-stage company than even buying a used car. Finding comparable transactions to base your price on is much more difficult because transactions are not widely reported, and every company is different.

For another thing, when you sell a car, you will (hopefully) never see the buyer again, and your "win" with a high dollar transaction is final. With VC investing, the first investment is just the beginning of a series of investments and a long-term relationship.

Recognizing why inflated valuation is bad for the founder

If you get an inflated valuation on an early-stage company from inexperienced angels, you may think that you've got a win. In reality, you've just set yourself up for failure. When you have a high first round valuation, you may not be able to keep up that pace in your next rounds.

If subsequent rounds are at a lower valuation, VCs will be scared away because you haven't executed the plans you claimed you would, and first round investors will be upset at having lost money already and will be unlikely to throw "good money after bad."

A valuation that is too low is also very bad for you. Not only do you have to give up equity at a lower price, resulting in greater dilution of your own ownership, but you have also limited the amount that you can raise, which puts you in the trap of being raising just enough to get some things done but not enough to hit all the milestones you need for a Series B round.

Your valuation should be high enough that you can raise the money you need to accomplish the benchmarks necessary to get to the next round and low enough to be attractive to investors. Investors want to see a 2X ("2 times") return on investment between the Series A and Series B rounds, and a 10X return on investment over the life of the deal.

Using Multiple Valuation Methods

There is no single spreadsheet that you can plug some numbers into to get your company's true valuation. In addition, traditional business valuation companies use all kinds of metrics and tools that are virtually useless for early-stage venture firms. They look at things like cash flow or assets on the books, neither of which your company is likely to have enough of to use in that equation. Rather than deciding that your zero asset, zero cash flow company is worth nothing, VCs use a few other methods.

Every valuation is different and there are multiple factors that come into play when determining a company's value. Because the process has so much uncertainty and subjective evaluation, we recommend using several different valuation methodologies and then use the various values to come up with and work out a final valuation that takes all or most of the methods into account. By using multiple methods, you can check yourself to see whether your thinking about the value is consistent and makes sense when multiple factors are taken into consideration. Additionally, using many models allows you to have a more transparent valuation discussion with your VC and shows that you understand their viewpoint for the investment.

The following sections take you through various valuation methods. To make the examples easier to follow, each valuation method is based on a company with the following characteristics:

- Projected year five revenues of $20 million.

- Year five profit — EBITDA (earnings before interest, taxes, depreciation, or amortization) — of 25 percent, or $5 million.

- P/E (price to earnings) average for rapidly growing businesses in this industry is 20X EBITDA.

- A VC return requirement of 60 percent.

- Risk profile:

Category	Risk Level
Technology	Moderate
Execution	High
Market risk	Moderate
Financial Risk	High
Regulatory Risk	High
Economic Risk	Moderate/High

- Burn rate of $45,000 per month with 18 months until achievement of milestones.

- Investment required to get to positive cash flow is $4,000,000.

- Typical valuations for similar companies in the area are around $3 million.

- Scorecard factors include

    - Team has CEO with two successful exits and excellent technical staff.

    - The exit is estimated at $100 million or more.

    - There is some competition, but nobody is in the space currently.

    - The company has several strategic partnerships.

    - The company will likely need further rounds of funding within 12 to 18 months.

The venture capital method

The venture capital method of valuation is perhaps the most common and is easy to calculate. This method is based on the VC's need to achieve a target return on investment for his limited partners (LPs). The VC starts by analyzing the business plan to determine the *terminal valuation*, or what the company may be acquired for some time down the road. Then the VC discounts that based on how much will be needed to invest, the amount of time required for the investment, and the desired return.

Most VCs want to return 25 percent or more to their LPs across their entire portfolio of investments. Because half of all their investments are likely to be worth zero in five years, and others may return no more than their original investment, their target needs to be more like 60 percent for an individual investment. That's 60 percent *per year*, not just one time for the entire investment period! The VC is really hoping for one or two big homeruns where he can make a lot of money to make up for all the losers.

The first step, then, is to figure out what your company will be worth in five years or whenever you think you will be ready for exit.

Many companies acquiring other companies determine value by using multiples of EBITDA and/or revenue. EBITDA is simply a standardized way of describing the profitability of your company that takes all of the various tax and non-cash impacts on the bottom-line out of the equation. In that way, EBITDA lets you compare apples to apples when you're looking at the profitability of several different companies.

To base valuation on EBITDA, start by researching exits in your industry. Yes, your company is unique and unlike any other, but you need to find similar transactions so that you can understand what a likely acquisition looks like in your industry. You can look at the big acquirers and their activity over the past three years. Ask these questions

> ✓ At what stage did they acquired companies.
>
> ✓ What were the strategic reasons for the acquisitions?
>
> ✓ What were the multiples of EBITDA or revenue?
>
> ✓ What was the total dollar amount of the investment?
>
> ✓ How are those investments going now?

The answers to these questions help you develop a good forecast about how your company is likely to be acquired. Of course, the VC has quite a bit of expertise in this area as well, but she will expect you to be extremely knowledgeable in your industry, so you need to do this homework. The more history you can tell about specific transactions, the better.

When you use this method, make sure that you think realistically about the information you gather. We recently had a company describe its likely acquisition in five years for $500 million. That's pretty impressive for a start-up, and although it's conceivable, it's also unlikely. After doing a little more research, we found that during the past three years, acquisitions in the industry had ranged between $25 million and $40 million and that the largest player in the industry had annual revenues of $3.5 billion. Had this company tried to impress a VC with its potential $500 million exit, it would have been laughed out of the room. A better strategy would have been to build the company to $8 million in revenues and exit at $36 million or 4X ("4 times) annual revenues, which was standard for the industry.

Using the example company outlined at the beginning of this section, the company predicts earnings in the fifth year of $5 million, and we know that the P/E ratio for similar companies from our research is 20X earnings, or $100 million for the example company. The VC needs a return of 10X his investment, so if the company were worth $100 million in five years, it would need to be worth $10 million today, including the value of the VC's investment. To calculate the pre-money value, or what the company is worth before the VC invests, take the $10 million value and subtract the VC's $4 million investment to get a pre-money valuation of $6 million. In this case, for the investment to work, the VC takes 40 percent of the company's equity because his $4 million investment represents 40 percent of the $10 million overall post-money value of the company. Table 11-1 shows the numbers.

Table 11-1	The Venture Capital Valuation Method
Item	*Amount*
Investment	$4,000,000
Exit year	Fifth year
Revenue	$20,000,000
EBITDA	$5,000,000
P/E for similar companies	20X
Terminal value	$100,000,000
Target IRR	60%
Target investment multiple	10X
Post-money valuation (after investment)	$10,000,000
Pre-money valuation (before investment)	$6,000,000

The scorecard method

The scorecard method begins by analyzing the average investment in similar early-stage companies in your area and in your industry. Your VC may be able to help you gather data on similar transactions, or you can find online reports such as the Moneytree Report (http://www.pwcmoneytree.com). In the example, the average is $3 million.

The scorecard method works by looking at the major factors in an investment such as strength of the team, size of the opportunity, and competitive environment. The investor assigns a weight according to which of these factors is the most important, with the total of all the factors adding to 100 percent. The investor then ranks the company by comparing it with other companies in the market. An average ranking is 100 percent, below average rankings are anywhere from zero to 99 percent, and above average rankings are 101 and 200 percent. The final column is calculated by multiplying the weight by the ranking.

You calculate the scorecard method by adding the values in the right-hand column to get an aggregate score multiplier which you multiply by the average company value to get an adjusted value based on both the market and the company's unique attributes. This method is similar to the way realtors use "comps" in real estate valuation.

In the example, the average company is $3 million, and the weighted scorecard multiplier is 1.675. Do the math: $3 million × 1.675 results in a value of $5,025,000, as Table 11-2 shows.

Table 11-2	The Scorecard Valuation Method		
Category	**Weight**	**Ranking**	**Value**
Average Similar Company Valuation			**$3,000,000**
Team	30%	200%	0.60
Opportunity Size	25%	200%	0.50
Product/Technology	15%	100%	0.15
Competitive Environment	10%	125%	0.13
Marketing/Sales Partnerships	10%	200%	0.20
Need for additional investment	5%	50%	0.03
Other factors	5%	150%	0.08
Weighted scoreboard multiplier			**1.6750**
Scorecard Adjusted Valuation			**$5,025,000**

The risk factor adjusted method

The risk factor adjusted method takes either standard risks (technology, execution, market, and regulatory risks, for example) or company specific milestones (breaking into a specific market or getting a beta website launched, for example) and assigns a value to those based on the likelihood of the company achieving success in that area. The multiplier is then calculated by multiplying each of the risk factors together to get an aggregate risk adjustment.

The risk factor adjusted method works by understanding the risks that stand between a company today and the milestones the company must achieve to get to its exit five or more years from now. The method begins like the venture capital method with an estimated exit. Then a list of the major risks are compiled and a probability is assigned to each.

In fact, most companies have hundreds of risks — or even an infinite number if you count things like asteroids hitting the earth as a potential risk. This method picks out the most likely risks that have the largest impact on the company. Typically the number of risks is between 5 and 15. The aggregate of all risks are multiplied by each other to arrive at a net valuation based on all of the risks together.

One thing we like about the risk factor adjusted method is that it makes the risks and their impacts transparent in the negotiation between investor and entrepreneur. Investors are always worried about unspecified and not clearly understood risks. Having a summary list is helpful in allaying their fears. After you have an agreed-upon list, all you need to do is negotiate the relative risk of each and the probability of success in order to arrive at a risk adjusted valuation.

In the example in Table 11-3, you multiply the numbers in the right column to get an aggregate risk factor of .04704. You get the valuation by multiplying this factor by the estimated exit value ($100 million) to get a current adjusted value of $4,704,000.

Table 11-3	The Risk Factor Adjusted Method
Risk	*Probability*
Technology risk	0.5
Execution risk	0.7
Market risk	0.6
Competitive risk	0.5
Financial risk	0.8

(continued)

Table 11-3 *(continued)*

Risk	Probability
Regulatory risk	0.8
Economic risk	0.7
Aggregate Risk Factor	0.04704
Exit Value Assumption	$100,000,000
Current Risk Adjusted Value	$4,704,000

This number can obviously be manipulated by the person doing the valuation, so the value in this (or any methodology) is that the VC and the entrepreneur can be transparent about what the risks are and can have a discussion about the risks and their impact on value as opposed to just picking numbers out of thin air.

The simplified net present value method

The simplified net present value method can be used as a quick rule of thumb valuation method. Although some NPV methods take variable cash flows into account, this method assumes that there will be only one cash flow at the exit. If the investor knows that her target return in this case is 20X her original investment and that the estimated exit is $100 million, she can divide the estimated exit by 20 to get a present value of $5 million, as shown in Table 11-4.

Table 11-4	The Simplified Net Present Value Method
Item	Value
Assumed exit value	$100,000,000
Desired ROI multiple	20X
Current value	**$5,000,000**

The burn rate method

The burn rate method is not necessarily a real valuation method, but it provides a way to think about valuation based on the equity needs of the business owner and the actual need for capital. You can use this method as a reality check when you use other methods. It works on the principle that the reason you need funding is to overcome some major risks and achieve significant milestones at which time your company will be worth much more.

To use the burn rate method, determine what milestones you need to accomplish and then assign a timeline and resources to each. Make realistic estimates for the costs to achieve each milestone; then address the milestones that create the most value for your company and do the most to prove your concept. For example, if you have a software company, figuring out how much money it would take to develop a working beta version of your software or an MVP (minimum viable product) would be high on your list of milestones.

The burn rate method takes the monthly burn from now until the accomplishment of major milestones. In this case, assume that the investor will buy 40 percent of the company and that the total amount of capital needed is $4,000,000. You multiply the total burn by 1/40 percent (2.5 times the burn) to get the value for the company, which in this case is $10,000,000 minus the investor's $4 million, resulting in a pre-money valuation of $6 million (see Table 11-5).

Table 11-5	The Burn Rate Method
Item	*Value*
Current burn rate (per month)	$100,000
Number of months to reach milestones	40
Total burn	$4,000,000
Equity percentage assumption	40%
Post-money value	$10,000,000
Pre-Money Value	**$6,000,000**

Summing it all up

After you have multiple valuations, you can compare and contrast the different numbers and come up with a final valuation, as Table 11-6 shows. Because these methods rely on different factors, ranging from exit value to average value in the market to how much money is needed to succeed, altogether they should provide a fairly holistic view. Note that a big range can exist between the lowest and highest valuations and that the story you craft will have a big impact on which end of the valuation spectrum you end up on.

Table 11-6	Comparing the Multiple Valuations
Method	*Estimated Valuation*
Venture capital method	$6,000,000
Scorecard method	$5,025,000
Risk factor adjusted method	$4,704,000
Net present value method	$5,000,000
Burn rate method	$6,000,000
Average	**$5,345,800**
Standard Deviation	**$610,400**
Median	**$5,025,000**

For the example company, you get an average of about $5,300,000. There is a standard deviation of $610,400, which allows for a bargaining range each way, depending on the terms of the deal. The aggregate method gives you a good range within which you know the valuation should fall.

Creating Your Valuation Story

The art of valuation is as much about picking winners as it is about finance. Ultimately the artful valuation approach takes the form of a story. Your valuation story is a way of holistically describing the path that your company will take on the way to making it big. If the worst thing you can do is to blurt out a number to an investor, the best thing you can do is to provide a story with your rationale that uses as many defensible case studies and industry standards as possible. The worst case scenario when you take this approach is that you and the VC will disagree on the value, but you'll gain bonus points for having extraordinary industry knowledge and awareness — something that VCs look for in the CEOs that they invest in.

The five parts of your story

Like many stories, valuation stories have several parts that must be described in order:

1. Your business model, your product/service, and the problem it solves. This part includes both your marketing plan (what channels you'll use, pricing, competition, and advertising) and your proof (what your beta or launch conversion rates have been).

2. Projected sales and EBITDA in five years.

3. Your research on acquisition values in your industry and your estimated exit value.

4. The major risks that you face between now and your exit, and the impact and likelihood of overcoming each.

5. Your discounted present value of the company.

Fleshing out the story

When you're asked for your valuation, don't say "$4 million," because the investor will be thinking, "I've seen a dozen similar deals with a $2 million valuation; this deal is overpriced." Even if your deal isn't overpriced, the flat valuation answer puts investors in a position of defensiveness. Try telling a story and see what the investors think.

Here's an example of a valuation story:

> Based on the current selling price of $100 per month for our SaaS product and our impressive 15 percent conversion rate in our marketing tests, we are confident that within five years we will have 10,000 subscribers, resulting in $1 million per month in revenues, or $12 million a year with an EBITDA of $5 million.

> In the past three years, there have been a number of acquisitions in our market. Some examples include ABC Corp., which sold for $75 million with $10 million in annual revenues, and ZYZ Corp., which sold for $50 million with $8 million in annual revenues. With these companies trading at 6X to 7.5X revenues, our projected value of 6X revenues, or $72 million, is highly realistic. We have identified QRS Corp. and LMNO Corp. as strong candidates for acquisition and have made contact with them last month.

> The major milestones for us to reach between now and our exit are hiring a top quality CMO to lead our marketing effort, building strategic partnerships and affiliate relationships for marketing, completing our 2.0 version of the application, and completing a Series B round for $3 to $4 million in 12 to 18 months. We are providing an opportunity for $1 million in early-stage investment for 20 percent equity in the company based on a $4 million pre-money valuation and $5 million post-money. This provides the investor with a potential 14.4X return on his or her investment in five years.

Instead of a flat valuation number, the investor is getting gobs of information with a story like this. A savvy investor is pulling out the following tidbits:

- ✔ The product is done, and the company has paying customers; therefore, technology and initial market risks are mitigated.
- ✔ This company has the ability to scale significantly, and the management team understands the need to grow quickly.
- ✔ The market is interested in companies like this and is paying high multiples of revenue for it. The management team has the discipline and maturity to research recent acquisitions and the foresight to identify and contact potential acquisition targets already.
- ✔ The management team is focused on the risks and has plans to mitigate them. The team is transparent about the company's weaknesses, which is a good indicator of coachability. The risks between now and the exit strategy seem reasonable and surmountable.
- ✔ The valuation is lower than expected, given the strength of the product and the potential for a strong exit. The management team understands that there are risks, and they respect that I am looking to achieve a significant return on my investment to balance the risks that I am taking with early-stage investments.

The value of your exit is what is going to drive the current value of your company. So how do you go about figuring out what your exit value will be? This is where those financial pro formas (financial projections of revenues, expenses, and profits) that you created come in (refer to Chapter 6 for details on creating a pro forma). If you have projected your revenues and expenses for five years, then you can start to use some traditional valuation methods based on the cash flows that you are projecting.

Chapter 12

Negotiating Your Terms

When you go into a negotiation with anyone about anything, you need to know what you want. You cannot argue for your goals if you don't know what they are. Therefore, negotiation is about self-discovery first and foremost. Although the mandate to "know thyself" seems like an easy task, deeply understanding your interests and the interests of your company isn't always easy. You have to do a lot of research. When people think that they are bad at negotiating, the real issue is that they haven't dug into the details of their own interests.

When you negotiate your deal with investors, you have to make guesses, predictions, and plans far into the future, and you have to understand the implications behind pricing your company and dividing the control of your business with shareholders.

Negotiation isn't about fighting, aggression, anger or acting rude. It's about trying to find out whether everyone at the table can be happy. It's also about maximizing the potential outcomes for everyone. This chapter describes the mindset of a good negotiator and helps you identify the parts of your term sheet that you should pay close attention to as you plan for negotiation.

Scoping Out the Negotiation Landscape: The Fundamentals

Negotiating a venture deal is unlike any negotiation you have done before. You may think that you just need to negotiate your price and then sell some stock to investors. But no — venture deals are much more complicated than that!

The items on the negotiating table

Before you enter into negotiations, you need to understand all the items you're negotiating. First time entrepreneurs looking for venture capital think the negotiation is just about price and percentage of stock sold. In reality, the negotiation involves myriad subjects, things that you'll want to agree on now, while everyone is friendly and things are going well.

Negotiating for venture capital is tough and requires significant preparation. You need to anticipate what these issues are and have a position on each one. Although you may not get exactly what you want in all areas, having a good starting position and knowing what you're getting into can help you during the negotiation itself. This is not the time to wing it or to learn as you go through the process.

- ✔ Determine which terms you'll be negotiating (the later section "Most-Often Negotiated Term Sheet Terms" lists the most commonly negotiated items).
- ✔ Research the norms for terms in your area.
- ✔ Determine your desired outcomes for each term.
- ✔ Understand which terms are flexible and which you will stand firm on.
- ✔ Prepare a simple rationale for each term that you want and include a few bullet points outlining why this is a good deal for everyone.

Developing the right mindset

Take a look at the language you use when you describe what you want out of the deal. If you are saying things like, "I'm giving away a piece of my company," then you may not be in the right mindset for negotiating a deal. The fact that you are giving up some of your company is an assumed part of the deal.

Negotiation is always a give and take between parties, with the ultimate goal being to arrive at what everyone hopes is a fair trade. So nobody is giving away anything in this process, and nobody is taking anything. You are exchanging. The VC gets shares in your company, which may potentially become successful. You get cold, hard cash, which the investor earned through years of hard work. Before you start the negotiation process, be sure to put yourself in the investors' shoes.

Thinking win-win

The fourth of Stephen Covey's Seven Habits of Highly Successful People and the best attitude to take in venture deals is to think win-win. Venture capital negotiations are not like any other kind of negotiations, where, when the negotiation is over, each party goes his or her separate ways. An equity round isn't the last time you'll deal with the VC. It's actually just the beginning of your relationship. Not only will the VC take a role on your board, but you'll probably seek future rounds of financing and then coordinate an exit strategy among various parties, all of whom may have competing interests.

In any negotiation, four outcomes are possible: win-win, lose-lose, investor win–founder lose, or founder win–investor lose. Because venture capitalists are professionals who understand deal structure, they rarely strike a deal that results in a founder win–investor lose outcome. The best VC deals are win-win and not just because that's a feel-good way to negotiate.

Generally, if the VC makes money on your deal, you do, too. However, depending on liquidation preferences, you may make a little money on your deal while the investor makes a lot. If you could not have made money without the support of venture capital, this outcome is probably still a win. It's just an unbalanced win-WIN.

Beginning with an open mind

Venture capital deals are incredibly complex, and the stakes are high for everyone involved. Before you assume that the VC is taking advantage of you or undercutting your success to boost his own, remain open-minded and ask questions before fighting back. Remember, VCs have been negotiating deals like yours for years and have devised a series of best practices, many of which are the result of mistakes that VCs don't want to make again.

Many of the terms in the term sheet have serious implications. The initial agreements may impact the survival of the company in ways you had not anticipated. Be sure to learn about what the terms mean and work with an experienced securities attorney who has a large number of venture deals under his or her belt, so that you understand what arrangements are generally accepted and why.

For information on what you can expect an attorney to do and what to look for in the attorney you hire, go to www.dummies.com/extras/venturecapital.

Negotiating founder shares

Imagine that, during negotiation, your VC says that, as a part of the investment, you and your two partners must give back the 33.3 percent of the company you each own into the *treasury stock* (stock that the company holds and that can be allocated for vesting so that founders get the stock over a period of time, for compensating key employees, or for raising additional capital.) In place of the 33.3 percent, the VC wants to provide you with a small amount, say 10 percent. The rest of your shares will vest over five years or may fully vest at exit.

If you're like most entrepreneurs, you are suspicious of this arrangement and not particularly excited about taking a step backward in your ownership stake, especially since these new VCs are coming on board with a 25 percent share of your company. If you delve into the reason behind this requirement, however, you'll see that this provision in your term sheet actually makes sense and, furthermore, protects your interests.

Here's why the VC wants to vest founder shares and why you should agree to it. Stock is precious and needs to be leveraged in ways that protect the interests of the company. Imagine three cofounders divide stock three ways. Then one of the cofounders leaves the company after VCs become involved. If the departing founder no longer works for the company yet continues to own 33 percent of company stock, this can cause serious difficulties for the company. The company needs to recruit a replacement for the cofounder's role, yet there is no stock to offer the replacement candidates because the cofounder took off with a third of everything. This is why the VC's demand to create an employee option pool and a founder stock vesting schedule makes a lot of sense.

Accepting that the relationship changes in negotiation

At a certain point during negotiation, your attitude toward the deal changes. You're no longer selling your deal but are moving into partnership mode. Emotionally, you may start out on the opposite sides of the table, but by the end of the negotiation, you and the VC are facing the same way, trying to work out problems together.

Your negotiation is not just a sale of equity; you're also entering into a partnership with a venture capitalist, one who will hopefully bring capital, connections, advice, and leadership to your board. For this reason, the focus of your negotiations should shift from your position versus the VC's position to what best benefits the company and represents your *shared* interests. After you and the VC are in partnership, everyone should be focused on working toward an exit strategy as quickly as possible. Your theme in negotiation at this point should be on alignment of interests rather than just getting the best deal for yourself. A deal that is aligned from the start makes working through the difficult decisions easier when the time comes.

Knowing your negotiation partner

Dale Carnegie wrote, "Knowledge isn't power until it is applied." In a tiation, you need to know not only what your own desires are, but also the desires and motivations of your negotiating partner. For this reason, your negotiation shouldn't begin at the conference table with all of the attorneys present. It should begin well before the big meeting as you get to know the VC and get to know the parameters of the fund.

Learning about the fund

Find out about the venture capital firm and the funds that it manages. This information gives you a better idea of what the firm has set out to accomplish and how your company can help the VC to achieve his goals for the portfolio. You may find that you are on the edges of where this fund typically invests, that the VCs are busy with three other deals, and that now is just not a good time to push for a strong negotiating position.

Spend time finding the answers to questions like the ones that follow. Note that in some cases, you will get more satisfying answers by talking to people in the community than you will from asking the VC directly. VCs are unlikely to share potentially sensitive details, but you may be able to get a wealth of information out of someone who works in or with one of the portfolio companies:

- What is the VC looking for?
- How have his deals been going lately?
- How much time does the fund have before the VC needs to wrap up?
- How much committed capital is left in the fund?
- How senior are your negotiators in the fund?
- How well has the negotiator done on his past deals?
- What other deals is the VC looking at right now?
- How well does your deal match the fund's typical investment? (Is your company in the VC's target industry or target business phase? Are you looking for an amount that is typical for this fund? And so on.)

Learning about the VC

If you have gotten to this stage, you've already determined that the VC works in your industry and invests in companies at your phase of development. But now you need to know some other things about the VC. What is he like to work with? How does he treat founders? Does he add value in the boardroom?

Because you're entering into a fast-paced, three-to-seven year relationship with the VC, it's important to know how he thinks and how well you communicate with each other. Arrange meetings that don't happen around a conference table — have coffee, lunch, or dinner, for example — and get to know your VC on a personal level.

VCs have pages and pages of due diligence checklists that they'll use to evaluate your company. They'll look at your contracts, your relationships with suppliers, advisors, partners and employees, and more. You should be doing the same with them. Here are ten things you can do to check them out:

- ✔ **Ask for contact information for four or five companies they've invested in.** Better yet, get a complete contact list for their entire portfolio, including deals that have closed down and those that have had exits. Call the CEOs and ask a lot of questions about the relationships with those companies.

- ✔ **Research your VC's investment portfolio and contact some of the companies that did not do well.** Talk to the CEOs of those companies and get as much information as you can about how the VC handles things when it's not going well.

- ✔ **Check out sites like** `http://www.thefunded.com`, `http://www.techcrunch.com`, **or** `http://www.venturebeat.com` **and search for articles or ratings of your VC.**

- ✔ **Do a background check on the VC firm to see whether it has a history of being litigious.** Law suits are a matter of public record, and you should be able to learn a lot by observing past legal behavior.

- ✔ **Check out how the firm treats founders.** Some VCs replace founders with new CEOs over 75 percent of the time. Find out what happened to the founding CEOs. Were they kicked out of the company, or were they placed in a more appropriate role for the individual, such as CTO (chief technology officer)?

- ✔ **Check out your VC's syndication record.** Does he take a lead position and bring in other VCs after doing the due diligence, or does he mostly follow? If he's a follower and your deal is likely to require syndication, you may want to continue looking until you can find a good lead investor.

- ✔ **Evaluate your communication style with the VC.** Do you clearly understand everything he's saying? Does he seem to get your drift?

- ✔ **What are the values of the venture fund?** Do they match with yours?

- ✔ **Research the VC's attitude toward follow-on funding.** Does he have a reserve for follow-on? What conditions dictate his decision to invest or pass? Will he support you going to other VCs for the next round if he doesn't fund the next round?

- ✔ **Ask about the VC's management style.** Are you comfortable with his level of involvement in your company? Some VCs talk with founders twice a week, others get in touch much less frequently.

Recognizing your own power

Going into negotiations with a big venture capital firm is intimidating. These guys negotiate all the time, and they're very good at it. They have all the money, which is what you need. Although it may seem like the VC has all the power in the negotiation, in fact, you may have more power than you think:

- ✔ **They need to strike deals in order to make that money.** Without entrepreneurs and their growing companies, VCs are out of business. To carry out their mission of investing their LPs' money in hugely profitable ventures, they need to work with founders.

- ✔ **They want to invest in your company.** By the time a VC sits down to negotiate with you, he has already decided that your company has the potential to go big. He is excited to invest because your deal is the kind of deal he has been looking for, and it probably represents the one out of a thousand deals that have come through his door. Yes, he has looked at a thousand deals, while looking for one like yours. Do you think he wants to get this deal done? Yes!

One way to be more certain of your competitive power is to go to every pitch event you can find for six to nine months before you start looking for money. Become familiar with the kinds of companies that are pitching and the kinds of pitches that seem to be most successful. Keep up with VentureBeat (http://www.venturebeat.com), TechCrunch (http://www.tech crunch.com), and other online media to see which companies are getting funded. Is your company similar to those in any way? Is it better? If you can objectively assess your company's potential, you may find that your company is going to be really hot, a position that may give you the upper hand in negotiating.

Having multiple parties negotiating with you at once is the best way to increase your power during negotiation. Your goal is to get three or more term sheets so that you can play the VCs off each other. Having more than one VC firm interested in your company doesn't just happen; you have to create this kind of interest over a period of time. Start nurturing your relationships early and get to know the VCs you think will be interested in your deal when you're ready. When the time comes, put out your pitch to all of them simultaneously. As you pitch to multiple VCs, keep these points in mind:

- ✔ Many VCs have no-shop clauses in their term sheets, and it'll be too late to go out and find competing bids after you've progressed down the road with the first VC you approach. The no-shop clause is reasonable for VCs to demand because the cost of due diligence is high, and they don't want to do all that work if you're not committed to the deal.

✔ Respect the time and effort a VC firm puts into due diligence. If you're not interested in a particular VC, don't waste his time and yours by pitching just to use his interest as a ploy to bolster your negotiating position with another VC. Doing so could hurt your reputation in the community. VCs generally all know each other. If you're shopping your deal, they'll know it, so be upfront about your process and share that several VCs are looking at your deal right now. Then watch what happens.

Knowing when to stick to your guns and when to be flexible

In negotiating your VC deal, you will encounter times when you need to stick to your guns and other times when you need to be flexible.

Before you either accept or reject a deal that you're unsure about or that strikes you as unfair, do your research on the VC. Interview some of the CEOs of his portfolio companies to find out how their experiences have been. If the other companies benefited from the VC's involvement or the requirements are valid or common, then you may be wise to accept the terms the VC is offering.

One of the most important principles of negotiation is to always be prepared to walk away from a deal you don't like. Know when you will walk away from a deal, and when you can still negotiate.

Having a plan B

Your negotiating position relies heavily on having options. Ideally, you'll begin the negotiation process months before you're ready to accept funding. You'll be proactive and establish relationships with several VCs and have all your documentation and research assembled and organized. Your goal is to have multiple options available so that you're not dependent on closing just one particular deal.

The important thing to know when considering your plan B is whether your plan B is better or worse than the deal you can strike with a VC. This is sometimes called your BATNA (best alternative to negotiated agreement). For example, if you think your company is worth $3 million, and the VC is willing to go with a valuation no greater than $1 million, then you have to ask yourself whether your BATNA is better than going with the $1 million valuation and getting VC funding. If it's not, then you may want to beg more flexible on the valuation before walking away from the deal.

You should also have a plan B ready in case your negotiation doesn't work out. Going into a negotiation in the position that if you don't close the deal you don't have any other options isn't a good idea. Plan out your options and rate them. Plan B may just be to continue bootstrapping your company at a slower pace. That's okay. Just make sure you understand when to walk away from the VC because your plan B looks like a better deal than the mediocre deal with the VC.

From Initial Interest to Negotiating Table: Identifying the People Involved

When you are negotiating with a venture capital firm, you may think you are negotiating solely with your primary contact, but in reality many people's interests are being represented, and your negotiation is anything but simple. The following sections describe the various people you are likely to encounter and the roles these people take in the deal.

The managing director — your lead investor

When you work with a VC, you have probably made contact with one of the managing directors. After you convince this managing director that your deal is a great investment, he still needs to convince the investment committee that it should invest. The lead investor serves a number of functions in getting the deal done:

- Initial screening
- Presenting to the committee
- Leading due diligence
- Negotiating the term sheet

The lead investor helps you to make your case to the investment committee, so you want to be sure to support him in that role:

- Provide him with all of the materials and background data that he needs to make a good argument for your case.

> ✔ If there are any surprises that you haven't told him about, come clean before the committee presentation so that the lead isn't caught by surprise.
>
> ✔ Support the lead and his analysts in due diligence by getting information back to him as quickly as possible. Try to make sure no more than 24 hours goes by before you get information back that has been requested.

The investment committee

In most funds, a managing director may have 50 percent or fewer of his recommendations accepted by the investment committee, so getting the buy-in from the managing director doesn't mean that you have a done deal. The best way to engage the members of the investment committee is to have done your homework and practiced your pitch.

Find out what you can about the investment committee by asking a lot of questions of your lead investor:

> ✔ Who will be sitting on the committee?
>
> ✔ What biases and predispositions does each member have?
>
> ✔ Who has the most persuasive power in the group?
>
> ✔ Are there any common mistakes that you can avoid (using terms like "conservative estimates," for example)?
>
> ✔ What similar deals have been recently negotiated, what deals have been declined recently, and why?
>
> ✔ How many deals are in play right now (that is, going through due diligence)?

If your lead investor is up for it, he may help coach you through your pitch and throw sample questions and objections at you so that you can anticipate the kinds of responses the committee may give you.

After you know the backgrounds of the people on the committee and what they look for, you can tailor your message to their needs, as long as you can do so without being insincere. Being yourself is far better than awkwardly twisting your story to match what you think they want to hear.

Herding kittens, er investors: Syndication

If your deal is very, very large, or on the edge of an investor's portfolio industry, the VC may have to work with other investors to complete your round. A large round may have four or five VCs working together. When multiple investors get together to do a deal it's called *syndication*. Angel rounds are almost always syndications of multiple investors. You may even mix angel investors and VCs in a round, although that scenario is less common.

Investors syndicate for a variety of reasons, ranging from diversifying risk to participating in deals that are bigger than their funds can normally carry.

After you get the go-ahead from your lead VC firm, your firm may contact other firms that they regularly syndicate with and share your package with them. Here are some things to know about how syndication impacts you:

✔ Due diligence goes much more quickly when the syndicating VCs have a strong trust relationship with the primary VC.

✔ Typically the VCs of the different groups will work together, but you may be required to conduct multiple pitches in multiple cities and answer dozens of due diligence questions.

✔ If you are working with angel investors, the lead investor may or may not help with syndication. The job of herding all the investors together, getting the term sheets negotiated and signed, and collecting the checks may all fall to you. Don't underestimate how much work this can be!

Handling the Valuation Question during Negotiation

A popular maxim in the negotiation field is that the first one to give a number loses. Although this statement may be true in many types of negotiation, it can backfire when you're negotiating for the stock price for your company.

Imagine this scenario: You get an appointment to pitch at a big VC's office. You're excited, and you practice your pitch deck and timing until everything is smooth and ready to go. You give your pitch, and the first question from the VC's managing director is "What's your valuation?"

What do you say? Basically, you can go wrong with this question in a number of ways. If you claim your price is negotiable, you won't be respected as someone who can answer the hard questions. If you confidently answer a solid value, you may also lose.

When you are asked for the valuation of your company, this is your big chance to steer the direction of the negotiation.

Providing a number — and a rationale

VCs are sophisticated and already may have a number in mind that they'll confirm during the due diligence process, if you get that far. At this point, they're testing to understand how you negotiate and what kind of a partner you may be.

Although many negotiation books coach you to backpedal with sentences about how you can't really share that information, or you'd like to discuss the deal more before you get to the price of shares, we recommend that you go ahead and provide a number while also providing your studied rationale for the valuation. The following sections provide additional advice on how to discuss valuation. (Head to Chapter 11 to read more about presenting your valuation.)

If you are negotiating with angel investors, the price negotiation is often more difficult. You will have done your research for your valuation story, and they may have a feel for what valuations in your region have been trending over the past few years.

Anchoring your request

Have you ever seen those late night TV commercials where you can get the product for "Not $59.95! Not $49.95! Not $39.95 but just $29.95.... for TWO!" What the advertiser has done is to play with the psychology of *anchoring*. When they start with a high price and then lower and lower the price, you're left thinking that the final price is an incredible deal.

Venture capital firms are a lot more sophisticated than late night TV watchers, but you may be surprised at how even trained professionals can be swayed by irrelevant anchoring information. Author Daniel Arielly describes tests where people are asked to write down the last two digits of their social security numbers (that is, a totally random numerical anchor). The researchers then asked participants how much they would pay for a variety of items. The people with the highest 20 percent of social security numbers said they'd pay an average of $56 for a cordless keyboard; those with the lowest 20 percent of social security numbers said they'd pay only $16 for the same keyboard. The social security numbers anchored the consumers concepts of pricing, even though the anchors had nothing to do with price or value of the item.

Adding rationale for your anchor

As an entrepreneur pitching to VCs, you don't want to use the random anchoring method (though that strategy seems to be disturbingly popular). Your best strategy is to do your homework and have a great rationale for your anchor and then you can deduct from that with discounts for "smart money" that the VC brings, the value of the connections they bring, the value of having them on the board, and so on.

So long as you have a well-researched valuation story when you state your number, that sets an anchor for the negotiation. If you choose a lower number, you may leave money on the table, and if you choose a higher number, that may change expectations to your benefit.

Keeping the end in mind: A little piece of a big pie or a big piece of a little pie

When you are negotiating the valuation of your company, keep the end in mind. Ultimately you want to make as much money as you can from your company. When you negotiate with VCs, you're negotiating for the capital that will possibly make your company huge and very desirable as an acquisition target for a variety of companies in your industry. If you find yourself arguing for an extra $100,000 of valuation one way or the other, ask yourself this question: Do I want a big piece of a little pie or a little piece of a big pie? Many entrepreneurs who are loathe to give up equity, end up with a big piece of a little pie. This can be a big mistake!

As founder percentage of ownership gets smaller with each funding round, the case value (on paper) increases. The true cash value is realized when the company undergoes a liquidity event. Note how, in Figure 12-1, the founder has only about 5 percent ownership of the company after the fourth funding round, but the cash value of that share is over $11 million. Compare that cash value to the founder's 30 percent ownership after the first round of funding, when the company's value was $2 million, and the founder's cash value was only $400,000.

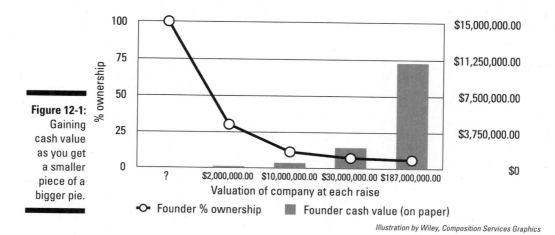

Figure 12-1:
Gaining
cash value
as you get
a smaller
piece of a
bigger pie.

Illustration by Wiley, Composition Services Graphics

Making sure your "great deal" doesn't kill your company

When you're thinking about the long-term strategy for your company, understand that getting a "great deal" can actually look good in the short run but ruin your company in the long run. The best deals are those that look far down the runway and address the changes — both planned and unplanned — that will occur in the future. Most VCs understand this and build contingencies into their negotiations to deal with "what if" situations, some of which are not so pleasant.

Most VCs are nice guys, but they didn't become successful by sticking their heads in the sand. They win by knowing when something isn't working and fixing it right away. These solutions may mean decisions must be made that are good for the company, but bad for you.

You need to take the long view, too. When you get your "great deal" — the one that provides everything you want, including total protection of your stock and your CEO role — it may not be such a great deal in the long run. If your deal hamstrings the board, taking away its ability to put the right person in the right role to help the company move forward, for example, your company loses out, and so do you.

The founder's share of post-money value is not always obvious at first. Consider the three term sheets shown in Figure 12-2. The pre-money valuation is the same in all three, and the VC's share is the same in all three, but the raise is $1 million more in Term Sheet 1, and the employee pool is smaller in Term Sheet 3. The term sheet with the smaller raise and the smaller employee pool is the one that gives the entrepreneur more money. In this scenario, the company has fewer shares to give out in future hiring rounds.

When negotiating the best deal, follow this principle: Focus on what's best for the company, not what's best for the investor, the management team, or for you. Focusing on the company helps to make clear that the goals of the parties need to be aligned and that nobody gets the great deal that ultimately kills the company.

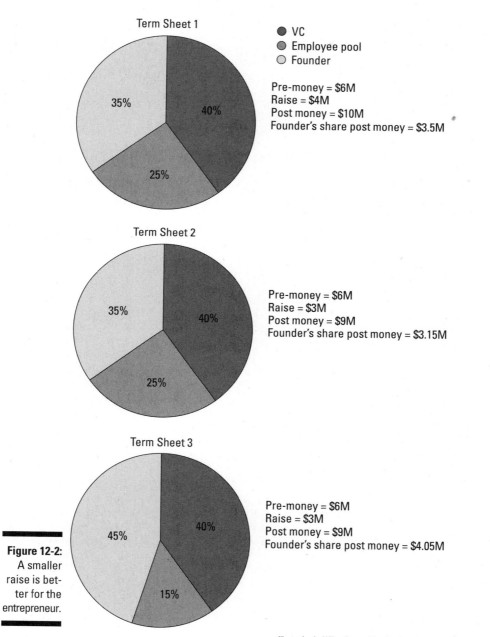

Term Sheet 1

- ● VC
- ● Employee pool
- ○ Founder

40%
25%
35%

Pre-money = $6M
Raise = $4M
Post money = $10M
Founder's share post money = $3.5M

Term Sheet 2

40%
25%
35%

Pre-money = $6M
Raise = $3M
Post money = $9M
Founder's share post money = $3.15M

Term Sheet 3

40%
15%
45%

Pre-money = $6M
Raise = $3M
Post money = $9M
Founder's share post money = $4.05M

Figure 12-2:
A smaller
raise is bet-
ter for the
entrepreneur.

Illustration by Wiley, Composition Services Graphics

Over-pricing leads to lose-lose situations

Say that you're able to negotiate a $6 million valuation for your company. The VC agrees to it, even though you may know that this valuation is too high. You figure "Hey, I got a high valuation, so everything is great!" Twelve months later, when you go for your Series B round, and your new investors feel that, even with the traction you've gained over the past year, your valuation is only $4 million, and they'll go no higher. You shop the deal all around town, and the consensus is that $4 million is the maximum anyone is willing to go. Now you have a *down round*, and everyone's shares get diluted as the new round re-prices everyone's investment at two-thirds of what they invested. Needless to say, your investors are unhappy with losing 33 percent on their investments, and trust is lost going forward. Coming to a fair and reasonable negotiation that will carry through the entire lifecycle of your deal is far better.

Adopting a strategy that gets you top dollar

As we note earlier (refer to the section "Recognizing your own power"), you want to be in a situation where multiple firms are bidding for your equity. Your ideal negotiating position is when you have three VCs all wanting a piece of your deal. When this happens, you can negotiate for the top dollar.

The thing to remember is that timing is everything in getting your best deal. Begin fostering multiple VC relationships three to nine months before you want to pitch your deal and then line up all of your prospects and make your pitch to all simultaneously. Then watch the term sheets flow in. Now, when you're negotiating, you can play the VCs off each other. This is how you get top dollar.

If you approached just one VC and didn't like the deal, you may be tempted to pursue a linear, sequential approach, going through the VCs one at a time. The problem with this strategy is you don't know who is going to offer you the best deal. Often the first deal you get is the best one. If you pass on the first deal in hopes that one of the other companies will offer you a better deal, how enthusiastic do you think the original company will be to invest after others have offered less or, worse, nothing at all? This strategy identifies you as a rookie and can end up wasting everyone's time. Your first offer is often your best offer, and it would be a shame to lose it by holding out.

Desperate deals and the kindness of strangers

A lot of desperate deals come across VCs' desks. These deals looked great six months ago, but some critical contract fell through, a round of funding never happened, or the technical development of the product suffered setbacks. In many cases, these events are death knells for companies, and everything shuts down quietly.

VCs don't often do desperate deals because they don't want to have to go back to their LPs and explain why they saw this deal going down the tubes but pursued it anyway because they felt sorry for the company and so tossed it a few hundred thousand dollars as a lifeline. Even if the general partner *is* inclined to feel generous,

his fiduciary duty to the LPs doesn't provide a lot of leeway.

Occasionally, the desperate deal does get done. Although it may involve generosity, the more likely reason is to protect a first-round investment. VCs make shrewd decisions about follow-on investments. Investing additional capital in this regard isn't a matter of generosity as much as a portfolio self-preservation.

Angel investors sometimes invest in the underdog out of generosity, but these situations are few and far between. To go for the sympathy vote, you need to have a great story and a clear path to success. That's about as far as "generosity" goes in the VC investment world.

Most-Often Negotiated Term Sheet Terms

Your negotiation outline is often driven by the terms on your term sheet. Make sure you have a solid understanding of how the terms work and what they may mean for you down the road, regardless of whether things go well or not so well. You'll negotiate these terms now when everything is going great and everyone believes that your company is going to be a huge success. Over the course of the next five or so years, divergences of opinion may occur between you and your board. The terms you agree to now lay out how decisions will be made when everyone is not in alignment.

Think holistically about the terms being negotiated because they don't exist in isolation from one another. Making a trade-off in one term may affect another term.

A lot of terms can show up on the term sheet; in the following sections, we focus just on some of the most popular ones. For a great detailed discussion of term sheets, we recommend *Venture Deals: Be Smarter Than Your Lawyer and Venture Capitalist,* by Brad Feld and Jason Mendelson (John Wiley & Sons, Inc.).

Valuation

Valuation refers to the act of declaring the price of shares in your company. Your best tools for negotiating the price of your shares include well-prepared valuation models that lay out your rationale in a transparent fashion; head to Chapter 11 for valuation models. These methods provide a concrete set of assumptions that can be discussed in support of your valuation. Ultimately, the higher your value, the more of your company you keep and presumably the better you'll do at your exit.

Pre-money valuation is what your company is worth before the VC makes an investment; *post-money valuation* is what your company's worth after the investment. For example, if your pre-money valuation is $2 million and the investor puts in $500,000, then the post-money valuation is $2.5 million. The VC then owns 20 percent of your company because he will have put in $500,000 of the $2.5 million valuation.

VCs use several valuation methodologies, and you should too. As your negotiation shifts, you can use different valuation methodologies to make your point. Not all of the valuation methods will return the same number; that's okay. Your final valuation should be somewhere within the range of what the various valuation models give you.

Valuation is an important part of your negotiation, but it's not the *most* important thing. Don't lose out on your negotiation by focusing only on valuation and neglecting the many other things you need to be focusing on!

Board seats

The size of the board is driven mostly by the size of the company and number of investors involved. If you're an early stage company in Series Seed or Series A, you may have a three-person board consisting of your CEO or founder, your VC, and an impartial third party who can contribute to the company's development and serve as a tiebreaker in any vote. Larger companies in their Series B or C rounds may have five board members, with two seats representing the investors, two seats representing the founders and CEO, and a fifth seat that is independent.

The board you start with is not likely to be the board you end up with at your exit, so make sure you have clear provisions about how and when board members are elected, how they are removed, and so on.

Consider these points during this part of your negotiations:

✔ **Balance power between investors and entrepreneurs:** As a general principle, the best tactic is to negotiate your deal in such a way that power and control are balanced between investor and entrepreneur. Even more important is ensuring that incentives are aligned so that everyone works toward the same goals.

The balance of power is important in venture-backed companies. If you find yourself grasping onto any semblance of control and fearing your own board will make decisions without your blessing, you're not going to be happy after your company is funded by venture capital. Still, entrepreneurs who aren't willing to give up some control should think about how to bootstrap their companies instead of pursing venture capital funding. Choosing the small business route can make you a lot of money as a principal owner. Consider steering away from venture capital, especially if you are intimidated by working with a board of investors and advisors.

✔ **Negotiate for "smart money" on your board:** Investors are nearly always included as representatives on the board. As an entrepreneur, your job is to respect the risk and contribution of the investors as equal to the ideas and execution labor that you bring to the table. Smart money is your ultimate goal when it comes to investor representation. Having investors who bring connections and experience to the table is often worth many times the cash that is invested into your company.

✔ **Ensure you always have an odd number of directors so that decisions can be made by majority vote.** The tiebreaker is typically someone outside of the company that is chosen by mutual consent. This independent director (you may have more than one) is someone who is both impartial and who brings some value to the table, such as industry expertise or contacts that can help the company.

Liquidation preferences

Liquidation preferences are typically negotiated in such a way that investors get their original investment back before founders and others get a share of any proceeds from a liquidation. (The liquidation event may include acquisition, IPO, or other change of ownership resulting in cash or equity payment to shareholders; refer to Chapter 8 for details on the exit possibilities.)

Liquidation preferences are a powerful negotiation tool. When you negotiate them, be sure to think of terms holistically and not as individual items to be negotiated. For example, if you and your VC cannot come to terms about the valuation of the company, you may be able to use liquidation preferences as a way to argue for a higher valuation while guaranteeing a certain share of the proceeds to the investors before the founders get paid.

We know of an investment group who often asks for a 3X ("3 times") liquidation preference when they are uncomfortable with the valuation. This is way out of the norm but can make sense if the investors are willing to stick with the company through follow-on rounds, since most VCs won't touch a deal where first round investors have a 3X preference. Normally a liquidation preference larger than 1X, when investors receive their money back before any money is distributed to common shareholders, would not be advisable. But if you are stuck on a certain valuation, you may be able to get it by offering a higher liquidation preference.

Be aware of the risks related to offering generous liquidation preferences, especially when they are also tied to provisions regarding decision-making about the exit. If your board decides to have an exit against your wishes and you have provided a 3X liquidation preference (that is, the investors get three times their money back before you receive a penny), then you could end up making very little for your efforts if the exit is at or around 3X the VC's initial investment. If investors put in $1 million, you won't get a penny back before the company reaches $3 million in exit value when there is a 3X preference.

Protective provisions

Protective provisions are important because they clarify the kinds of decisions that are made by a majority of the board rather than by management alone. These provisions protect both investors and entrepreneurs from randomly changing the rules in the middle of the game. They are important because they affect decision-making about your exit strategy, obtaining new funding, creating or selling stock (which could dilute current shareholders), changing the size and makeup of the board, borrowing money, and so on.

Most of the time, protective provisions make sense and simply clarify that you cannot make unethical changes to the company structure to the benefit of the founders or investors, and that major changes can be made only by mutual agreement. Make sure that the limits on decisions aren't onerous or require day-to-day intervention, though. The limits on borrowing should be high enough so that you can make quick, short-term decisions without having to call a special board meeting just to get a corporate credit card, for example.

In successful negotiation, the outcome of the negotiation creates transparency with regard to decision-making. The protective provisions may seem obvious in some cases, but they are very important with regard to maintaining good investor relations and alignment.

Employee pool

Setting aside some stock for the employee pool is customary. This pool often holds about 10 to 20 percent of the company stock and can be used as a sweetener for compensation for early employees, consultants, and contractors.

You want this compensation plan to anticipate both the type of people you'll need to hire along the way and how much stock you'll need to so that you can keep good people on board.

Set up this plan in the beginning, so that it doesn't end up as a negotiation point when you're closing the deal and investors will be loathe to have 20 percent come out of their share.

Anti-dilution clauses

Anti-dilution clauses are terms that protect investors in the case of dilution. Dilution occurs when you raise money with shares at a specific price and then raise a subsequent round at a lower price. In this situation, the company loses value, and early round investors lose value along with it — unless an anti-dilution clause is in place.

Investors are increasingly worried about their shares being diluted on future rounds of financing. And, just to clarify, we're not talking about the kind of dilution where you own 10 percent of the company and a new series of investors comes in and buys a big new chunk of the equity, resulting in your owning only 5 percent of a much bigger and better capitalized company. No, we're talking about the kind of dilution where the Series A investors bought stock at $2.00 per share and now, 18 months later, milestones have been missed and the company is going back to raise more money at just $1.00 per share. This event dilutes the original investors' value to half of its original amount.

As an entrepreneur, make sure you thoroughly understand anti-dilution clauses. When they kick in, the result is anti-dilution for your investors and forced dilution of your common stock. Because of this, anti-dilution clauses have a big effect on the founder's bottom line, so this term will be a key part of your negotiation strategy.

When you're negotiating with VCs, anti-dilution clauses are almost inevitable. You're certainly free to discuss them, but you're unlikely to get them removed from your term sheet. Here's what you should focus on:

> ✔ Make sure that the terms are not so onerous that you are unable to raise future rounds of financing, which could result in the closure of your company.
>
> ✔ Keep your options open by insisting on a weighted average method rather than a full ratchet so that you can make a smaller raise in a down round if things are going poorly and get yourself back on track so that your next funding will be an up round. For more about weighted average and full ratchet anti-dilution clauses, look to Chapter 9.

An anti-dilution clause clarifies what will happen in the future when things don't go according to plan. If everything goes well, then the anti-dilution clause will never kick in. If things go poorly, the clause protects investors at your expense. Because you're not likely to be able to avoid these terms, put a lot of effort into making sure that your company is successful and that all of your future rounds are up rounds. For more on anti-dilution clauses, see Chapter 9.

Vesting of equity

Vesting refers to the promise of equity at some future time in return for founding the company or working as an employee, board member, or consultant to the company. Stock is one way that new companies can print their own currency and offer something that may have future value in return for services rendered now.

Equity can vest in a number of ways; triggers can be based on achievement of milestones, passage of certain periods of time, or the occurrence of certain events, such as liquidation or a departure from the company. The variety of vesting options and their tax consequences make them an important part of your negotiation strategy.

When you're negotiating vesting, obviously the shortest vesting for you, as a founder, is best. You want to secure ownership of your stock as fast as possible to avoid future situations where vesting doesn't occur. If you have partners as founders, consider devising a vesting schedule for everyone, including yourself, so that your company's equity doesn't walk out the door if someone leaves in the short term. Also keep in mind that that a large percentage of VCs end up removing the CEO (possibly you) from that role before the company exits. If removal means leaving the company, you could lose your chance to vest and, as a result, lose a significant portion of your stock. Table 12-1 lists a few possible situations and your negotiating strategy to mitigate the potential losses.

Table 12-1	Negotiation Strategies to Protect Vesting
Situation	**Strategy**
You are the sole founder.	Try to negotiate immediate vesting for yourself.
You have two or three cofounders.	Set up a vesting schedule so that founders have to stay for a specified period of time or until exit to fully vest.
You may be removed as CEO and put in another role.	Ensure that this change will not change your vesting schedule or amount.
You may be removed entirely from the company.	Negotiate for immediate vesting upon your involuntary removal (this one may be tough to get) or for the option to buy out your shares at the price of the last round.
You may voluntarily leave the company before exit.	Negotiate for the option to buy out your shares at the price of the last round.

Dividends

If you have an early-stage company, you may want to negotiate hard against the payment of dividends. If you are a pre-revenue or pre-positive cash flow company, paying dividends could rapidly diminish your runway to the next round of funding or even push you into insolvency if your next round doesn't come in time. Even if dividends are potentially paid in equity, then this is a forced dilution of common stock shares that you probably don't want.

Dividends do make sense in certain circumstances:

✔ You're at a later stage deal where the multiples to exit will be much smaller, and dividends can have a greater impact for investors' returns while having relatively smaller impact on your cash situation.

✔ You, the founder, are reluctant to pursue a quick exit. (This is rarely a good idea from the business perspective, but some founders have personal reasons for not wanting to pursue an exit.) If you have a dividend payout, then the investors can get their money back over time, thus reducing their risk, but also reducing their upside. You would want to pair this unusual strategy with some kind of redemption rights to cash out the investors at an agreed-upon schedule. Remember, most VCs have a ten-year fund lifecycle, so they need to divest the money at the end of the cycle so they can return it to the LPs.

If this is your first venture round, avoid dividends if you can. A better approach is to come up with a fair valuation that everyone agrees on and a clear roadmap to an exit that returns significant multiples to the investors.

Redemption rights

Redemption rights are the right of the preferred shareholders to demand that their shares be redeemed or exchanged for cash, typically in the amount of the original investment plus any unpaid dividends. There may be provisions for payment of this over a period of time, or it may be a lump sum.

Redemption rights are tricky. They can either allow for some flexibility in exit options for the investor, or they can bankrupt your company. Be sure you have clear provisions for when redemption rights can kick in so that there are no surprises, and you aren't operating with a gun to your head throughout the investment period.

Other terms

There are quite a few other terms that can show up on the term sheet that you'll want to negotiate. Table 12-2 summarizes some of them.

Table 12-2	Other Terms to Negotiate
Term	**Description**
Pay-to-play	Forces investors to continue investing pro rata in future rounds or see their preferred shares converted to common.
Drag-along agreement	Stipulates that, if a majority of preferred shareholders want an exit through sale or liquidation, then the remaining preferred and common shareholders must either agree to go along or be dragged along in the process.
Conversion	Allows preferred shareholders to convert their shares to common stock at any time or at a pre-defined trigger such as an IPO at a certain price.

Term	_Description_
Information rights	Provides investors with access to information about the company, such as budgets and audited financials at pre-agreed periods of time.
Registration rights	Allows investors with preferred shares to have those shares registered in an IPO under certain circumstances.
Rights of first refusal	Gives investors in earlier rounds the right of first refusal to invest pro rata to their initial investment in follow-on rounds.
Voting rights	Defines the rights of common and preferred shares in voting.
Restriction on sales	Gives existing shareholders in a privately held company a right of first refusal to buy shares before they are sold to new investors outside of the company.
Proprietary information and inventions	Ensures that key employees sign documents acknowledging that all intellectual property is the property of the company and not the employee.
Co-sale agreement	Gives preferred shareholders in a privately held company the right to sell shares pro rata if and when the founders sell their shares.
Founders' activities	Clarifies roles outside the company, if any, for the founders in order to ensure that full efforts are put into running the company.
IPO shares purchase	Gets underwriters in an IPO to offer investors a portion of the discounted friends-and-family shares that are typically carved out for the investment bankers' best clients.
No-shop agreement	Stipulates that founders will not take their deal to other VCs while the deal is in negotiation.
Indemnification	Indemnifies investors and board members in the company's bylaws and may also require directors and officers (D&O) insurance coverage for all board members.
Assignment	Allows for investors to assign their shares over to another party, usually subject to the terms and agreements in the original purchase.

Chapter 13

Due Diligence: Preparation and Fundamentals

*O*riginally the term *due diligence* was used by broker-dealers to describe the proper standard of care in investigating companies they took to market. Now the term is used everywhere — in the grocery store, on TV, and in other non-investment–specific situations. Nevertheless, the meaning is the same. *Due diligence* just means getting to the bottom of something in a very organized way. For venture capitalists, due diligence is the process of researching a company prior to purchasing shares.

Sound like fun? In this chapter, we explain the process and its purpose so that you'll know what to expect.

Due diligence is not just for VCs. Angels (covered in Chapters 4 and 9) should — and probably will — perform due diligence. And even your Aunt Jenny should spend 20 plus hours looking at your company before she invests in you, despite believing that having changed your diapers back in the day means that she knows everything she needs to know.

Peaking under Rocks and behind Trees: An Overview of Due Diligence

Due diligence occurs at many levels. Most people use the term to refer to the behind-the-scenes research that VCs do on you when they think they may be interested in your company. But really, due diligence starts with the first interaction between you and the VC firm.

The entire due diligence process is like searching for a needle in a haystack, and what VCs find and where they look differs for every company. First they'll check out all the standard points to make sure all *i*'s are dotted and *t*'s are crossed. Then they'll look for the unknown. The VC may work on one or two hunches and dig deep to find out more about the situation. When this happens, your best strategy is to be as open as possible and share everything. In the following sections, we outline the kinds of information you can expect VCs to investigate.

Knowing what VCs look for

The venture capital firm will have staff members and third-party consultants (occasionally referred to as "hired goons") carefully research the following:

- ✔ Your company's finances
- ✔ Your (or the founder's) personal finances
- ✔ Criminal backgrounds of the founders
- ✔ The history and relationships that your company has with all strategic partners

Due diligence information is collated by the company and given to the investors generally in the form of digital documents. Some info, like financials, is printed out because they can be hard to read digitally. Investment firms also make phone calls and look through any publicly available materials.

When VCs ask for all this information, they're looking for a number of things:

- ✔ **To see whether all your documents are in order.** They'll dig to uncover whether you've filed for incorporation, have the necessary employment agreements, or have filed for the necessary patents. They'll also look to see what strategic partnerships you've formed.

- ✔ **To see whether something bad exists that may kill the deal.** Here they look for things that can be damaging to your company's reputation (like the CFO having a criminal history of embezzling, the company filing for bankruptcy, or any problems related to fraud misrepresentation), intellectual property (IP) problems, and any lawsuits your company is involved in.

If the investigation reveals something bad, the VCs will stop the due diligence process. They will not expend further resources on your deal so that they can spend time on other companies instead.

✔ **To see whether any opportunities exist that you may have missed.** Examples include things like identifying a previously untapped key distributor that you need to work through or discovering whether you have a second product that may be on shelves quicker and with less expense than the one you're currently focusing on.

During this part of the investigation, VCs try to find something they can enhance. If the due diligence team can uncover a new revenue stream or a quicker, cheaper, and easier way of doing anything with your company, your deal becomes even sweeter. It's not unusual for VCs to change a company's strategy to take advantage of a bigger and faster growing market.

Understanding your role

Due diligence can ultimately take months and fill multiple binders of info as the VC firm digs deep into your background and your company. Throughout the process, you are expected to help gather all the information that the VC firm needs in order to conduct its investigation. Your help enables the firm to find what it needs more quickly.

Don't feel put-off when a great deal of information is requested. The first time a company is asked to gather all of the necessary personal and business information, the company owners/officers can be downright offended. Remember, due diligence is normal. The more information that the VC wants to gather about you, the closer you are to getting an investment.

Going Step by Step: The Phases of Due Diligence

From the moment a VC sees your deal, the due diligence process in one form or another has begun. If the investor finds something serious that she doesn't like, then due diligence is over, and your company has no chance of being funded by that particular VC. Sometimes due diligence uncovers a small flaw that can be fixed — a great situation because the end result will be a company that's stronger, and the VC will likely be willing to move forward on the deal.

When a VC likes your deal enough to devote full-time resources to perform due diligence on your company, you will be in *full due diligence*. In the next sections, we explain the entire due diligence process from the initial stages to the final, full due diligence stage.

Investigating with eyes open and fingers crossed

The challenge of due diligence is that the investor works very hard looking for something bad while simultaneously hoping not to find some deal-killing information. After all, VCs want to do your deal, and they hope yours will be their next big thing, but they also have to make sure that your deal is not their next big dud.

As due diligence gets deeper, the VC will have invested a lot of time and resources into your company. Having to give up on your deal because of something found in deep due diligence is a

real drag. It happens all the time, though. Most VCs will tell you that a large percentage of their firms' time is spent on due diligence in companies that they never fund.

The worst case is when a VC spends months performing due diligence and finds a flaw that can't be fixed. The VC has lost time, and the company has to figure out whether it's going to try to raise money again or needs to rethink the business.

The initial vetting

The initial vetting process is often done by an administrator in a VC firm. He checks to see whether your company fits the VC's criteria, and he may ask around for a reference to understand your reputation in the community. Generally, the initial vetting occurs shortly after you send your pitch deck or application to the VC.

How the initial vetting process proceeds depends on the venture capital firm itself: how large it is and how many companies want its attention. A small firm may have only one general partner and see only 150 pitch decks per year. A large firm can get thousands of pitch decks per year.

Many venture capital firms encourage founders to send an executive summary or short business plan to them via e-mail. If you do this, an analyst or a junior VC will screen your application. VCs call this stage of their work *sourcing*. Who performs the initial vetting and what happens at this point depends on the size of the venture capital firm:

- ✔ **In large firms:** In large firms, the process may start with a junior VC. If the junior VC likes your executive summary, you may then meet with an associate, either in person or on the phone. If the associate thinks your company is ready for investment and is appropriate for the firm, he'll then alert a general partner (GP) — a senior staff member — about your deal. If the GP likes your potential, then you move on to the pitch.

- ✔ **In small firms:** In smaller firms, the initial screening may begin with the GP. If you pass muster, the partner will show your materials to the investment committee and invite you to give a pitch.

The investment firms also send associates and analysts into the field. In this case, the field isn't a grassy pasture; it's wherever entrepreneurs are found. The point? You may be vetted by a VC before you even intend to be. Think about how you want to portray your company's image in public because you can meet a VC at any time.

Learning more by having you pitch

The pitch is a relatively formal way for an investor to learn as much about your company as possible in a short timeframe. It may not feel formal in the way that people are dressed or the words that they use, but there are strong conventions used during the first meeting between a VC and a founder.

Although the purpose of the pitch is to tell the VC about your company and the investment deal that you are offering, he's learning more than just the details of the company in this meeting. The VC is looking for signs that he likes you and that you'll be a good person to work with in the future. Specifically, VCs are looking for evidence of the following (refer to Chapter 6 for details on what makes a company attractive to VCs):

- ✔ You are highly coachable; that is, you take advice well.
- ✔ You have the experience to take the company through good times and bad.
- ✔ You and your company fit the strategic objective of the venture capital firm's portfolio.
- ✔ Your company is in a big or rapidly growing market.
- ✔ Your product or service is truly disruptive and unique.

Your pitch will be most powerful if your business is strategically planned, your deal is structured, and the due diligence materials are compiled before you set foot in the VC's boardroom. Head to Chapters 14, 15, and 16, for details of the investor pitch.

If the pitch goes well, you're that much closer to getting capital for your business. Many VCs will then invite you back to talk at greater lengths about your company and the deal, or they'll want to meet your team if they haven't already. The deep dive or second meeting isn't about negotiation yet, but it's headed in that direction. Read on.

Deep dive meetings

If you are invited back to meet with an investment group for a second time, this next meeting goes deeper into your deal than the quick pitch meeting did. During a deep dive meeting, you really get into the nitty gritty details, you're expected to have data on financials and market research, and you'll talk more about your technology.

During this meeting, you'll include a rehearsed pitch that lets the new people in the room catch up on your company details and your deal, but beyond that, you really want this meeting to be interactive. Encourage questions. Your goal is to get the investors so engaged that they're interrupting each other to ask you questions.

 Make sure you have a lot of information that you can make available for the investors to look at immediately after the meeting. You can put your materials on a thumb drive that you can hand out, or you can pass around a branded flier that tells potential investors how to access the online folder where you've been storing your due diligence files.

 At this point, it's unlikely that anyone will sign a non-disclosure agreement (NDA), so keep your secrets hidden. Don't include them on the thumb drive you pass out or, if you're giving investors access to your online folder, place your trade secrets in a separate, password-protected file. Don't share them yet.

Entering into full due diligence

If the venture capital firm is still interested in your company after the initial vetting, the pitch, and the deep dive meeting, the firm will take a much closer look, devoting full-time resources to ascertain whether your company is really one to invest in. This stage is called *full due diligence* and it has six phases:

- **Phase 1 – Materials collection:** The investor takes a general look at the company and team.

- **Phase 2 – Main questions:** The investor formulates a list of questions that have come to mind after having perused the basic information from Phase 1.

- **Phase 3 – Site visit:** The investor goes to visit the company's office or facility.

- **Phase 4 – Reports and commitments:** The investor creates a report to highlight the findings in the due diligence and commits to proceed or not.

- **Phase 5 – Deal closure:** The investor and company enter final negotiations and close the deal.

- **Phase 6 – Investment management:** The investor engages in ongoing contact and updates, which continue for the length of the investment.

The full due diligence process can take a month or many months, although some angel investors may rush through due diligence much quicker. A VC typically does a lot more research than an angel investor because she needs to justify her investment recommendations to a committee and ultimately to her limited partners (LPs).

Sometimes when the due diligence process seems to take forever, the VC is doing another type of due diligence: watching to see how you're performing on your short-term goals. Are you accomplishing what you said you would? Is everything moving along smoothly? By taking extra time, the VC gets to know you and your team and is able to sniff out any problems that may not have shown up in the first few meetings.

Phase 1 – Materials collection

If you get to this first phase, then it's time to celebrate, even if just a little. Believe it or not, this first step is progress! It means that a firm or investor is interested enough in your deal to devote time to determining whether your company will be a good investment.

In this phase, the VC initially digs into your business to make sure that you've been doing everything right. Also, you'll likely be given a point of contact in the VC's firm. If you're dealing with an angel group, you'll be given the name of an administrator or lead investor who will act as your point of contact for the group. Here's what you can expect:

- **The due diligence team leader (DD) looks at the whole company superficially at first and then begins to dig deeper.** Remember, his challenge is to find the bad thing about your company without spending months doing it. If something bad exists, he wants to know about it as soon as possible.

  The DD's first step is simply to start gathering all your information, like financials, patents, and other intellectual property. You can make the whole process go more quickly by compiling a lot of this material in advance. Head to the later section "Preparing Documents for Due Diligence" for information about the specific due diligence materials.

  In the past, due diligence materials were hard copy documents that filled giant binders. Now with the ease of transferring documents digitally, most due diligence materials are stored online on a server that's password protected. You can give the password to investors as they become interested in your deal. If an investor requests additional files, you can simply upload them to the server.

During the materials collection phase, disclose the relationships, situations, and anything else that may or may not come to light in the future. If two founders are married to each other or have a parent/child relationship, disclose that important piece of information. Mention any run-ins with the law, bankruptcies, and close relationships with shady characters. If your brother-in-law is in the Mob, tell your DD early on. By sharing information up front and forthrightly, you have the opportunity to explain mitigating circumstances around the event. If the VC finds out this information on her own before you disclose it, she'll wonder what else you're hiding, and the vetting process may end right there — or take much longer due to an apparent breach of trust. Although you don't need to share everything in the first meeting, after due diligence has started, full disclosure is best.

For advice on how and when to inform your VC of familial connections between founders, go to http://www.dummies.com/webextras/venturecapital.

Phase 2 – Main questions

After the DD has gone through a lot of your information, he may still have questions. Depending on how communicative your DD is, he may contact you regularly as he goes through your materials.

Some of these questions may simply be technical questions to clarify the investors' understanding of your business, and others may be broad questions about risks in your industry. As you provide the answers, keep in mind that the VC wants to see how deeply you are connected to key issues, key players, and the trends in your industry. The more knowledgeable you are, the better you look during this phase.

Phase 3 – Site visit

The site visit is an important part of the venture capital due diligence process. Many VCs like to visit your office, even if you and your partners all work out of your basement. The VC can tell a lot about your business by the way you have organized your space, files, and physical resources.

VCs aren't looking for you to have a fabulous designer office with expensive furniture (in fact, that can be a negative because the VC will question your allocation of scarce resources), but they will be looking at how you work, what resources you have available, and what decisions you have made about working together.

In companies where retail space, kitchens, manufacturing, or scientific labs are involved, the site visit can be critical because it gives you a chance to demonstrate your sophistication in building out your particular type of company.

Peter recently took a site visit to a very sophisticated lab at a life-sciences company and was impressed not only by the organization of the lab, but by the stories the CEO told him about how he had acquired a $50,000 machine for $5,000 from a defunct bioscience company and how other items in this lab that looked brand new had been sourced used or near-new from companies that had shut down. These choices showed that the CEO was going to use investor's money wisely and get a lot done with relatively little capital.

Phase 4 – Reports and commitments

At this phase, the VC has completed his research and prepares a due diligence report. In this report, the VC needs to demonstrate that he's looked at everything that a prudent person would have considered. He also either commits or declines the investment, based on the information available. Given the virtually infinite number of factors that may be considered in an investment deal — factors ranging from verifying the educational backgrounds of the principals to understanding macroeconomic trends that may impact the particular industry — VCs want to produce a document that provides a solid argument for their go/no-go decisions.

Although you may ask for a copy of the report, don't be surprised if the VC isn't willing to share it with you. Some will share, and others won't because of potential liability issues.

Here's what you can expect in either case:

- ✔ **A go decision:** If the VC makes a commitment to invest, he'll typically present you with a term sheet, which succinctly describes all the important aspects of your deal. For more detailed information on the term sheet, head to Chapters 9 and 12. In addition, you can be sure that he'll help you with any areas of concern outlined in his report.

- ✔ **A no-go decision:** Your VC may decide not to go ahead with your deal. In that case, most VCs are willing to provide some helpful advice and will describe, in general terms, their reasons for rejecting your deal. If this happens, it's probably too late to continue to argue your case (you should have been working on this during the due diligence process). The best tack is to take his advice and move on to the next VC.

Phase 5 – Deal closure

After the investigative part of your due diligence process is complete, the time comes to close the deal. At this point, your lawyer works with the VC to agree on the terms and the timing of funding. Your job is to get to work to achieve all the milestones that you and your VC agreed upon during the negotiation process!

Phase 6 – Investment management

The VC's contribution doesn't end at the deal closure phase. He needs to continue to understand what's going on in your company, even after the investment has been made. To that end, he'll want — and you should be prepared to provide — monthly or quarterly updates. In addition, plan to meet face to face at least annually and probably more frequently if you and your VC are in the same geographic region.

The VC has a fiduciary duty to his LPs not only to make great investments in companies like yours but also to manage those investments for as many as five or ten years. Part of that management process includes reviewing your financials, updating your strategic plan, ensuring that you're meeting milestones, and beginning on your exit strategy. Your VC may even have control provisions written into your agreement to ensure that you provide him with timely and accurate information.

The investment management phase is the time to show your VC that you and he are great business partners because chances are you'll be coming back to him for more funding in 12 to 18 months. If your relationship with your VC is good, and you're achieving your goals, the likelihood of getting funded in the next round is good. Just remember that due diligence for your Series B financing round starts the day after your Series A closes! Head to Chapter 9 to read more about multiple rounds of funding.

As Time Goes By: Knowing the Due Diligence Time Frame

A lot must be done in the course of due diligence. The people on the investigative team are not just reading your documents and checking boxes. They're really thinking about your company, comparing it to other companies that they've seen, and making go or no-go decisions each step of the way.

Each iteration of due diligence that the company performs has costs: employee time and money in the form of credit checks, and hired consultant fees. In addition, most investors use external firms for at least some of the due diligence process.

How long your due diligence process takes depends on a number of things. We go into details on the situation-specific factors in the next section, but two general factors are also important:

✔ **The firm's eagerness to invest:** Firms can be more or less eager to invest, and your due diligence process length can be attributed in some way to their internal desires. Ask upfront how long a firm anticipates due diligence to take. If the answer is six months, you better believe them!

✔ **The type of investor:** Friends and family due diligence often is very low. Angel investors may put in a week's worth of hours researching your deal, but VC's can do months of due diligence. Mergers and Acquisitions (M&As) private equity groups will do even more due diligence (see Figure 13-1).

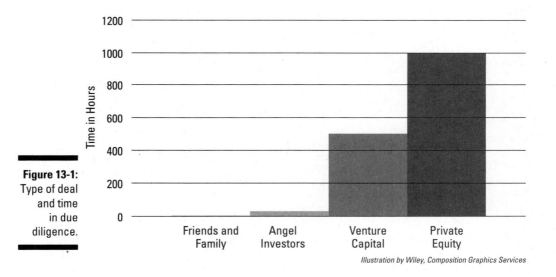

Figure 13-1:
Type of deal
and time
in due
diligence.

Illustration by Wiley, Composition Graphics Services

Understanding why it can take so long

The due diligence process can take weeks or even months to complete. We have seen deals done in as few as five weeks (angel round), and others that take six months or more. The amount of time the due diligence process takes varies, depending on the size, age, and complexity of your company. Also, each venture capital firm has a set of procedures that it follows, and these vary a great deal from company to company. If your VC is the venture arm of a large corporation like Google, Pfizer, or Johnson and Johnson, due diligence may take even longer. Those VCs will need to get buy-in at the corporate level, which takes time.

Beyond that, some factors reliably increase the amount of time spent on due diligence:

- **Extreme documentation:** During due diligence, you have to provide a lot of documentation (hop to the later section "Preparing Documents for Due Diligence" to see a list of all the things you may have to provide). Although some of the documents may take just a few seconds to review, others can take days and weeks.

  If your company's value rests primarily on your patents, expect patent reviews to take a long time. The VC may need to hire an outside consultant or law firm to assess the quality of the patent. He may also need to hire technical consultants in the field to ensure that the process or product you have patented actually works. Just because you can patent something doesn't mean that it can actually be made and sold!

- **Shenanigans:** Occasionally, due diligence takes so long because the VC doesn't actually have any money to invest. Although not common, these VCs may use this delay tactic to keep your company out of the hands of other VCs while the investors finish raising the needed funds. They may view this tactic as a way to efficiently do two things at once (raise capital and perform due diligence), but the delay isn't really fair to you. No fund can guarantee an investment until it has raised its minimum or it actually closes (that is, has raised the required capital and has completed the legal steps required to invest). The risk is great that something could prevent that fund from investing in your company, in which case you'll have wasted your time waiting unnecessarily.

  When you talk with a VC, do your own due diligence to see how long ago the fund closed, which companies are in the portfolio ahead of you, and how much money the firm has left to invest.

- **Getting to know a young or inexperienced company:** Some types of due diligence have nothing to do with the extensive document list. To get to know you and your team as people, VCs watch to see how you interact with them and with each other. They look at your short-term plans and whether you're achieving your goals on schedule. They look at your communication style and how well you keep them updated on your progress. In cases of young and inexperienced companies, the VC may want to watch you for six months just to get a feel for how you operate.

Speeding up the process

The faster you secure investment, the more quickly you can begin to grow your company. Here are some ways to speed things along:

 ✔ **Be prepared:** Being prepared is the most effective way to make sure that due diligence goes quickly. If your company drags its feet collecting materials, you add more and more time to the due diligence process.

 ✔ **Be organized:** If your files are well organized and stored in folders that make sense, and you've made available a table of contents that allows an outsider to follow your filing system, everyone can easily find what he or she is looking for.

Imagine that you're the new junior VC, a recent hire, and have been assigned to a company half way through the process. What kinds of maps and tools would you like to have when digging through a company's documents? Provide those for the people who have to look through your documentation.

 ✔ **Be available:** Staying in touch is important during due diligence. If investors misunderstand a document or start to get the wrong idea, they can lead each other down the wrong path in conversation. Even smart people get confused sometimes. Call fairly often to check in. When you call, ask whether the VC needs any documents and try to create a rapport with the person that you are calling. When you're friendly and helpful, the person you're talking to may share that the mood surrounding your deal is moving in the wrong direction. Sometimes you can turn it back to positive, and sometimes you can't.

Preparing Documents for Due Diligence

The due diligence checklist is an extensive list of documents that you'll want to be able to provide to investors. We've divided the many, many documents and bits of information into various categories: general business documents, financial details, tax matters, and so on.

As you go through this list, keep in mind that not all the items listed will apply to your company. If your company doesn't have patents, don't worry if you don't have patent filing documents, and if your company has only been around for two years, don't worry about having three years of financial statements. The main thing is that you are able to provide to the VC all the information that he wants as he analyzes your company. The next sections describe the documents often requested during due diligence and share preparation pointers.

In case you're feeling that putting all this documentation together is a pain and the VC may never ask for it, you should know that VCs are impressed when you have a package together. Because it's rare to find companies that are so prepared, the VC is likely to think, "Hmmm, who else is looking at this deal?

This team has the due diligence package together already. Other firms must be competing for this investment." Bottom line: The more you have prepared before you go into negotiations, the better.

Going through the due diligence checklist

Each company is different. Some companies may have a lot of materials in the real estate part of the checklist but very little in the way of employee documents. Life science and engineering companies may have a lot of intellectual property filings and regulatory documentation. If you find that your company simply doesn't have much documentation in one of these areas, that's okay. Collect what you can.

You will likely find that you don't have some documentation that you really should have. If you've done two friends and family fundraising rounds, for example, but you still don't have a capitalization table (refer to Chapter 9), then you may have to stop everything and put one together. Doing so is a normal part of growing your company! Investors are more interested in how you recover from the realization that you've been missing something.

General business documents and information

General business documents are really fundamental. They show that your company is real and that federal and local governments recognize it as an independent entity. These documents also show that you're organized and thinking like a big company, not like a start-up working out of the founder's basement (even if you are):

- Articles of Incorporation with all amendments
- All the company's assumed names and copies of registrations
- A document listing all states where the company is authorized to do business and annual reports for the last three years
- Bylaws with amendments and a meeting minutes book (including all minutes and resolutions of shareholders and directors, executive committees, and other governing groups)
- Organizational chart
- Capitalization table listing the shareholders and the number and type of shares held by each
- Agreements regarding options, warrants, convertible securities, calls, voting trusts, and subscriptions

- ✔ Certificate of Good Standing from the state where the company is incorporated

- ✔ A document listing all states, provinces, or countries where the company owns or leases property, maintains employees, or conducts business

Financial details

Your financials will be scrutinized for a number of reasons. Potential investors need to understand your business and how much revenue you can draw compared to expenses. But that's only the beginning. Investors also want to determine how well you are growing as a company. They want to see whether you're developing more efficient ways of doing business as your resources increase. Further, they want to see how well you organize your financial data and whether you are using it to glean important information for future decision-making. Here's what you need:

- ✔ Financial statements for the current and past three years

- ✔ For any financial statements that were audited or reviewed, the auditor's letters and replies for the past five years

- ✔ Statement of assets and liabilities

- ✔ Documentation for all indebtedness and contingent liabilities

- ✔ Inventory list

- ✔ Statement of accounts receivable and payable

- ✔ A description of depreciation and amortization methods and changes in accounting methods over the past five years

- ✔ Fixed assets and their locations

- ✔ Sales and purchases of major capital equipment during the last three years

- ✔ All Uniform Commercial Code (UCC) filings

- ✔ All leases of equipment

Tax matters

Your company's tax materials are very important. Having audits or liens in your past is not a deal-breaker, but investors want to see that you were able to handle the situation well. Gather these things:

- ✔ Federal, state, local, and foreign income tax returns for the last three years

- ✔ States sales tax returns for the last three years

   ✔ Employment tax filings for three years

   ✔ Excise tax filings for three years

   ✔ Any audit and revenue agency reports

   ✔ Any tax settlement documents for the last three years

   ✔ Any tax liens

Real estate assets and leases

Whether you have real estate assets or leases, your company's ties to buildings or land will be important to investors. VCs will want to see these items:

   ✔ A schedule of the company's business locations

   ✔ Real estate assets owned by the company.

   ✔ Copies of all real estate leases, deeds, mortgages, title policies, surveys, zoning approvals, variances, or use permits

Intellectual property

Intellectual property can be a tricky subject. Your company's patents can be a large asset, but if you're using technology owned by a founder — or worse, a founder's spouse — investors may want the company to buy the intellectual property before they move forward with investment. Gather this information:

   ✔ Domestic and foreign patents and patent applications (include patent filing documents)

   ✔ Trademark and trade names

   ✔ Copyrights

   ✔ Copies of all consulting agreements, agreements regarding inventions, licenses, or assignments of intellectual property to or from the company

   ✔ Summary of any claims or threatened claims by or against the company regarding intellectual property

   ✔ Descriptions of technology assets

   ✔ Descriptions of methods used to protect trade secrets (but don't give up the trade secret!)

   Treat trade secrets with the utmost of care during due diligence. Trade secret details should be known by as few souls as possible.

   ✔ Any work-for-hire agreements

   ✔ Patent clearance documents, if any

Employees and benefits

Employees may come and go, but each one leaves his or her mark on the company history. Gather the following:

- ✔ Employees, including positions, current salaries, and bonuses paid during last three years, and years of service
- ✔ Description of all employee health and welfare insurance policies or self-funded insurance
- ✔ Document detailing all difficulties with employees within the last three years, including alleged wrongful termination, harassment, and discrimination charges or complaints
- ✔ List of any labor disputes, requests for arbitration, or grievance procedures currently pending or settled within the last three years
- ✔ Worker's compensation claim history
- ✔ Unemployment insurance claims history
- ✔ Collective bargaining agreements
- ✔ All stock option and stock purchase plans
- ✔ All employment, consulting, nondisclosure, non-solicitation, or noncompetition agreements between the company and any of its employees
- ✔ Resumes of key employees
- ✔ The company's personnel handbook and a schedule of all employee benefits including holiday, vacation, and sick leave policies
- ✔ Summary of retirement plans
- ✔ Material information about the founders, including marriage or family relationships among principals, major health issues, past issues with bankruptcy, criminal or civil convictions, or other issues that the VC will turn up during due diligence.

Licenses, permits, and regulatory issues

Regulation can include different issues for different kinds of companies: methods of dumping waste, Environmental Protection Agency (EPA) documentation, Federal Drug Administration (FDA) requirements, or United States Department of Agriculture (USDA) permits.

- ✔ Copies of any governmental licenses, permits, or consents
- ✔ Any correspondence or documents relating to any proceedings of any regulatory agency
- ✔ Environmental audits, if any, for each property leased by the company

✔ Hazardous substances used in the company's operations

✔ Environmental permits and licenses

✔ Any environmental litigation or investigations

✔ Any known superfund exposure

✔ Any contingent environmental liabilities or continuing indemnification obligations

✔ A description of the company's disposal methods

✔ All FDA regulatory process documents if applicable

✔ Copies of all correspondence, notices, and files related to EPA, state, or local regulatory agencies

Material contracts

This category includes contracts from all the different firms and companies that you have worked with in the past and are working with currently:

✔ A schedule of all subsidiary, partnership, or joint venture relationships and obligations, with copies of all related agreements

✔ Loan and bank financing contracts, line of credit, or promissory notes to which the company is a party

✔ Security, mortgages, indentures, collateral pledges, and similar contracts (including guaranties to which the company is a party) and any installment sale contracts

✔ Distribution, sales representative, marketing, and supply contracts

✔ Any options and stock purchase contracts involving interests in other companies

✔ Nondisclosure or noncompetition agreements to which the company is involved

✔ Copies of all contracts between the company and any officers, directors, shareholders, or affiliates

✔ Any letters of intent, contracts, and closing transcripts from any mergers, acquisitions, or divestitures within the last five years

✔ The company's standard quote, purchase order, invoice, and warranty forms

✔ All other material contracts

Product or service lines

Investors want to know about your products more concretely than just what you propose in your business plan. These documents contain detailed information about (current, future, and past) products, product lines, and services:

- A list of all existing products or services
- Products or services that are planned for future development
- Copies of all correspondence and reports related to any regulatory approvals or disapprovals of any of the company's products or services
- A summary of all complaints or warranty claims
- A summary of results of all tests, evaluations, studies, surveys, and other data regarding existing products or services and products or services under development

Marketing and customer information

Customer base is the cornerstone of revenue. If your company has one customer that buys $3 million in product every year, your business is very different than one that has 3 million customers who buy $1 in product every year, even though the revenues are the same. Gather the following:

- The company's ten largest customers and their sales volume for the past two years
- Unfilled orders other than those in the normal course of business
- Any supply or service agreements
- A description or copy of the company's purchasing policies
- A description or copy of the company's credit policy
- A description or copy of the company's major competitors
- A list and explanation for any major customers lost over the last two years
- All surveys and market research reports relevant to the company or its products or services
- The company's current advertising programs, marketing plans, budgets, and printed marketing materials

Litigation issues

Litigation is not always the death knell for a company; it's sometimes just a part of doing business in the United States. We've got to give all those lawyers something to do, right? Don't leave anything out. This part is extremely important. Gather these items:

- A schedule of all pending litigation
- A description of any threatened litigation

✔ Copies of insurance policies possibly providing coverage as to pending or threatened litigation

✔ Documents relating to any injunctions, consent decrees, or settlements to which the company is a party

✔ A list of unsatisfied judgments

Insurance coverage

All companies should have insurance, but many different kinds of insurance are available. Investors want to know whether you need to change your coverage before they invest. Gather these items:

✔ Schedules and copies of the company's general liability, personal, and real property insurance; product liability, errors and omissions, and key-man insurance, if necessary; and directors and officers, worker's compensation, and other insurance

✔ A schedule of the company's insurance claims history for past three years

Professionals

Include a schedule of all professional firms engaged by the company in the last five years:

✔ Law firms

✔ Accounting firms

✔ Other consulting firms

Articles and public relations

Include copies of all advertising and marketing articles relating to the company within the past three years:

✔ Press releases and clippings

✔ Analyst reports

✔ Advertisements

Planning documents

These are the internal documents used for management and administrative planning:

✔ Projections, operating budgets, and capital budgets

✔ Strategic plan and related documents

- ✔ The company's credit report
- ✔ Analyst reports
- ✔ The company's general ledger
- ✔ A description of the company's internal control procedures

A few final pointers

In many cases, you'll be preparing these documents for the first time, and many of them will simply be a one-page description of the issue or situation. Here are some pointers to keep in mind:

- ✔ **Be thorough:** This is your chance to present any skeletons in your closet, along with your explanation of the specifics and mitigating circumstances.

- ✔ **Decide how you want to present the information:** Some companies print all of their due diligence documents and present them to the VC in a binder. Others store the documents electronically and make the folders available to the VC. Whichever method you choose, your organization and clarity in the folder/tab structure and document naming is an important part of making the documents easy to find and understand.

Make a table of contents that identifies the location of the many documents. This reference enables VCs to rapidly find the documents they are looking for. As we note in the preceding section, a table of contents list also helps you shorten the amount of time due diligence takes.

Part IV
Pitching to Investors

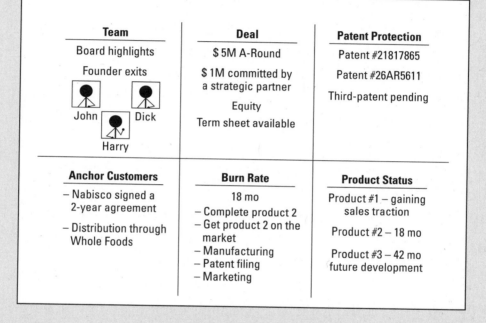

Team	Deal	Patent Protection
Board highlights Founder exits John Dick Harry	$ 5M A-Round $ 1M committed by a strategic partner Equity Term sheet available	Patent #21817865 Patent #26AR5611 Third-patent pending
Anchor Customers	**Burn Rate**	**Product Status**

– Nabisco signed a
   2-year agreement
 	
– Distribution through
   Whole Foods
	18 mo
	– Complete product 2
	– Get product 2 on the
	   market
	– Manufacturing
	– Patent filing
	– Marketing
		Product #1 – gaining
		sales traction
		
		Product #2 – 18 mo
		
		Product #3 – 42 mo
		future development

Learn how local culture dictates attire and how what you wear impacts the success of your pitch at www.dummies.com/extras/venturecapital.

In this part...

- Create a powerful pitch — one that's full of both factual data and emotion — that brings investors to the edge of their seats and leaves them wanting to know more about your company and your deal.

- Cover all the key topics in a professional-quality slide deck that connects with your audience.

- Incorporate presentation tactics that keep your audience interested and avoid distractions and easy-to-make mistakes. Hone your message over the course of the fundraising process.

- Follow up and position yourself for future success, whether you get the deal or hear "No, thank you."

Chapter 14

Planning Your Pitch

An investor pitch is the standard way that investors learn about you, your product, and your company. The pitch is meant to be short — always under an hour and almost always under 20 minutes. You are expected to convey tons of information in this short presentation, which is why pitching is an art form that you must practice.

In this chapter, we discuss the convention of the investor pitch. Even though the invitation to pitch to an investor may seem informal, there are definitely rules and traditions associated with the pitch. We outline the importance of the pitch, explain how to plan the pitch, and talk about the best attitude leading up to giving your pitch. (For a review of the process from initial screening to the party you plan after you close the deal with the VC, refer to Chapter 13.)

Communicating a Lot in a Little Time

The pitch is a technical presentation with carefully chosen points. These points include things like how you'll make money and how you'll scale your company. Keep in mind, however, that in many cases the purpose of the pitch is not to tell everything possible about your company; the purpose is to build interest and score an invitation to a follow-up meeting. In the following sections, we explain what to focus on in your pitch so that you can convey the key ideas and engender the interest you want in the time you have.

As we note in the chapter's introduction, you may have only 2 minutes or you may have the luxury of over 20 minutes to deliver your pitch. In either case, you have a short amount of time to get across enough information to let the VC know what you're doing, how you make money, how much money he can make from the deal, and whether you are capable of executing your plans.

Balancing thoroughness and brevity

Pitching to a VC isn't a single event; it's a process. Your goal at each step is to move along to the next phase of the process, and so, in a sense, you're pitching at every encounter you have with a VC. But when you're making your first pitch to a specific investor, you want to hit the high notes of your company. Although you need to have done your homework and know all the details to support your claims, you want to save the finer details for the follow-up meetings, when you'll have the opportunity for a deeper discussion and can go into more detail.

Limiting the product discussion

An investor pitch is not designed to go into great detail about the product or the technology that inspired the product. Whereas a sales pitch is very product focused, an investor pitch is meant to sell the company, or at least company equity, to an investor. For that reason, your product line has only a cameo role in this presentation — even though it may be the bread and butter of your whole company or highly complex and a great improvement over anything ever created.

So don't give it a lot of screen time in this particular show. If you find that the product is more than 25 percent of your pitch, then you're probably missing something else that is equally important. If you have a particularly novel technology, discuss it very briefly and encourage questions about it for the question-and-answer segment of your talk. (Refer to Chapter 6 for advice on the role your product plays in your efforts to secure venture capital.)

Saving the mission and values for another day

You don't need to expound on the company mission and values unless you know your company's values align particularly well with the values of the investors in the audience. In that case, mentioning the values alignment quickly should suffice. For example, "People in close-knit neighborhoods have better health overall and are concerned less about crime when compared to otherwise identical neighborhoods. Our work on product X is driven by the desire to fundamentally tighten the relationships between people in their own neighborhoods." Under usual circumstances, there's no need for a whole slide about values and mission in the pitch.

Although your pitch isn't the time to focus on your company's values and mission, you should discuss this topic with your investor outside of the pitch. If you have strong stated values surrounding local manufacturing, for example, you may think twice about taking money from a VC who outsources all manufacturing overseas as a matter of course.

Keeping financial predictions short but believable

You don't need to go into depth on your financial predictions in the pitch. Investors at this point just want to understand whether your company needs to raise $2 million or $20 million to get to profitability. During the pitch, stating when you plan to break even and when your company will become profitable and then defending your points is enough. For example, "It takes about 2 months and costs $C to sign each new client. Each client is worth $R in revenues per year. At the rate we're going now, we will be profitable in 11 months." That level of detail is impressive and takes very little time to convey.

Although you don't need to go into exhaustive detail during the pitch, be sure to have very detailed pro formas (Chapter 6) and other predictive financial documents available for a deeper discussion immediately thereafter.

Having multiple pitches ready

You should have multiple pitches in your back pocket so that you can gain interest in just a few words or a few minutes. Creating the one perfect pitch will simply not cut it. You'll need to adapt your pitch to different audiences and different amounts of available time.

Follow these guidelines to adapt your full pitch to the time you have available:

- ✔ **When you have time for only a few words:** Focus on identifying your industry, your product, the problem you solve, and the way you make money. For example, "Company X is in the Medical IT space. We have a SaaS (software as a service) software product that helps medical professionals share medical records for an affordable monthly subscription rate."

- ✔ **When you have a few minutes:** Touch on the following topics at a high level: the industry, the problem, the product, the market, the pro forma, how you scale, your timeline, your deal, and so on. Five minutes is plenty to cover everything at a high level.

- ✔ **When you have 20 minutes or more:** Focus on all the same things you would discuss in a 5 minute pitch, but go in to deeper detail on each one.

In the next section, we explain how to build a pitch from scratch. By following that process, you automatically create pitches for each of these scenarios.

If you're unsure of how long you are expected to pitch, then ask! The difference between a five minute pitch and a ten minute pitch is huge. No one can wing it successfully, and a VC will respect the fact that your pitch matches his time expectations. Over prepare and then expect to go with the flow. You may be cut off before you can finish your pitch. Don't let it phase you. Be flexible and genuinely interact with the VC throughout your meeting.

Creating a Pitch from Scratch

Whether you've never pitched before or you already have an extensive pitch deck (head to Chapter 15 for more on those), you'll benefit from creating a new pitch from scratch. Taking a long pitch and shortening it to 5 or 10 minutes is really hard. Important information tends to get lost, and the main points may be hard for your listeners to understand.

We've found that starting with the world's shortest pitch (only 4 words) and building up in scope is the best way to create a pitch from scratch. Here's how:

1. **Create a four-word description.**

   This description isn't a tagline. Nor does it have to be catchy or even a sentence. Just find four non-technical keywords that describe your company accurately. Be sure one of the words describes your field, for example, focusing on hardware, software, clothing design, culinary, travel, energy, and so on. And be specific: "World changing technology transportation" is less effective than "Bicycle tires never puncture" or even "Stronger rubber tire technology,"

2. **Expand your four-word description into a tweet (140 characters).**

   In just 140 characters and using reasonable phrasing, describe your company. When well-honed, this statement should be on your website and at the top of all your executive summaries. Make it memorable, to the point, and easy for someone to paraphrase when describing your company to another investor. Here's an example:

   > Bicycle tires puncture. Our new manufacturing methods with 300X stronger rubber for a tire that doesn't puncture. Made for racing experts.

3. **Build rough pitch deck slides.**

   Create a digital slide show for your pitch deck by using Microsoft PowerPoint or Apple Keynote. When you create your pitch deck, begin with basic slides as placeholders for the elements of your company's specific story. Make a slide for each of the following: problem, product, business model, team, funding needs, competitive advantage, market, and accomplishments. These slides are only the beginning.

4. **Develop your pitch deck more fully.**

   In this step, you expand some of the points listed in Step 3 into multiple slides and relegate other points to verbal communication.

Asking yourself key questions

Use these questions to think about your company in investor terms as you create your slides.

- ✔ What does your company do?
- ✔ What problem do you solve?
- ✔ How big is the problem you will solve?
- ✔ How do you make money?
- ✔ How much money can you make and can you rapidly scale up?
- ✔ How will you overcome the risks associated with your company's ability to make money?
- ✔ Have you completed any major milestones so far?
- ✔ Why are you raising money, what will the money be used for, and how long will the money last?
- ✔ How much money will you need?

You need to incorporate all the subjects listed, but feel free to change the order or to focus on your strategic strengths to put your best foot forward.

Tips to follow when creating a pitch deck

This pitch deck format has become standard. Expect to create one if you are raising money from VCs. You can present the digital file in person (a pitch) or send it in an e-mail. Here are some pointers to keep in mind as you create your pitch deck:

- ✔ **Notice that many of these questions in the preceding section include the word *money*.** The investor pitch is a conversation about how you plan to use a great product and a great company to make money for yourself and the investors who join you in developing your company. Focus your pitch on making money, and you'll stay on the right track.

✔ **Avoid pitch deck templates, which may hamstring you into a format that doesn't work for your company.** The most successful pitches tell stories that engage the audience; they're interesting, have a purpose, and include beginnings and ends. And each company has its own unique story. Standard templates may not do your company justice.

✔ **A well told story, like a great piece of music, has a "hook" that runs throughout the presentation.** Your story should have a brand and a feel that matches your company and makes it memorable. If you are presenting at an event, pitch events have from 5 to 40 companies pitching. If you have an invitation to pitch in a VCs office, remember that VCs see hundreds of pitches in a year. You need to stand out so the VCs remember your company and follow up.

Knowing When to Pitch

Finding the perfect time to raise capital and start pitching to investors is tricky. You need to raise money before your current funds are completely exhausted. However, pitching before you have fully prepared to raise capital is dangerous. Your lack of preparation will be apparent. For that reason, strategizing your fundraising efforts is like a game of chess, where you have to balance being prepared with the need to act quickly.

Aiming for the beginning of a high-growth phase

Investors seek companies that are on an extremely steep growth curve. Because extreme growth in a company is rare and only semi predictable, VCs look for hints that indicate your company is capable of doubling in value every year for the next three or four years. Therefore, the best time to start pitching your company is when you are really busy with the beginnings of big growth. Sure, pitching during a high-growth time when you have so many other things to do is inconvenient, but investors love to invest in a company that's picking up momentum. Use the following guidelines to decide whether your company is in that sweet spot:

✔ **When it's too early to raise investment capital:** If you company has these characteristics, you're probably not ready to make your pitch to VCs:

 • The product is still in concept phase.

 • The company's main assets are a good idea and a business plan.

- Only one or a few people are in the team.

- No go-to-market strategy has been developed yet.

✔ **When it may be too late to raise investment capital:** Companies with these characteristics may find that they've missed their prime opportunity to raise money:

- The company is out of working capital.

- Team members are leaving the company.

- Revenues are high, and taking capital no longer makes sense.

✔ **When the timing is just right for a fundraising round:** If your company has these characteristics, now's the time to raise capital:

- You need capital to meet sales demands.

- You need new key employees for the next business development phase.

- Your company is successful in one market, and you need to ramp up marketing development so you can break into a new market.

Planning for future development

Sometimes you may feel like your company has to be totally built, successful, and flourishing before you can even talk to VCs. Although investors like to see you positioned for great success, you don't need to have everything wrapped up in a bow to start the conversation.

VCs are experts of early-stage companies, and they know that you can be poised for success even if your product is still a prototype or you have only two customers. Different kinds of companies have different kinds of risk hurdles. If you've tackled enough of your risk hurdles, then still having a lot of work ahead of you is okay. The key is to know what you don't know and to know which weaknesses are surmountable.

Knowing what you don't know

You don't have to have the answers. Start-up companies aren't expected to have accomplished everything yet. Instead, you have to be forward thinking. In other words, identify the big unknowns that are still looming ahead for your company. By identifying the risks and decisions you'll have to make in the future, you effectively demystify the unknowns.

Consider a company named GrowX, for example, that's developing a therapeutic drug. The company has to get through a lot of regulatory hurdles with the FDA before it can sell its product to customers. GrowX still has to run many experiments to determine whether its drug is effective against disease, and it runs the risk of the drug never getting to market. For GrowX, FDA approval is a big unknown. To get a handle on the FDA approval process, GrowX has hired an expert who knows how to work with the FDA. It also has developed a backup plan to turn the drug into a research tool for non-therapeutic use (meaning it would not need FDA approval), in the event that the drug fails to treat the disease. GrowX is doing its best to get a handle on the things that, at the present, remain unknown.

Identifying acceptable weaknesses in your company's development

Depending on the type of company you have, being weak in some areas of company development may be completely acceptable. Companies based on highly technical hardware, software, or novel science, for example, are unlikely to have a completed product or paying customers when they approach VCs. In fact, if a life-science company had a drug completely developed, tested, and approved through regulatory channels, the company would be too advanced for VC funding.

However, you must fix these weaknesses before you talk to VCs:

- ✔ You have no pitch deck.
- ✔ Your team consists of only one or two founders.
- ✔ You have no promotion strategy.
- ✔ You have no pro forma prepared.
- ✔ No revenue plan has been developed.
- ✔ No prototype of your product has been developed.

Assessing whether you're ready for investor capital

Use the assessment form in Table 14-1 to determine whether your company is ready to pursue investment capital. *Note:* This assessment assumes that your company is a venture company capable of doubling in value every year for the next three or four years.

Table 14-1	Investor Capital Assessment Worksheet	
People (0–10 points possible)		
Give yourself 1 point for each high-caliber person associated with your company up to 10. Founders, management-level employees, advisory board members, executive board members, and mentors all count as part of the start-up team.		
Plan (0–5 points possible)		
A business plan is no longer something that you send to investors, but it's still really important to write (refer to Chapter 6). It has become a primarily internal document that the team continually refines, changes, scraps, and rewrites. Give yourself up to 5 points for a plan you refer to and update regularly, but only 1 point for a business plan that collects dust on a shelf somewhere.		
Pro forma (0–5 points possible)		
Judge for yourself how well-validated your pro forma numbers are. Give yourself 1 point for a "conservative estimates" pro forma or up to 5 points for a pro forma with numbers that you can support with field research and experience. Chapter 6 has more on pro formas.		
Product (0–5 points possible)		
Give yourself 1 point for a prototype.		
If the prototype has some functionality, add 1 point.		
Add 1 point if it's completely functional but not ready for purchase yet.		
If the product is complete, manufacturing or user interface is complete, packaging is complete, and the product is ready to put in the hands of customers, add 2 points.		
Promotion Strategy (0–5 points possible)		
If you have a plan to sell your product directly to users, give yourself 1 point.		
If you have a plan to sell your product to a distributor in large quantities, give yourself 4 points.		
Strategic Partnerships (0–10 points possible)		
Give yourself 1 point for each strategic partner that is willing to write a letter of intent showing formally that he or she wants to work with you.		
Give yourself 5 points for each strategic partner that is willing to invest liquid capital in your company.		
Give yourself 5 points for each strategic partner that is interested in purchasing your company in the future.		

(continued)

Table 14-1 *(continued)*

Paying Customers (–5 to 10 points possible)	
If you have sold your product to a few customers (includes beta test sales if money changed hands), give yourself 3 points.	
If you've sold to 10–50 customers, then give yourself 2 more points.	
Add 3 more points if you've sold your product to more than 50 customers.	
Add 2 more points if your customers are thrilled with your product and willing to give testimonials.	
If you have a completed product and you have not sold it to a single customer, deduct 5 points. Having a finished product with no sales is a red flag suggesting that you have not been connecting with your potential customer throughout the product design phase.	
Pitch Deck (0–5 points possible)	
Give yourself 1 point for a pitch deck that you have put together but never given publicly.	
Add up to 4 more points if you have a well-designed and practiced pitch deck that you have rehearsed many times in front of other people, gotten honest feedback on, and made extensive changes to based on that feedback.	
Total points	

Add up your points for the assessment, giving yourself only the maximum allowed for each section. For example, if you have three or more strategic partners (each worth 5 points), you would calculate more than 10 points on that section, but you may record only 10 points. Here's what the scores mean:

- **0–10 points:** Your company is very early in development and therefore not ready to seek investment capital. Keep building your product, company, and customer base.

- **11–20 points:** You are not yet ready to start talking to investors. A little more development can go a long way for your company. Identify where your scores are weakest and work on those aspects of your company.

- **21–30 points:** You can start fundraising now. Although you still have a lot of work to do in the development of your company and product before investors will be interested, you'll probably make great headway in the next six months. Let investors watch you grow.

- **31–40 points:** Your company is in a sweet spot of venture development. If you haven't begun talking to investors, you should consider it now.

- **41–55 points:** Investors will take your company seriously now if they haven't before. You have overcome many of the hurdles of company development. If investors are passing on your deal, take a hard look at the reasons for their lack of engagement. Company stage is not the problem.

Measuring the Success of a Pitch

If you've landed a meeting with a VC or been invited to pitch at an investor conference, how can you judge whether your pitch goes over well or not so well? A successful pitch is measured through something more than the speed at which money is wired to your account. In fact, don't expect immediate investment at all.

Managing expectations

After you pitch to investors, do not expect anyone to hand you a check. If your pitch was well received, you'll be invited to take the next step, which may be a personal discussion with a decision maker or board of decision makers or an invitation to begin due diligence (refer to Chapter 13). Alternatively, you may not hear back from the investors at all.

No news is not always bad news. Your company may be a little too early-staged, and the investors want to watch you for the next few months to see whether you make progress. Or the investors may be holding off on making an investment until some event — like a fund close or a liquidity event — occurs on their end.

It may be difficult to have put your blood, sweat, and tears into a company and devoted a huge amount of effort into the investor pitch only to hear nothing back for weeks or months after a meeting. But this is, unfortunately, the reality. Don't take it personally. The investors may have put you on a watch list (which is a really good thing!) without saying a word to you about it. And if a VC does call to tell you that he's not interested, take heart in the fact that you got a solid answer from an investor and now you don't have to worry about staying in touch with him anymore.

Although VCs sometimes invest quickly, the best outcome that you can usually expect after giving an investor pitch is to be invited back for a deeper discussion and to meet the other partners in the firm. This deeper meeting may focus on a live demo of your product; it could be a formal negotiation; it may be a literal hike in the woods or invitation to a baseball game — all investors do this meeting differently. Whatever form the meeting takes, investors all want to know more about the deal and about you. Remember, they have to be able to justify every investment they make to their limited partners, so they seek to collect a lot of information to show that they have exercised their fiduciary duty.

A tale of two companies

Two companies pitched side by side at an investment conference. Both were companies run by enthusiastic founders who had been building their companies for about four years. Both companies worked hard on their pitches and gave well-practiced talks to interested investors. Further, both had conversations with investors after the pitches that led to some due diligence. Then their paths diverged. One company closed its seed round three months after the pitch event. The other company never raised capital. The differences were in the details of the deal. One deal captured the interest of the investors, and the other one simply did not.

Tracking progress after the pitch

Every pitch does not end in funding. Your job is to line up meetings with the investors that you think will be most interested in your company. Meet with them all and start a conversation about working together. If the investors like your company and consider investing, you will have to work closely with them over the next few months while they perform due diligence. Your job is to stay in touch.

In some cases, A+ pitches don't get funded, while B– pitches do. Why? The fact is you can raise money with a mediocre pitch, and you can fail to raise money with a stellar pitch. Although the pitch is very important, so is the investment deal. No amount of preparation on the pitch will overcome a weak investment deal. Your pitch needs to be sharp enough to attract attention and clear enough to avoid any confusion about your deal.

Staying Positive through the Process

Fundraising is hard and includes a lot of ups and downs. You'll be on cloud nine when you're invited to pitch to your first investor and in the dumps two weeks later when you've heard nothing back. You can help your team stay positive by managing everyone's expectations. In the following sections, we outline some of the challenges of staying positive and tell you how to keep an optimistic attitude.

Although investing involves several technical aspects, the field relies heavily on gut feelings and relationships. If you lose track of your positive outlook, consider stepping back for a little while. No one wants to hear a pitch from someone who's feeling gloomy.

Focusing on something new when optimism wanes

Fundraising will provide you with some of the highest highs you can ever imagine. Think about how great you'll feel after you sign a contract for a multi-million dollar deal. But it can result in long slumps of lows, too. Getting turned down by one VC after another or — worse — simply not hearing back from anyone can be hard on the whole team.

If you find yourself complaining, grumbling, or venting more than occasionally, it may be time to focus on some other aspect of your business for a while. Turn inward to develop a new product or focus on creating a more efficient manufacturing method, for example. Refocusing can recharge your enthusiasm and put you in a better position in the long run. If there is a real problem with your company, a short break may help you discover what the problem is. Plus VCs commonly see companies actively fundraise, then take a break, and then come back to get funded six to eight months later.

Even if there is no real problem with your company, sometimes you find yourself working too hard and too long, and you can feel burnt out. We suggest looking to *Startup Life: Surviving and Thriving in a Relationship with an Entrepreneur,* by Brad Feld and Amy Batchelor (John Wiley & Sons, Inc.), for some guidance on real personal issues that can arise during the lean years for start-up CEOs.

Taking positive steps to stay on investors' radar

Venture investing is a field of work like any other, and venture capitalists know each other and talk about the hot new companies on their radar. When fundraising, you can (and should) spread the word that you're seeking investment capital. If you are doing everything right, your company will start to become known in VC circles.

Just like marketing to customers, you can market to investors. Make it easy for investors to gossip about you over their lattes when they run into each other in the local coffee shop. Create a monthly newsletter that has one or two tidbits of good news about your growth and development. If you get any kind of press coverage, help spread the news article through your own website, Twitter, and e-mail blasts.

Cultivating the attitude of a life-long learner

One of the hardest parts of fundraising is handling the immense amount of advice you'll get. And like all advice, some will be good, but the rest will be useless and maybe even a little insulting. Having the attitude of a perpetual student lets you absorb, learn, and grow while ignoring — and not getting worked up about — the unhelpful stuff.

As annoying as advice can be, you do need to request and take advice from certain people. Your team members, potential customers, strategic partners, board members, and the VCs that you pitch to will all have constructive criticism that you need to hear. Listening to criticism, especially after you've worked very hard on something, is never easy. However, you must become good at taking criticism and turning it into progress. If you bristle at unsolicited advice, people will stop offering it, and you may miss a gem of very useful information.

Using confidence and coachability to attract investors

Investors want to work with someone who listens attentively to new direction and then has the confidence to use that advice wisely. Insecurity can cause shoot-from-the-hip reactions that undermine your chances to attract venture capital. Investors need someone who engages in a rational course of action, is a strong leader for his or her team, and can be a good partner. Coachability is actually a combination of traits that indicate a person is open to advice and able to take that advice and transform it into action that eventually leads the team to success.

See how many of these traits you possess (and if you don't possess them already, don't fret; they can be learned and honed):

- **Humility:** You know things need to be done and you know that you're not capable of doing them alone.

- **Action-oriented:** When faced with two choices, to act or to wait and see, the coachable person tends to act.

- **Purity of purpose:** Your actions are all pointed to the single goal of making your company grow well and grow quickly.

- **Ability to surrender control:** Giving up some control over your company means tapping into the resources that a VC can offer: liquid capital, experience, and powerful relationships, for example.

- **Faith:** You trust that everyone invested in the company wants what is best for the company and will act accordingly.

Chapter 15

Visualizing the Deal: Creating Your Pitch Deck

In This Chapter

▶ Creating pitch decks for different purposes

▶ Uncovering the secrets to a stellar pitch deck

▶ Converting pitch topics into visual slides

*P*itch decks, also called *slide decks,* are important tools for fundraising. Along with the pitch (which we explain in the preceding chapter), the pitch deck has become the standard method for conveying information about an investment deal. In the past, people would submit their business plans to VCs for consideration. Now, the digital pitch deck has become the normal communication device for entrepreneurs to share company details with investors.

Your goal with your pitch deck is to convince a VC to engage you in further discussion and due diligence. Your pitch is like a profile on a dating site: You don't add your entire life history, just enough to get someone to agree to meet for coffee.

Countless types of pitch decks are designed to communicate all different kinds of information. In this chapter, we focus on pitch decks designed to sell your company to investors.

Designing Pitch Decks That Work

Pitch decks are not one-size fits all. Expect to make a few different pitch decks for different purposes. You'll need decks for short presentations, for long presentations, and for times when you won't be around to present the deck. In fact, you should expect to alter a deck quite a bit each time you present it. Personalizing the deck to highlight the specific desires of the VC office is a nice touch.

In the following sections, we offer general guidelines you can follow to ensure that your pitch deck is a compelling representation that makes VCs sit up and take notice. For blow-by-blow guidelines on the topics your pitch deck should cover, hop to the later section "Covering the Important Pitch Topics."

Creating a pitch for every occasion

You need to have many investor pitch decks when you are fundraising. Short pitch decks are perfect for times when you aren't sure you'll be able to hold the attention of the room. Longer pitches are great when you're presenting to investors who've asked for more information or are taking a second look at your deal. (For details on what goes into your pitch — and how to modify it for different audiences — refer to Chapter 14.)

When you're beginning to fundraise and starting to create your pitch, plan to make more than one pitch deck. You will need a deck for short (5 minute) pitches, for long (20 minute pitches), and one to use when you can't pitch in person (the absentee pitch). Also, target your pitch deck to each different audience.

Following are a few pointers to keep in mind as you create your pitch deck:

✔ **When designing multiple pitch decks, start with the shortest pitch deck first.** High-quality pitches are easier to create when you build from a small framework to a larger framework.

Some of the worst pitches we've witnessed came from people who tried to cut a 20-minute pitch down for a 5-minute presentation. Your pitch needs to have a logical progression and a great story, and you just can't accomplish either of those tasks by cutting half of your slides out of your pitch deck. So start with your shortest pitch and build from there.

Keep your pitch deck's goals in mind while you design the deck to ensure that you stay true to your purpose. Doing so is especially helpful if you find that you need to make other kinds of pitch decks, too. As your company gains traction, you'll likely pitch to strategic partners and customers; you may even pitch to federal or state government agencies.

✔ **Have your backup information available if needed.** Your pitch deck represents only the tip of the iceberg, if the iceberg is all the planning and research you have put into your business. Be sure that you have all the backup information readily at hand so that when a VC asks for deeper materials, such as your detailed financial pro forma (go to Chapter 6 for more on those), you have one all ready to go.

✔ **Craft your pitch and then get feedback from others.** Everyone needs outside perspectives to create a stellar pitch deck.

Knowing what the pitch deck should contain

Your slides are designed to support your statements, clarify your comments, and give deeper meaning to your pitch. A well-designed pitch deck is an extremely powerful tool.

Your pitch deck is meant to support your presentation, not overshadow you. You can use images, graphs, and a few words to really add punch to your verbal presentation. You want to stand out as a great investment deal, not as the oddball pitch that the VCs giggle about afterwards. Stick to the standard pitch deck topics that you can find in the following sections and on the Internet. Watch other companies pitch to see what a standard pitch looks like.

No matter how long your pitch is meant to be, make sure that each slide contains no more than one or two thoughts. In the following sections, we outline the form those thoughts can take.

Using images to clarify points

Infographics are visual representations of information. These graphics can be simplistic cartoons, highly complex drawings, or photographs with information attached. The best infographics are aesthetically pleasing, fairly simple, and instantly understandable.

As Figure 15-1 shows, an infographic shows data in a way that is instantly recognizable because images are combined with traditional data-describing methods such as charts or graphs. In addition, slides with infographics don't have to remain on the screen for very long to convey their point. They often allow you to move through information more quickly.

Consider using infographics in the following situations:

- **To convey challenging information.** Some ideas are hard to get across verbally — a difficulty that especially plagues groundbreaking products that an audience has never experienced before. In this situation, you may find yourself struggling to convey to the VC exactly what your customers can buy for the retail price. If any confusion exists, your audience will decide that you don't have a good product. You can use images to pin down loose ends in your description and show to the audience exactly what your product offers.

  Whenever you find yourself stumbling over something that is difficult to describe, think about whether an infographic could help clarify things.

✔ **To show growth:** A map could be used to describe a company that is planning to expand services across the country over the next two years, for example, with color coding to show how many states were served last year, how many were served this year, and how many you plan for next year. This quick visual drives home the point that your company successfully expanded through a number of states last year and has reasonable growth plans for the near future.

✔ **To describe details of the deal:** If you are raising $5 million and you have $2.3 million committed from one VC, you may put up a pie chart showing the amount raised already. VCs hear a lot of numbers, but that visual representation of a fundraising round that is nearly half committed will stick with them after you leave the room.

✔ **To distinguish yourself from other presenters:** If you are pitching at an event where multiple companies are presenting, you use images to make your pitch stand out and be memorable above all the other pitches.

Infographics allow your audience to visualize data in a deeper way. To make an infographic, begin with real research and data, find a way to express those numbers in pictures. Be careful not to get too fancy; the point is clear communication. In the example in Figure 15-1, the point is that children average six shoe purchases per year whereas men purchase two new pairs per year.

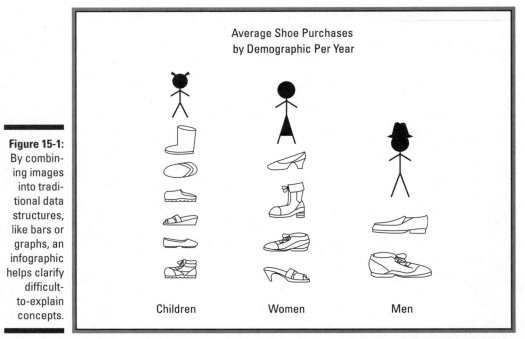

Figure 15-1: By combining images into traditional data structures, like bars or graphs, an infographic helps clarify difficult-to-explain concepts.

Average Shoe Purchases by Demographic Per Year

Children   Women   Men

Punching them with data

Investor pitches tend to be very forward focused: You talk about revenues that are two years in the future, for example, or products that aren't manufactured yet and customers who don't know you exist. To give weight to your assertions about the future success or growth of your company, you need to flaunt in your pitch any hard data you have that backs your assertions up. This data can be from things like data from field research, past product performance, and regulatory experiments.

Your own data is a true mark of experience and traction. You may think that your little 50-person survey, for example, is not worth mentioning, but the data can be really important. Say that you put up a slide that says, "80% willing to pay $49/mo" while you talk briefly about the scope of your survey. From this slide, the audience gets the idea that your price point is acceptable to your customer and that you are making an effort to talk to your customers before you try to sell to them.

You can combine data with graphics to make your slides both informative and interesting. With the survey example, imagine that the slide has images of your potential customers with the results of your survey as a caption.

Showing off your branding and style

Your pitch deck is a great opportunity to introduce your audience to your brand. You can use graphics and style to help the audience understand the feel of your company. Are you focused on a young, sporty market? Make sure the feel of your slides matches your branding. Maybe you have a highly sophisticated customer base that is populated by women who are used to the creature comforts. Classic fonts and Victorian curlicue lines may be appropriate as a style for your pitch deck. If your company is in the business-to-business (B2B) sector, then your pitch deck may be more Spartan and industrial.

When you sell a product, branding and image can boost sales. The same thing is true of the pitch deck. You are selling investors on the company. By branding yourself, the pitch deck, and any handout materials with the look and feel of your company, you create a cohesive impression in investors' minds. No matter what kind of pitch deck you create, you want the slides to convey your company's branding and personality. Consistency is key.

Knowing what to include on an absentee pitch deck

Many VCs will ask you to e-mail your pitch deck to them. Other times you may mail a print version of your pitch deck to an investor. In cases such as these where you won't be able to present the pitch deck in person, you need to include *more* information than you would for an in-person presentation. Because you won't be in the room when the VC looks at the deck, your slides have to be self-explanatory.

With an absentee pitch deck, length isn't an issue because your reader can move through the "presentation" at her own speed, settling on some slides and completely ignoring others. You can use smaller font size (we don't recommend going smaller than 14 point, though), lots of words, and detailed data on each slide. If you plan to send this document digitally, you can also include hyperlinks to websites, other documents, and other supporting information. (Keep in mind, though, that although you need to go into greater detail, you still need to keep your message concise. More words aren't necessarily better.)

If you plan to send an absentee pitch deck, make sure you do the following:

- ✔ **Capture the investor's attention on the pages you think are the most powerful.** Remember, people won't always look through the deck from front to back; they will flip through randomly. In addition, we have heard stories of VCs who flip to the back of the deck to see the deal and then read the rest only if the deal looks good!

- ✔ **Make your information thorough enough so that people can make sense of it out of context.** You can't be sure who will read it so you make sure every concept is crystal clear.

- ✔ **Do not expect this document to be confidential.** Because you can't be sure whose hands it will fall into, leave out any secrets.

Following best practices for a great presentation

There are a few best practices regarding pitch decks that can separate the pros from the newbies. Look like a pro by following these rules:

- ✔ **Make sure your slides are visible:** Some pitches occur in a small office with you and the VC hunched over a computer; others may be in front of a small investment team in a conference room; still others may require giving a pitch at an investment conference in a theater designed for 600+ people. Regardless of the setting, keep your slides to the 20/20 rule:

Include no more than 20 words per slide and use fonts at 20 points or larger.

✔ **Provide simple, concept-based images and a few compelling words or numbers to focus on.** If you have a slide with revenue and earnings projections, for example, limit yourself to no more than three or four rows by four or five columns. Save any more detail for due diligence and your backup documents.

Slides are free! You can always add another slide to your deck. Sometimes flipping quickly through two or three slides can convey something better and faster than a single slide.

✔ **Practice your pacing:** Some slides need only be up on the screen for a few seconds to convey a point powerfully, whereas others need more time. A rule of thumb is to show each slide for at least five seconds and spend no more than one minute on any one slide.

✔ **Avoid common mistakes:** If you aren't careful, your pitch deck can steal the show. Avoid these common traps:

- You have too much stuff on one slide, forcing your audience to read and comprehend many things while you talk.

- You use stunts just to be different; sure, you'll be memorable if you get your 10-year old nephew to yodel before the pitch. You'll be remembered, but not taken seriously.

- Your deck is sloppy, full of animations, or hard to see, making it impossible for your audience to focus on you while you present because they'll be busy squinting and trying to decipher your poor visuals.

Covering the Important Pitch Topics

Your goal with your pitch deck is to tell a powerful story. Although every company's story will be different, the key points are about money: how you make money, how much money you need, and how much money you can make in the long run with this company. The rest of the pitch is there to define and support your money story.

In this section, we describe the topics that you need to include in a pitch deck, whether your pitch is 5 minutes or 20 minutes. If hitting all this information in 5 minutes sounds impossible, take heart: After you have each point identified, perfected, and practiced, you'll be able to cover everything just fine.

Because each company's story is unique, the order of the topics will be different for each company. In addition, the number of slides that should be in the pitch deck also varies. There is no magic number of slides because every pitch is different. Some companies will have more than one slide on a single topic; others may decide not to include a slide on a specific topic. The key thing is to make sure that your presentation covers all the topics described in the following sections.

We've arranged the following sections in the general order in which most pitch decks are presented. Keep in mind, however, that no single "right" order for your pitch deck exists. After all, you're telling the story of your company, and no two stories are the same. Just make sure yours is arranged in a way that leads listeners to the conclusion that they should invest in your company. The two most important parts of your pitch are the first 30 seconds and the last 30 seconds. The rest of the pitch should build gradually, but you really want to hook your audience in the beginning and excite them at the end for the potential of your company and your deal.

The very first slide

At a minimum, your first slide should include your company name, company logo, contact info and website URL, and the name of the event.

When you're pitching — and especially if you're participating in a pitch competition — every second counts. Why not get the most out of your first slide? Your first slide may be up for 30 seconds or more before you even begin to communicate your message. Use this "free time" to your advantage! Think about what you want to convey beyond your company name and company logo. Consider including product shots, your company's tagline, your company's Twitter username, or other items that will set the stage for your pitch.

An overview of your company

With the company overview, you create a context for your message. After you have set the context, you can start getting into the details about your company. Put your company in a conceptual box so your audience knows very basically who you are. Give them the 500,000 foot view of your company by saying, "We are a software company," "We make medical devices," or "Our company makes educational toys."

This tactic may seem as though you are stating the obvious, but this simple, declarative statement lets you make sure that the audience doesn't mistake you for a different kind of company. If audience members are confused upfront, half your pitch may go by before they get straightened out. Think of all the information they'll miss!

After putting your company in a conceptual box, you need to tell the listeners what exactly you do. Very clearly. This is much harder than you think. To be totally sure that your message is clear, talk to people who don't know your industry or your company. Tell them in two or three sentences what you do. Ask them to use their own words to describe your company. Until they get it right, you haven't gotten it right.

Some companies describe themselves by saying that they are the X for Y: "We are the Facebook for Airline Pilots" for example, or "We are the Big O Tires for bicycles." If you use this method, be careful, that you aren't diverting attention away from your own company and confusing the audience more. In one pitch we heard, the company described itself as being a Rebel Mouse for Google. We didn't have any idea what they were talking about until later in the day when we finally had a chance to look up Rebel Mouse!

As part of the company overview, you can also mention a little about your company history if doing so gives you clout. Some companies have an impressive lineage to tout, and doing this upfront can set the tone for the rest of the talk. If your company has spun out of a well-respected company, share this information as part of the company overview. Similarly, if two founders came from high-level positions in well-known companies and joined up to create your company, you want to flaunt that powerful history. If you can point to a household name (think Microsoft, Nestle, Wal-Mart, or Toyota) and say, "We came from there," do it early.

The problem your product solves

Your company has likely created a product that fulfills a need in the world. Your audience needs to understand that your target problem is a big deal for a couple of reasons. This problem may have global implications, like energy, communications, or information management, or it may address a small local need, like the need for fresh food in your neighborhood fulfilled by a grocery store. The nature of the target problem directly affects the type and size of company you will create.

Because venture capitalists work with companies that have large growth potential, you need to show a VC that the problem you solve allows for plenty of accessible revenue possibilities and high growth. The following sections outline the kinds of information to share related to this topic.

Market size, scalability, and dynamics relative to your product

The size of the market is limited to the number of people who are pained by the problem that you solve and how much money they are willing to dedicate to a solution. You must tell VCs that your target problem is shared by a large number of customers who have the money to pay for the solution — your product. (**Note:** If you don't have access to a huge market — think 1 billion and more — VC funding is probably not the right solution for your company. Head to Chapter 4 for alternative ways to get the financing you need.)

Potential value of the market

It's pretty hard to judge the potential of a market, but that's what you should try to do. A growing market is more likely to have room to adopt your technology. Think about the smartphone market. There are around 310 million people in the U.S. and 235 million of them use mobile devices. Eventually most of them will switch to smartphones. Because there are about 114 million smartphone users now in the U.S., you can see that this market is only half penetrated.

If your company has a product that requires a smartphone, your market is still growing. In the next few years, more people will have adopted the technology that will allow them to use your product. Venture companies are built on growing markets such as the smartphone market.

Customer return on investment

Be sure to let the VC know what the return on investment (ROI) is for your customers. In other words, if customers buy your product, how much money will that save them? What pain are you solving? When you can show how big the problem is and how much your clients can save by implementing your solution, you'll get a lot of interest from investors.

Is your customer an individual or a business? Businesses buy for only two reasons: to make money or to save money. People buy for lots of reasons, only some of which are logical. Identifying that you know your customer will make the VC feel a lot better about your pitch.

Your competition

Your goal in discussing your competition is to show you know who is working along side of you. You have to keep your eye on anyone who may come out with your product a month or so before you do. In news media, this is called "getting scooped." When you discuss your competition, note two things: how you will avoid getting scooped by a competitor, and what your company has learned by studying your competitors' successes and failures.

Describe your competitive landscape. If you were describing the beer industry, for example, you'd say that the U.S. beer industry has a few mega players — Anheuser-Busch InBev (50 percent), SABMiller (18 percent), and Coors (11 percent) — and all the little craft breweries that together make up only 4 percent of the total U.S. market.

If your company were a little craft brewery, you would then describe your closest competitors in a positive way: "Our competitor brewery X started two years ago, and it has grown to sell Y gallons more per week than they did last year." (Because a little brewery cannot compete with the giants in the industry, it's important to show successes in the artisan realm.)

Competition is often a positive thing. Competitors that came before you prove your model works if they are successful. You can improve upon their model as you grow.

One red flag for VCs is your telling them that you have no competition. Although having no competition may sound great at first, such a claim may indicate that you haven't thoroughly investigated the market in which you'll be selling your product. You must consider all types of competition, not just those that compete directly against what you offer. There is always *indirect competition* — substitutes in other product categories or similar ways of solving a problem. Your biggest competitor of all may be apathy for your product — potential customers who continue to do what they have done all along without buying your product.

Your product or product line

You need to describe your product so your audience knows what you plan to sell. When describing your product, be as visually accurate as possible. Instead of listing the product as text on a slide, show a photograph of the actual product. If your product is a component for a larger product, show how it fits into the user's world. If your product isn't manufactured yet, you can have a photorealistic rendering made for you so people can see the product without having to use their imaginations.

For example, a home-use diesel engine heater may look like a bunch of coiled up wires, but a picture of an engine, a picture of your product, and then a photo of a person in a hat and gloves sitting in a car gets the point across quickly: Everyone can clearly see that your product warms car and truck engines when it's cold outside. As you progress through these slides, you can verbally describe how this product is better than all the other engine heaters because it's faster or cheaper or easier to install.

It's also nice to show progress. If you have a slide with an ugly prototype, followed by a slightly nicer prototype, followed by a slide with a minimum viable product, the VC can get the point that you've worked quite a bit on this. In this case, for sure, show is better than tell.

Take care not to let the product dominate your talk. If your product is simple and easy to understand, you may not spend much time on this topic at all. At the very most, you should keep the product discussion under a quarter of the total presentation time.

Barriers that reinforce your company's value

If your company seems too easy to start and run, the VC will be concerned that any Tom, Dick, or Harry can start a competing company and surpass your progress in a short time. You need to show that your company was challenging to create and that you are the right team for the job. The best barriers are the ones you have already overcome and your competitors will have trouble mastering.

A couple of things help reiterate to VCs that you indeed have an unfair advantage to successfully grow your company:

- ✔ You own patents that prevent others from using your technology.
- ✔ Your team developed a technology that would be extremely hard to copy.
- ✔ You or your teammates have industry connections that get into the right doors.
- ✔ You have rare and specific industry training that is critical for success.

Figure out what gives your company an edge. If you can't think of anything, then you better consider adding someone to the advisory board who can help add an edge.

Your business model

After your audience understands what your company does, the next thing they want to know is how you make money. The business model is a combination of company stage and development, product development, revenue model, and product distribution models.

A business model has many parts. Don't try to put all of the parts on the same slide. Multiple slides are much more clear. You can describe a revenue model with a pie chart on one slide, for example, show your product development plan on another slide, and devote a third slide to company stage.

Company stage

The company stage is a big part of the business model for companies with a long product development phase. Initially, the company's resources are entirely devoted to R&D. Then the company devotes effort to product development, after which the company shifts focus to business development, until finally the company becomes primarily a sales- and customer-support–focused business. These transitions can take many years and require significant changes in company structure.

Include the following information:

- Tell investors how much time you think your company will remain in each stage of development. For some companies, the product development stage may take years; for others it may take only a short time.

- Clearly state what stage your company is currently in and let investors know that your team is able to manage your company while it is in this stage.

Product development

Tell investors whether your company will be revenue positive while you focus on product development. Some companies have a consulting side, which financially supports the product development side. Other companies make proposals to the federal government to win grant money to develop their product. Having a positive revenue stream means that the company is not entirely reliant on investor capital, which lowers the company's risk of failure significantly.

Revenue model

Your revenue model may be highly complicated and subject to change over time. You don't have time in the pitch to discuss nuances of your revenue model. Instead, break it down:

- Describe where the majority of your income will come from over the next few years.

- Show a financial summary with five year projections. Include totals for revenue, cost of goods sold (COGS), earnings before interest, taxes, depreciation and amortization (EBITDA), and net income.

- Share what your product costs and profit on sales are. In many cases, VCs want to know your pricing strategy and, to some degree, base their opinions on whether they would buy your product or service if they were a target customer. VCs are very interested in gross margins.

Let investors know whether you've validated these revenue streams. Companies that have run market tests before approaching VCs have the upper hand because they can point to their test marketing data to demonstrate customer acceptance.

- Point out how much investment (raised in how many rounds) you will need to get to profitability.

Target market

This topic lets you convey your market understanding and sophistication. The most important point is to show that your product is part of a large or rapidly growing market. Investors are waiting to hear a few key points when you talk about your analysis of your market:

- ✔ **Identify your addressable market:** Investors want to know that you have identified your addressable subset of the market. When you start an organic soda company, for example, your addressable piece of the market is not the $100+ billion world soft drink market, but more like the $21 million bottled, carbonated, organic U.S. soft drink market. The top slide in Figure 15-2 shows the addressable market for a company focused on organic carbonated beverages that are sold in bottles but not as fountain drinks. Make each circle relative to the size of the market and add market values.

- ✔ **Traction in the market:** To show traction as related to addressable market, you can discuss the piece of the market that you have touched to date. In the organic soda company example, your company's share of the market may only be the Whole Foods-shelved subset of the bottled, carbonated, organic soft drink market. How long have you been available in that market, what percentage share of that market have you captured, and how does that fare for current sales?

If your company is pre-revenue you cannot pretend to know what your market share will be in the future. Instead, show the market share growth for your competitors, as the bottom slide in Figure 15-2 does. Investors will average the success of your competitors and assume your market share growth will fall somewhere in the middle.

- ✔ **Pre-revenue market capture:** If you have not yet sold your product, discuss which piece of the market you plan to touch first. How will you go about it? You can build a mailing list of future customers who are interested to hear about your progress in developing your product. Some companies hold events or promote other products to get consumers interested in their products before they're even available.

Your marketing strategy

You've no doubt heard the saying, "Create a better mousetrap, and the world will beat a path to your door." We're here to tell you that nothing could be further from the truth. It is much easier to make a product than to sell it. Selling your product necessitates a buyer, whose behavior you can't predict or control.

As excited as entrepreneurs may be about their idea or product, in a world of media bombardment, getting the word out about your solution can be difficult and expensive. Investors see many good ideas, but they get really excited when they see a good idea paired with a great marketing strategy.

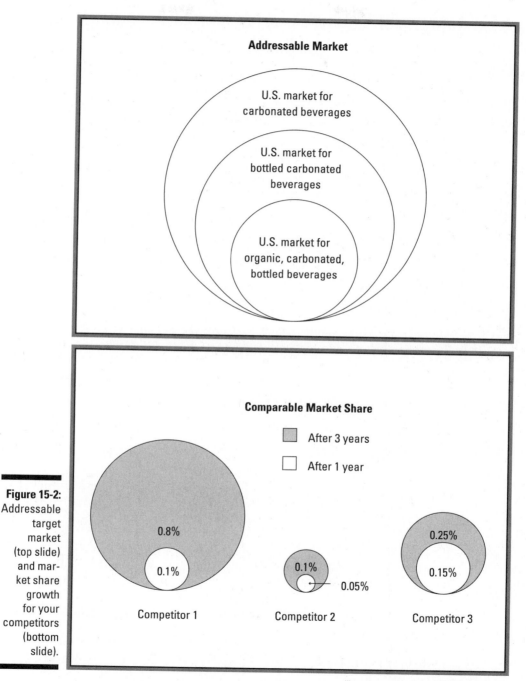

Illustration by Wiley, Composition Services Graphics

Venture capital investment requires that you be able to scale up quickly. For that reason, your marketing strategy can't rely on your knocking on a thousand doors and selling your product. Instead, when you present this portion of your pitch, you need to describe a strategy that leverages strategic partnerships, distribution channels, social media, and traditional advertising channels. Basically, you want to have a strategy that will result in thousands of sales with minimal intervention from you or your employees. Leveraging the capacity of partners makes it so that you don't need to build out a substantial sales force, which is very expensive. By leveraging your resources, you are more efficient with your capital.

A strong marketing strategy includes the results of any marketing research or test marketing exercises you've done. Including data that support the cost to acquire a customer versus the lifetime value of a customer makes your marketing strategy slide even more compelling. You'd be surprised how casual many entrepreneurs are when addressing their marketing strategy and how negatively VCs view that approach.

Your future milestones as risks

Any milestone that is key to achieving your goals is also a risk. Any major milestone that you have completed can be considered traction or track record. Communicating these together allows investors to understand your ability to execute.

Investors are always thinking about risk. If you don't tell them in your pitch about your real risks, they'll imagine even worse risks. The trick with this topic is to acknowledge the upcoming milestones while at the same time show that you are purposefully working toward them, one at a time. Include the following information:

✔ **Lay out a few of the major milestones that stand between now and your exit.** Communicate your milestones in a way that illustrates your current hurdles and shows that you are approaching them with thoughtful planning.

Be prepared to talk at great length about your plan to overcome difficult aspects of growing your business if investors want to discuss this aspect in more detail during the Q&A session that follows your presentation.

✔ **Discuss past milestones.** By mentioning a few challenges you and your team have overcome in the past, you give credibility to your company and your future plans. Highlighting past milestones that you've overcome helps VCs see that you're capable of great progress in the future.

The risk stairs shown in Figure 15-3 are a clear way to communicate your plans, path, and progress all in one slide. (This image is an adaptation from Adam Rentchler's risk stairs shown in Chapter 10.) Be sure to include the risks that your team has already overcome. This helps your investor understand your progress to date and the effectiveness of your team. Use this slide as a conversation starter.

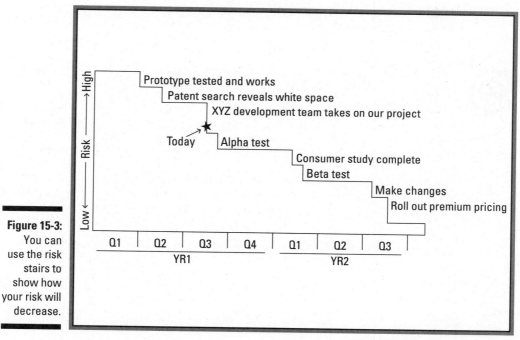

Figure 15-3:
You can use the risk stairs to show how your risk will decrease.

Illustration by Wiley, Composition Services Graphics

Following are some examples of common milestones:

- ✔ Hiring a key person with specific skills
- ✔ Securing a patent
- ✔ Signing your first big customer
- ✔ Overcoming or addressing regulatory challenges associated with making or selling the product (FDA, USDA, EPA)
- ✔ Finding an affordable manufacturer
- ✔ Creating the working prototype
- ✔ Being first to market

Your traction

Traction broadly describes how far your company has come. It encompasses product development, sales, strategic partner relationships, marketing, and intellectual property. Each company measures traction differently, based on the challenges that company has faced and will face in the future.

Your company is likely to be stronger in one or two of these areas. As you design your message to investors around traction, focus on your company's areas of strength.

You can show traction in your market without having made a single sale. By plotting user adoption of a free version of your product, as the slide in Figure 15-4 does, you can show that people are connecting with your product more and more over time. The bars represent downloads per month, and the line graph indicates data points collected per month. Notice that some traction was gained prior to the public version of the software being rolled out. A small batch of test users was providing data points and downloading the software.

Be creative about the data you use to show traction, but remember that the point is to clearly communicate that people are interested in your company or your product.

Figure 15-4:
A bar graph and a line graph together show traction with users over a one-year period.

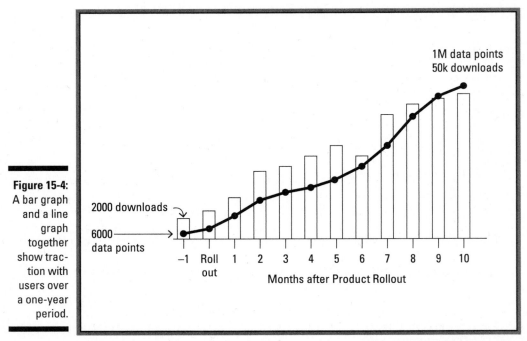

Your valuation story

Valuation is a touchy subject. You can do tons of research and analysis to determine your valuation, yet if you simply state a valuation to investors, you may come off sounding inflexible, and if the number is much higher than they expected, you can be shown the door immediately. If you're asked to share your valuation during a presentation, answering with a valuation story rather than just stating a number is a wiser approach. Turn to Chapter 11 for more about valuation.

Valuation does not have to be a slide on its own, but you do need to discuss it. Keep your conversation about valuation relevant by discussing it along with risk, traction, and the ask.

Telling your valuation story in five chapters

Your story should have five "chapters" that lead the investor to accept the logic of your assertion:

- ✔ Chapter 1 – Your marketing traction and well-supported rationale for sales

- ✔ Chapter 2 – Your projected future earnings within a three to five-year horizon

- ✔ Chapter 3 – A future valuation based on your industry research of recent exits

- ✔ Chapter 4 – The milestones that you face between now and your exit horizon and the likelihood of success for each one

- ✔ Chapter 5 – Your current valuation based on discounting the future cash flow based on your risks

Valuation is tied tightly to risk and traction. When you discuss the value you've already put into your company (not the cash or time you've put in — the value), investors will be more likely to nod along when you give a valuation.

In reality, most people have a valuation range. Under certain conditions, they would be happy with one number, and under other conditions they would require a different valuation. For example, if one particular VC firm is well-known in your industry, and you really want to work with that group, you may accept a lower valuation for the clout that the firm can bring your company.

Determine what conditions you would prefer and identify the range you'd be comfortable with. Let investors know that the valuation is negotiable, but remember that if you say your range is $1 million to $2 million without stating the conditions under which you would accept the $1 million valuation, then you really haven't given a range; you have just set your valuation at the lower end of your range!

When working with angel investors, size up the investors to determine what they bring to the table. If you'll take a lower valuation for a "smart money" or strategic investor, then you need to find out whether the person you're talking to fits that category before providing her with the adjusted valuation.

A VC is going to develop her own valuation regardless of what you tell her your value is, so be prepared for negotiation. Just like selling anything else, your company is only worth what someone will pay for it.

Your team

The number one cause of failure in early stage companies is a failure to execute. Pique the VC's interest by proving that you have an all-star team that is able to get the job done. In other words, this topic is your chance to explain why a VC should believe that your team is able to succeed in growing your company. Just describing team members' roles, titles, or job descriptions is a time waster. That information is better put in an executive summary.

If you have a very large, very strong team, you may not have enough time to go into great detail about why all ten (or more) are perfectly suited to help your company succeed. Choose five people to highlight and discuss them more than the others. These five may be founders, employees, or people in advisory roles. For each of the five, identify one stellar thing that person has done that makes him or her stand out as a great team member for your company. List the rest of the team on the slide to show the many other people on the team, but don't spend time discussing them.

Give specifics and be sure to highlight team member achievements relevant to the needs of your company. Here are some pointers to keep in mind:

- ✔ **Name drop and tout impressive achievements when you can, but only when they're relevant.** If an advisory board member won a gold medal in the Olympics for downhill skiing, for example, he or she would be an impressive addition to the roster for a company associated with the ski industry, but not for a company that makes machinery for alternative fuels. However, a board member who was an executive in a Fortune 500 company is an impressive addition to any company's roster even when your company and the Fortune 500 company are in unrelated markets. The bottom line: You are trying to establish credibility for the team members. Be relevant.

- ✔ **Highlight venture capital experience and successful exits.** Working with VCs is unlike any other business experience, and those who have been through it before understand how to work with a VC and are more likely to be successful in the relationship. Having team members who've been part of successful exits is another strong asset because it shows you know how to scale up big and become attractive as an acquisition or initial public offering (IPO).

Some people like to start their presentations with a slide about the team, but we suggest that the team slide be shown closer to the end. If you introduce the team early in the talk, VCs don't know yet whether they care about your team. If you wait until the end of the talk, when the investors know what you're doing and are fully engaged in your presentation, they can pay better attention to the qualifications of the team members and make more informed decisions about whether your team can accomplish the goals that you have described in your presentation.

Your exit strategy

Exit strategy is a controversial topic. Many people in the start-up world insist that you cannot build a good company if you are constantly trying to find a way out of it. We argue that VCs are interested in giving you their money for a short amount of time, five to seven years, and they're obligated to return money to their limited partners in usually no more than ten years after the fund is established. Because their primary goal is to get their money back and their secondary goal is to get their money back tenfold, they want to hear that you are already thinking about how to return their investment (and then some!) to them.

Looking at your options

At the very least, acknowledge that the VC wants a return on investment and that you are working to meet that goal. You can increase your credibility by mentioning details about how you can do so.

You can provide many kinds of exits for your investors.

- **IPOs:** Back in the late 1990s, the IPO was the popular way to cash out of venture investments. IPOs are few and far between today.

- **Mergers and acquisitions (M&As):** Most exits these days involve larger companies acquiring a start-up company to gain a strategic advantage. Big companies often use acquisitions as their R&D departments, and your payoff comes from solving their big problems.

- **Royalties and revenue sharing:** Some companies are not good targets for either M&A or IPOs but they still have venture potential. These companies can return multiples of VC investment through royalties or revenue sharing. Many oil and gas or movie deals are structured this way.

Building a case for a potential exit

Follow one of the Seven Habits of Highly Successful People: "Begin with the end in mind." If you are developing a company for acquisition from the very beginning, you are much more likely to have a desirable company at the end.

To build a case of a potential exit, follow these steps:

1. **Identify three companies that may be interested in purchasing your company in the future.**

   Indicate why they would buy you out in three years, and be sure you have a very good reason. Remember, M&As don't happen unless the purchasing company has a solid reason for the purchase.

2. **Find recent M&A history for those three companies.**

   Be able to answer these questions: In the last three years, have any of these companies acquired other companies? If so, how much did they pay for the acquisition and what kinds of companies did they buy?

3. **Find data on three companies like yours that were purchased in the last three years.**

   Look for this information: How much the companies sold for, the stage they were in when they were acquired, whether early investors from those companies saw a good ROI, and the typical multiples that were paid by acquiring companies — for example, 2X ("2 times") revenues or 10X EBITDA (earnings before interest taxes, depreciation and amortization).

The ask and the deal

You must ask for investment. Doing so can feel uncomfortable the first time, but keep in mind that investors spend most of their time with people who are asking for money. It doesn't faze them; it's part of their jobs.

As part of the ask, you should tell investors the following information:

- How much money you're raising

- How much equity you're offering (for an equity investment)

- What interest rate and discount percentage you're offering (for convertible debt)

- How much of the round has been committed

- What the money you're raising will be used to accomplish

- How long the investment capital will last (your *burn rate)*

- How much money you will need overall to get to profitability

Your ask should include an invitation for those in the audience to discuss the deal and the project further after the pitch. You can also invite them to take an executive summary handout or to join your online due diligence materials folder. Here's what you shouldn't do:

✔ **Don't raise your voice an octave and tell VCs about your *amazing opportunity*.** They'll judge for themselves whether it's a good opportunity or not.

✔ **Don't try to close the deal in your pitch.** If you ask for a show of hands for those interested in investing with you, you'll be met with blank stares and awkward silence. Private equity simply doesn't work that way.

Act matter-of-factly when talking about your fundraising round. Investors are used to dealing with people who need money. They may invest with you and they may not. If you accept that this is just one of many conversations with investors, then you will embody the appropriate balance of nonchalance and hope.

Your summary slide

When you finish giving your presentation, you often have your last slide sitting on the screen behind you. Make this slide do more than just convey standard contact information. To make the best use of this screen, create a summary slide highlighting all the things that make your company exciting. Break the slide into four or six divisions and fill each with reminders of your strong points (see Figure 15-5). Highlight the important points you want the audience to walk away with. Don't worry about repeating yourself here. Your goal is to remind the audience of all the great reasons they should invest in your company.

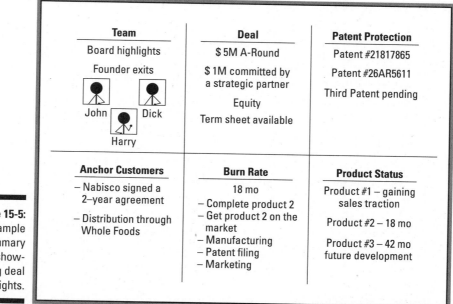

Figure 15-5:
A sample summary slide showing deal highlights.

Illustration by Wiley, Composition Services Graphics

Each company has different strengths. Think about why your company stands out and add those points to the summary slide. Always include the team and terms of the deal. Options for other highlights include all the topics in this chapter: distribution partners, intellectual property, exit strategy, current revenues, current growth rate, recently overcome risks, use of funds, and size of the addressable market.

Using back pocket slides

After your live pitch, you'll have a question and answer period. You can impress your audience by having a few slides to pull out of your back pocket when relevant questions are asked. Think about what investors are likely to ask and add four or five slides after your summary slide.

If nobody asks questions relevant to these slides, then nobody will know they are even there. However, if you get questions that reference these slides, having these slides at the ready shows that you anticipated the investors' questions and prepared thoughtful responses to them. Investors want to believe that you have thought things through carefully, and this is your time to show them that your thinking goes much deeper than the high level information you have provided in your pitch.

Make sure your audience has your contact information. Pass out cards if the group is small enough. Put your e-mail address and website on your first and last slides. You want to make it easy as pie for the VCs to get in touch when they have a question.

Chapter 16

Show Time! Making Your Presentation

....

In This Chapter

▶ Choosing the person who will deliver the pitch

▶ Connecting with your audience

▶ Working with presentation technology

....

*A*fter you spend the time and effort putting together an outstanding pitch deck for your presentation, you're ready to prepare for the pitch itself. You want your pitch to come off as professional, heartfelt, smart, and ahead of the curve. But here's a secret: The key information and data points you've amassed to describe your company and support your growth projections alone aren't enough to generate the interest and enthusiasm you want from the VCs in the audience. The fact is that many of the elements that you want to convey are impossible to put into words or graphics. These are the emotional and human elements of your pitch.

In this chapter, we tell you how to prepare for the practical aspects of the pitch — things like how to work with the acoustics in the room to ensure everyone can hear you, to how to test your equipment to avoid snafus — as well as how to give your presentation the emotional heft that will hook a VC's attention.

Choosing the Lead Presenter

Like the lead singer in a band, the pitch presenter sets the tone for the company. Choosing the person to present your company to investors is challenging for many companies because the person you may automatically assume *should* present — the founder or a key partner who's helped the founder realize the company's potential, for example — may not be the best choice. Say that your company consists of a founder whose technology is the basis for the whole product line and that this founder eats, sleeps, and lives this company. His dedication makes him the perfect presenter, right? Not so fast.

If he has trouble communicating with an audience — has difficulty speaking in front of large groups, for example, or struggles to convey ideas in layman's terms — then the founder may not be the right person to pitch the company.

Listing the traits of a great pitch presenter

Following are the traits that an ideal pitch presenter has; look for these in yourself or in whomever you choose:

- **Well-spoken:** Some people are better at speaking in front of an audience than others. Good public speakers choose their words in the moment to suit the mood of the room, and they use powerful communication tools like the *pregnant pause* (in which you use pacing and silence to build interest or suspense) and matching voice inflections with hand gestures. Do a little role-playing to see who in your team has the best public speaking style.

- **Charismatic:** Charismatic people possess a quality that draws others to them and inspires interest or devotion in their activities or causes. Charismatic people are rare, and they can be rather powerful because of the devotion they inspire. If you have a charismatic person on your team, you may want to consider having that person pitch, even if he isn't at the top of the company's organizational chart.

- **The right age:** The "right" age is different for each company. A company may seem more innovative if a young person gives the pitch. Similarly, a company may seem more capable of accomplishing difficult tasks when a mature leader delivers the pitch. The key is to ensure that the person pitching embodies the company's personality, whether it's innovative, mature, cutting-edge, or anything else.

Obviously, you can't change your age, but you can try to embody the qualities of the age group most appropriate to lead your pitch. Use your clothing, hairstyle, word choice, and your pitch deck to portray the age you want. Be careful not to overdo it, though. Subtlety goes a long way.

- **Able to take feedback:** Pitching is a difficult task that requires a lot of trial and error, and a key way to hone a pitch is to rehearse it in front of many people who can give feedback. Criticism, even when constructive, can be hard to hear and even harder to act upon. A great pitch presenter takes all the feedback, determines which parts are important, and creates an improved pitch after each rehearsal.

If you are not a natural-born public speaker, you can still play the role when you pitch. The trick is to practice. Doing so helps you develop many of the preceding traits. Also check out *Credibility Code: How to Project Confidence and Competence When It Matters Most,* by Cara Hale Alter (Meritus Books), to understand the body language traits that people tend to take seriously and which ones can get you into trouble.

Getting everyone pitch ready

Even though we spent the last section explaining how important it is to choose your presenter wisely and listing the characteristics you should look for in the person you select, the fact of the matter is that everyone — all team members and founders — should be prepared to pitch at any time. Here are the times when you'll be glad your whole team is ready to pitch:

✔ **Your usual presenter isn't available.** Only occasionally are you invited to give a formal presentation to investors and are offered weeks to prepare. More likely, you'll have a few days to prepare your pitch after you secure a meeting with an investor. If the usual pitch presenter is out of town or has the flu, you don't want to give up an opportunity to present your company to an investor.

✔ **You face a scheduling conflict.** Pitch events (where many companies are invited to pitch to investors on the same day) are often seasonal, occurring in the fall and spring. You may be invited to pitch at two different events on the same day on different sides of the country (a pretty common occurrence, in fact, because attractive venture companies become very popular when they are poised for investment). If multiple members of your team are prepared to pitch, you can divide and conquer both pitch events. Half the team can make waves in the Bay Area while the other half takes a bite out of life in the Big Apple.

✔ **You want to take advantage of any spur-of-the-moment opportunities to pitch your company.** When you're seeking venture capital for your company, you must act opportunistically. People who may invest in your company are all around you, and they don't wear signs identifying themselves as investors. You may get an opportunity to pitch your deal in an odd place without a PowerPoint presentation or any preparation time at all. You could bump into an investor in an elevator, at a networking event, in the bathroom . . . even at your child's 4th grade presentation of *The Nutcracker*. By preparing all team members to present your company's deal whenever they bump into someone who's interested, you can ensure that your company is getting all the exposure possible.

When your company is fundraising, everyone on the team must be ready to pitch all the time.

Wowing Your Audience

You have a lot of information to convey in a short period of time. It's easy to get caught up in the idea that details, accuracy, and timeliness are your pinnacle goals here. In reality, your real goal is to connect with your audience.

Be especially careful if you are a technical founder pitching your company. You will most likely get wrapped up in discussing the details of your technology. Take the human element of this pitch to heart. You need the audience members to like *you* just as much as you need them to like your technology.

In addition to the advice you can find in the following sections, you should also pay attention to how you dress. Fitting into the culture is important, and the accepted style differs in each city and may be specific to the type of company that you are representing. For information on how to decide what proper attire is in your situation, go online to `http://www.dummies.com/webextras/venurecapital`.

Making a connection

Few things are more moving than someone on stage who can connect with the audience. This is true in the theater, in dance, and also in business presentations. In the following sections, we outline some ways that you can connect with the investors during your pitch.

There is a big difference between speaking *to* an audience and speaking *at* an audience. Your goal is to see the audience members' faces as you speak. You need to look at each person as you deliver a sentence or two of information. If you can get their heads to nod as you tell them about your company, you know that you are making a connection.

From the heart

Robert's company had a platform technology that could be used for many different types of products. Although his product could be used in sports, education, or even video game entertainment, he had chosen to start his product line by developing a therapeutic product that would benefit disabled army veterans returning from war.

The initial product in the pipeline didn't make sense as the most strategic first product to investors. There was a more established market for the sports product, and the video game product seemed like it could bring in more sales revenue. It wasn't until Robert told the story of his early career work with one particular disabled veteran that it made sense to begin with the therapeutic product. Robert's heart was in it, and it's hard to argue with that. He had seen a powerful therapeutic need that few people knew existed. By adding a heartfelt story to the pitch, he was able to connect with his investor audience on a very human level.

Some groups, such as TED (a non-profit devoted to ideas worth spreading that puts on short, inspiring talks), have gotten connecting to the audience down to a science. TED, for example, requires that speakers offer something truly personal to make the audience see them as human. Then, the speaker requests a call to action. This method — a personal connection followed by a call to action — inspires audience members to get involved. And that's exactly what you want to happen when you ask a group of investors for money. You want the investors to understand you, your message, and your company. Then you want them to take action by initiating due diligence.

Go to ted.com to see hundreds of formulaic TED talks. They are short (under 18 minutes), draw on inspiration and emotion, and always involve a call to action.

Speaking the message

Identify the one fundamental message that you want your audience to remember and then keep that message in mind, both as you create your pitch deck (go to Chapter 15 for more on that) and as you rehearse. Your message will come through.

By focusing on one central theme as you create all your materials, you will naturally bring your points together in a way that supports that theme. Doing so helps you avoid getting distracted as you create the pitch, which can result in your arguing various points that confuse the main message.

Practicing to make perfect

You will go over and over your pitch deck before calling it finished, so much so, in fact, that you may know all the points and the order in which you plan to deliver them by heart. Even then, you still need to practice.

When you have settled on a version of the pitch that you'll present to investors (whether it's the 5-minute, 10-minute, and 20-minute version), practice it a minimum of 20 times, start to finish. Practice it in front of your business mentors and practice it in front of your team. Videotape yourself giving the pitch and then practice it again, concentrating on eliminating any awkwardness that you noticed in the video. Even then you won't be done practicing. You'll probably do your pitch 100 times or more before you close the funding round. At each practice opportunity, you have a chance to make your presentation even better, and your pitch will evolve over time. After a while, you will know this pitch so well you could deliver it backward.

The danger with a well-practiced pitch is that it can become a word-for-word memorization of a script. We've seen pitch presenters forget the next memorized line and simply blank out. Believe us, watching someone repeat the last two lines as a way to remember the next ones is hard; imagine what it must be like for the person who's presenting. A way to avoid this trap is to memorize the concepts and let the words come naturally. For example, if you know the order of your slides — that is, you know that your addressable market slide leads into your market study slide which leads into your product adoption strategy statement, for example — you can speak confidently and naturally about the key information in each even if you blank on one particular word.

Even though you know the pitch backward and forward and could deliver it in your sleep, don't forget to deliver your pitch to your audience with genuine desire for them to hear and receive it. Don't just go through the motions. Imagine you are delivering words and meaning to each audience member as though you were passing them each a bagel or cup of coffee. Did they receive it?

Honing an elegant performance

To ensure that you'll be well received by VCs, add one more level of preparation: identifying and eradicating any bad habits or behaviors that can be distracting.

When getting to know VCs, you need to make a great first impression. Bad habits can turn investors off before they really have a chance to get to know you. Remember, VCs are people who meet tons of entrepreneurs; they tend to get a little jaded and can be quick to judge presenters after seeing a couple hundred pitches.

Eradicating your physical and verbal tics

Everyone has little gestures and habits that are magnified in a presentation. Your presentation style can attain a certain polish if you identify your own quirks and avoid them during the pitch.

When speaking in public, people display quite a few really common nervous habits. You can videotape yourself giving the pitch and then watch the video. These ticks will become apparent to you when you see yourself on the video:

- ✔ **The leg slap:** With every point that a leg slapper makes, he slaps his thigh. The sound is loud enough to bug the people in the front rows, and once it becomes apparent to the audience, they begin to listen for the slap rather than to the presentation.

- ✔ **The lip smack:** The lip smack is a *tsk* sound that some people make at the end of sentences. It's the oral equivalent of the leg slap.

✔ **Playing with hair:** If you know you are likely to play with your hair (both men and women exhibit this foible), style it or cut it in a way that makes you leave it alone.

✔ **Flailing:** In an effort to be enthusiastic and energetic, some people wave their arms and bob their heads a lot. The cure comes with being conscious of your movements and practicing to eliminate them.

✔ **Looking back at the slides:** Some presenters actually turn their backs to the audience and talk to the slides. Practice the pitch so that you never have to look over your shoulder or turn your back to the audience.

Turning your head when using a lavalier or podium microphone can be especially frustrating to the audience. The audience will experience big changes in volume as you move your head in and out of the microphone's range.

✔ **Saying "um," "ah," and "er" a lot:** Using a verbal pause like this is so common that Toastmasters, a public speaking organization, designates a person in every meeting to count the speaker's "ums," "ahs," and "ers." The best way to avoid reflexively using these breaks is to practice your pitch so that you know it backward and forward.

Being "on" even when you think you're "off"

You are always being interviewed. Sometimes VCs invite prospective companies to lunch, dinner, or some other social affair, like a baseball game. They may invite your spouse and children as well.

Even though these situations feel more casual, you — and your family if they're invited — are still being interviewed. Keep alcohol consumption to a minimum and stay on your best behavior the whole time. Just because your tie has come off does not mean that you get to relax.

Being on time

It looks terrible if you are late to pitch to an investor. Scout the investor's office ahead of time. Determine where you might park. Identify where the office is in the building. Equally important is to avoid being early. Most people have tight schedules, and if you arrive even 20 minutes early, you will probably be in the way.

Whereas being on time to the meeting is a no-brainer, many people don't think of being prompt in other critical situations. You should be prompt in correspondence with the due diligence team or any contact leads that the investor may give you. If the investor requests any information at all, get back to him within 24 hours, even if the only thing you can say is that you need a few days to collect the information.

Investors may take three weeks to respond to your requests; unfortunately, that doesn't give you a pass to do the same.

Mastering the Technology

Technology can be your best friend and your worst enemy. When your audiovisual system, slideshow presentation, and physical presentation work together seamlessly, you have the appearance of confidence and mastery. When you have a glitch, your presentation turns to an uncomfortable experience at best. Investors have short attention spans. Any itty-bitty technical mishap that derails your pitch for even a few seconds can kill the connection between you and your listener.

In the following sections, we describe a variety of tools that people use during presentations and explain how to avoid — or recover — from any problems that may occur. For help choosing and using the right microphone, go online to www.dummies.com/extras/venturecapital.

Using remote control clickers to switch slides

You can purchase an inexpensive sensor to plug into your laptop that enables you to use a remote control clicker to switch slides while standing across the room from your computer. The little controller fits in your hand, often invisibly, and gives the appearance that the sides are switching by magic. Using a remote control is better than calling "next slide" to an assistant. It's also better than standing behind your computer the whole time or running back and forth between the computer and the center of the stage.

Buy your own remote control clicker and practice with it. Know how far you can walk from the computer. Understand all the buttons. Check the batteries. If the clicker fails to work properly, the effect can be worse than if you just switched slides manually.

Running live demos

Some presenters run live demos in the pitch. Demos are generally walk-throughs of software products or demonstrations of hardware products. We *strongly* recommend that you not take this tack unless you have been specifically invited to give a demonstration and not a pitch.

A demonstration is different than a pitch. In the pitch, you need to connect with your audience the entire time, which is impossible when you're controlling a working product. Whether you're demonstrating software or a tangible product, you're looking at and focusing on the demonstration, not the audience, and you can lose their interest very quickly.

If you feel that some sort of demonstration is important, consider showing a short series of screenshots from a video demonstration. Put them in your pitch deck and talk while you flip through them. This approach keeps the flow of your presentation and your contact with the audience consistent. If you think that a live demo is absolutely necessary, schedule one after the pitch for those who are interested.

VCs might invite you to bring your product to their office so you can all play with it together. This is a great time to do a demonstration of the product. You can geek out about the technology and let the VCs touch or manipulate your product. Do not confuse a demonstration with a pitch.

Including a video in your pitch

Some presenters play video during their pitches. If you have created a video for your product, you probably put a lot of thought and maybe money into it; as a result, you're probably pretty proud of it. You may also feel like using a video will take some of the pressure off of you in the pitch because the video gets the point across really well (you think). Our advice? Avoid using video during the pitch unless you absolutely have a very good reason for it.

Putting a video in your pitch can be really risky. Murphy's Law states that your video will self destruct as soon as you hit the Play button in the vicinity of an investor, crash your hard drive, instantly result in a bad hair day, or otherwise undermine your efforts. Even when the video plays correctly, it can ruin the mood. Here are two particularly problematic issues related to integrating videos into your pitch:

- **Audio level:** The audio on the video must be the same loudness as your voice and appropriate to the venue. Whereas you can control the loudness of you own voice in the moment — modulating your voice in a small room or using a microphone in a large room — getting the sound level right in the video is quite a bit more challenging. You've got to make sure that the audio is mixed properly when going through the speakers. Too loud or too soft, and you run the risk of upsetting the flow of your talk. If you have a mixing board in the auditorium and someone skilled to run it, you may be able to overcome the hurdle. If, on the other hand, your plan is to hold your microphone up to your computer's speakers so that everyone in the audience can hear — don't do it!

✔ **Timing:** If you're going to include a video, you need to segue into and out of it seamlessly, without any delays or awkward pauses. If you have more than a few seconds of time between your discussion and the start of the video's audio, you run the risk of losing the attention of your audience.

If you choose to play a video in your pitch, be sure to set it up ahead of time. Check the sound and projector color quality. Practice how you will introduce your video and how you will end it.

Depending on Internet connections

Store everything that you need for your presentation on the computer that you plan to use in the pitch. Relying on a VC's office guest wi-fi can be risky. If you bring your own hotspot, you have a better chance at getting an Internet connection, but some buildings don't have great mobile service, and you may get spotty reception, depending on how deep you are in the building.

Picking presentation file types

In an ideal presentation world, you would always be able to create your pitch deck on a computer and then use that same computer and software to present your pitch. Unfortunately, this capability is not always possible. If you are invited to pitch at a conference, for example, you may be required to put your pitch deck on a master computer that runs the pitches of all the participating companies. In this case, the conference managers will let you know which file types to use. You may be required to create and submit the pitch deck as a PPT file made in a certain version of PowerPoint, for example.

If you are not required to use a certain format, create your file in PowerPoint, Keynote, or another type of presentation software you prefer, and then save it as a PDF file. The PDF file type is stable, meaning that the layout of your slides won't be affected by any differences in the software or hardware you use to play the slides. Also, have your slides available in two different file types and have them backed up on a thumb drive incase something happens to your computer.

In general, over prepare and be flexible. You have no idea what might be thrown at you in terms of questions, format, technology, or accommodations. For the most part, VCs will not be testing you with last minute curve balls, but sometimes they are.

Chapter 17

If at First You Don't Succeed — and Even If You Do — Try, Try Again

. . . .

In This Chapter

▶ Staying on investors' radar

▶ Making regular and consistent progress

▶ Assessing how investors really feel about your deal

. . . .

*I*f you have a venture company, you'll go through the fundraising process pretty regularly. Even if you're successful, you'll probably engage in more than one funding round. Most venture companies expect to raise one angel round and two or three VC rounds before their companies are acquired or have another kind of liquidity event.

The days of meeting one VC and completing the round three weeks later are simply over. Expect to undergo a fundraising campaign for a few months and interact with many investors before you're successful. Why? For lots of reasons: Some investors can't invest in your company because it's in the wrong industry. Others will have completed their portfolio building and stopped investing altogether. A few investors simply won't be interested. Perhaps some of the people you've talked to who claim to be able to connect you with investors have wasted your time. (It takes experience to be able to predict how good a contact will be in helping you with lead generation; head to Chapter 7 for information on the ins and outs of networking.)

Raising investment capital is like riding a horse. When you fall off, you figure out what, if anything, you did wrong, make the necessary adjustment, and then try again. This chapter gives you the details on how to pick yourself up, dust yourself off, and start all over again.

Understanding Why Investors Say "No"

To raise money, you will spend a lot of time preparing your company, explaining your deal, and making sincere friendships with investors and other people in the community. By expending this time and effort in fundraising, chances are you'll be less frustrated by the process.

You can lose an investor in several ways. We've seen everything from simply being forgotten to shear personal disdain between investor and founder. Here are some of the main categories:

- ✔ **You underwhelm them.** If your team doesn't seem capable of executing on the great idea that you set forth, you can permanently lose investor interest. Refer to Part II for advice on how to position your company for maximum VC interest.

- ✔ **You confuse them.** A confused mind says no. So make sure your pitch conveys what you want it to. Chapters 14 through 16 tell you how to prepare and present an effective pitch in any situation.

- ✔ **You are a jerk.** Arrogance simply turns people off. Yes, you have a great company, but you have to be a great person to work with, too.

- ✔ **You act cheesy.** Don't use overly flowery marketing language or make inflated claims to investors. They are wary of scams and people making the hard sell.

- ✔ **You fall off the investor's radar.** When an investor doesn't hear your name or the name of your company for a few months, you are effectively out of the picture. Head to Chapter 7 for suggestions on how to build and maintain a good relationship with potential investors.

If you find that you're fundraising endeavors aren't going anywhere, take an honest look at how well positioned your company is; how effective your pitch is, both in terms of content and delivery; and how sincere you are in your relationships; and then make the necessary improvements. The following sections explain how to maximize your chances for success and what to do if things don't go your way.

We worked with a company that had a great product, a strong track record, and an unpopular founder. His personality was brash, insolent, and off-putting. After years of very strong product development progress, he had not raised capital, and it was due to the fact that no investor wanted to work with him. He found a personable and perfectly seasoned CEO to take over the company and pitch to investors. The best thing this founder did for his company was to step down to an internal, technical role (which he liked better anyway) and stay out of investor meetings. The company closed a funding round only a few months after the leadership transition.

Communicating after the Pitch

Your actions after you pitch to investors are almost as important as the preparation leading up to the pitch. Raising capital is very much about creating relationships with investors over a period of months. If you do a good job of staying in touch and communicating your company's milestones, you'll be more likely to secure your funds in the future.

Sometimes investors don't act as quickly as you'd like them to. After you pitch to a VC or angels, you may expect a whirlwind of due diligence and meetings shortly thereafter. Depending on investors deal flow, the time of year, and a ton of other variables, they may not hustle to get your due diligence done. Instead of assuming they're not interested or getting put off by the delay, keep talking with them. Don't be a pest (e-mailing a bunch and asking to "grab coffee," for example), but offer new information as it arises and generally make an effort to stay in touch.

VCs are always looking to make a good investment. Sometimes they don't see you as a good investment the first time they meet you. As your company makes progress, their tune may change. So even though a VC turns you away today, she may beg you to come back tomorrow, if you follow the advice we outline in the next sections.

VCs look at your investment in comparison to other similar deals but also in comparison with all current investment opportunities. When there are top-notch deals on the table, your deal may fall third or fourth in line for attention. Months later, when the high-quality deal flow has slowed, you may be on top of the heap.

Showing regular progress

Nothing increases your attractiveness to an investor more than progress. Over time, if you can show that you are doing the things you said you would do, people will start taking you and your company more seriously. At some point, investors who were only mildly interested before will start to see you as a potential valuable asset in their portfolios.

Of course, certain types of progress are more compelling than others. If you were invited to pitch at an event or present at a trade show, which means you were probably vetted by a committee and invited over other companies, mention that to investors. They may want to stop by your booth at the event to see how you handle the crowd. They also may want to follow up the pitch to see whether you've made any important connections. Similarly, if you close on a large customer account, you have effectively proven that a market exists for your product. Investors want to know about that kind of news.

Examples of a good investor PR strategy

The Good, the Bad, and the Ugly is not just a Clint Eastwood movie from the 1960s. It's also a smart investor communication tool. Carly Gloge, CEO and founder of Ubooly, is extremely good at communicating with investors. She keeps track of all the people who have invested or have talked seriously with her about investing. Each month she sends out a newsletter for investors that categorizes the news about her company as "The Good," "The Bad," and "The Ugly." You can adopt her strategy by doing the same. Here are the details:

✔ **The Good:** This part outlines the positive things that have occurred throughout the month. Describe your progress in development, marketing, or sales through trade shows, pitch events, customer acquisition, strategic partnerships, and other good news.

✔ **The Bad:** Not everything will go your way. If the big meeting with a new customer fell flat, share that news coupled with a mitigation strategy or a lesson learned.

✔ **The Ugly:** These are fundamental issues that need to be solved before the company can be a success. Your advisors and investors can often help you solve these problems. Sharing troubles early allows everyone to feel engaged and less blindsided when the challenges come up.

Here are some other types of news that you should share with investors:

✔ Release of new products

✔ New key hires

✔ Funds raised

✔ Deadlines for fundraising rounds that are closing soon

✔ Major changes that improve the profit potential for your company

If you could choose the perfect timing for fundraising, you would find a time when you'll be knocking off one amazing milestone after another. You are always working hard on your business, but sometimes your team is "heads down," working hard in the back office, and other times, that hard work is coming to fruition. Choose to fundraise in one of those fruition-rich times in the calendar. Also, keep an eye on the external forces in the larger economy. If the stock market takes a hit, you may want to wait until the dust settles before you try to raise capital. Also check the calendar; after mid-November, all new investment activity grinds to a halt until the new year.

Using e-mail wisely

When you start a campaign to stay in touch with investors, you need to choose wisely which VCs to put on your mailing list. Not all of them will be happy to get regular news about you. Set up a free mass e-mail service that has an unsubscribe button on the bottom of the page. By offering the unsubscribe button you and the VC get the following benefits:

✔ When you include a unsubscribe button, you give the investor a way to drop out easily. If one does unsubscribe from your mailing list, you know you don't need to stay in contact with him or her anymore.

✔ Many of these mass e-mail services let you track who clicked on links in your e-mail and who opened the e-mail in the first place. This information can be very enlightening because it lets you know whether an investor is actually reading your message or just tossing it in the electronic trashcan.

When writing e-mails to potential VCs for the purpose of staying in the forefront of their minds, give information; don't ask for things. Don't ask s VC to grab some coffee with you. This invitation, although sweet and probably genuine, is a request for the VC's time, which is a precious resource for any VC. She'll happily spend time with you when she's ready.

Assessing and Fixing What Went Wrong

If you pitch to investors and they don't dive into your deal immediately, you have to determine why. The most common reasons for a lack of immediate due diligence are that the investor didn't understand the company or that the investor will never be interested.

If the issue is that the investor didn't understand the company, don't just jump to the conclusion that the investor didn't *get it*. If you do, you may be missing out on some valuable information. Here are some things to look for when getting feedback from an investor who has not invested:

✔ The company is valued too high for its risk stage.

✔ There is too much risk left in the company.

✔ The team is not right, not complete, or contains someone that the investor doesn't like.

✔ Your business plan has a fundamental flaw.

✔ A regulatory law or upcoming change in legislation may put the company in jeopardy.

✔ The market is at risk from a competitor.

✔ The company is just outside the VCs industry expertise area.

Sometimes investors really aren't interested and never will be. That happens. But other times, just one thing may be causing the investor to feel lukewarm on your deal. If you find out what the problem is, you may be able to turn the investor's tepid feelings into something much warmer.

If you have spent time connecting with a specific VC and then you blow her off because she doesn't enter into due diligence immediately, you just wasted your time. You must follow through with the investor until you get a clear message that she is not interested or not able to invest in your company. Listen very closely to all comments and feedback. You will probably have to read between the lines a little bit. VCs really do like entrepreneurs and have no desire to squash anyone's dreams. It's hard to give advice, rejection, and support all at the same time. Ask for clarification if you are confused.

Be careful not to make changes blindly in response to potential investors' advice. Hear the advice and really use your judgment to determine whether the suggestions make sense for your company and the direction you believe you should go. Investors don't know everything, and they don't know your company as well as you do.

Following Up on the Different Outcomes

After talking with investors, four outcomes are possible: You engage in due diligence; you hear "No, thank you"; you hear nothing; or you hear "Come back after you hit certain milestones."

Possibility 1 — You enter into due diligence with a VC firm

If your efforts lead to due diligence, congratulations! What you do next depends on the type of agreement:

- ✔ **You have to sign a no-shop agreement.** In this case, you agree to stop talking to any other investors.

- ✔ **You don't have to sign a no-shop agreement.** In this case, you should keep talking to investors. If the first investor passes on the deal, you'll be happy you were talking to the other investors. Alternatively — and depending on your deal — your investors may want to work together to fund your round.

Possibility 2 — You hear the words "No, thank you"

Good news! You know not to bother with that investor or investor group anymore. Getting a clear "no" is rare. If you get one, you can consider it a successful answer. You can focus your time elsewhere. Move on.

Possibility 3 — You hear nothing at all

Unfortunately, not hearing anything at all is the most common of the outcomes. Radio silence is not only annoying; it's hard to work with. You can't make decisions when you know nothing about whether investors are interested or not. And if you don't know that, how can you know how to best approach them?

The answer is to analyze your interaction with investors. Doing so can help you ask the right questions so that you can get responses that help you figure out your next move in fundraising.

You may hear nothing for a variety of reasons, some of which relate to things on the investors' end (they've seen too many deals at once; they don't currently have the due diligence bandwidth; their capital isn't liquid; they're waiting for another deal to close; and so on). In other words, there are a myriad of reasons that investors may not invest right away in your company that have nothing to do with the quality of your deal.

Possibility 4 — You hear "Come back after you hit certain milestones"

In this case, the VC wants to see progress before she goes any further, and she typically specifies, directly or indirectly, the kinds of progress she's looking for. Your task at this point is to go back to building your company. Later, after you hit a few more milestones, you can start the fundraising campaign again.

Don't expect this message to be totally clear. Occasionally, a VC will give you a clear directive to accomplish one or two things and then come back and talk to them. Generally, the VC's wishes aren't going to be so concrete. She's not being difficult on purpose. There are probably a number of different milestones that you could accomplish, and then your company will be more attractive as an investment. Any one or two could tip the scales in your favor.

Sometimes investors aren't interested yet. But they could be if certain things were to happen on your end:

- ✔ Investors would like to see more traction with customers

- ✔ Investors would like to see a specific person or type of person added to your team or would rather your team be led by a more experienced CEO

- ✔ Investors think that your valuation is unreasonable.

- ✔ Investors are concerned about regulatory hurdles and are waiting to see whether your product passes FDA, EPA, or other regulation.

- ✔ Investors are concerned that you are too broadly seeking customers instead of focusing on one market vertical.

Overcoming Common Obstacles

One thing to keep in mind is that VCs see deals all day long. It's unlikely that your company's warts are unique. They've seen it all. If you are brave, ask point blank what they think the weakest part of your company is. The answer may be very enlightening. Use this information to overcome obstacles that may be slowing or undermining your ability to secure funding. The following sections have the details.

Experiencing personality limitations

You may think that a founder's personality is something that is pretty fundamentally ingrained in a company. Personalities don't change, and if the founder is still involved with the company, he's pretty closely tied to investor relations. However, you'd be surprised how quickly investors can warm to new management and forget about the founder behind the curtain.

Raising money too early

If you've talked to a number of investors and none of them are interested enough to commit capital, you may be trying to raise money too early. Go back through the preparation checklist (Chapter 14) to determine whether you jumped off the starting block prematurely.

Look out for the symptoms of raising money too early:

- ✔ Investors are very interested and enthusiastic at first, but then cool after they talk with you and ask you questions. In this case, VCs may invite you to call them back when you've met a series of milestones.
- ✔ Angel investors who hide behind the notion of a lead investor. In this case, you may end up with a stack of business cards from angels who will be interested as soon as you secure the lead investor.

If you think you are raising money too early, not all is lost. Go back to building your company and start the fundraising campaign again later after you hit a few more milestones.

Pivoting frivolously

Pivoting means that you change something significant about the product, target market, or end user after you come to the conclusion that your business plan isn't quite right. It's quite a bit different from iteratively designing your product and making little changes along the way. Because it often entails rebranding of the product and maybe even the company, pivoting is not something to undertake lightly.

Companies can be open to pivoting at some point as the business develops, but pivots should be rare and based on a lot of evidence that the company needs to follow another path. Pivoting can be extremely expensive and can require a lot of time to do well. Tread lightly if you plan to make a big change to your original product or target market. Although doing so may be necessary, do it in a very calculated way, not frivolously.

Being in too many markets

You may think that having a technology or product that can do lots of different things in lots of different markets is a great thing. However, having too many market possibilities for a platform technology or product is a death knell for many companies. Why? Because the team often finds it difficult to focus on customers in one industry. When a technology can be applied to many industries, choosing which one you will pursue first can be hard.

Investors will get excited about different verticals, and you'll feel drawn to follow the money instead of following your plan and, as a result, inadvertently compound the problem. Unfortunately, this desire to exploit all market opportunities simultaneously leads to founders spinning instead of focusing. After a few months of fundraising, the company can end up less focused and farther away from success than it was when it started fundraising.

You must choose one market vertical to pursue first, even though doing so means you have to sacrifice access to all the other possibilities, markets, and customers for a time. As a start-up, you simply can't pursue all opportunities simultaneously, so don't try.

Your message to investors? You've got a lot of growth potential in many different verticals. You're starting with this one because you're confident you can be successful here, and you'll begin pursuing the others in the future. Then you have to stick to it.

Treating Fundraising as a Process

The process of fundraising is much more complicated than creating a pitch deck and securing an invitation to pitch (covered in Chapters 15 and 16). A fundraising campaign is a long-term relationship-building process that can take a long time and a lot of man hours.

Plan your fundraising to take a minimum of six months, a timeline that assumes your company really is ready for investment (refer to Chapter 14 for information on knowing when to begin approaching investors). By setting up your fundraising campaign over a long period of time, you can ensure a financial runway for new milestones that investors request or a drawn-out due diligence process.

Beggars cannot be choosers, as your mom always said. If you are out of working capital, and you need investment to keep the company alive, you're in a tough situation. Broke companies have no leverage in the term sheet negotiation (Chapters 9 and 12) and have a hard time turning away an investor, even if that investor doesn't have the company's best interest at heart.

Planning for regular pitch opportunities

A good fundraising campaign strategy starts with a focus on building relationships. Then the campaign peaks with many pitching opportunities, a time period during which you may find yourself flying around the country like a presidential candidate as you try to meet all your potential investors. Finally, the campaign rolls into a quieter time when investors are doing due diligence, and you can focus on follow-up phone calls and e-mails.

After you've prepared your company and worked hard on your pitch deck message and pitch presentation, you may as well pitch everywhere that you can. Pitch to your friends, pitch to 600-person theaters, pitch to VCs around beautiful oak tables. Just keep pitching and be sure to include the following in your pitch-a-polooza:

- ✔ **Community groups:** Most cities have entrepreneur-focused community groups. Some of these are entirely made up of entrepreneurs who help each other get ready for investment or grow without investment. Some community groups are associated with angel or VC clubs and serve to directly connect investors with entrepreneurs who are fundraising. No matter the focus of the group, it can help you make connections and get invited to pitch at a local event.

  Community groups are great places to start spreading the word that you are fundraising. They are often very supportive of fellow entrepreneurs in the community and will do everything they can to get your campaign launched. In addition, many community groups have pitch classes and pitch events where you can either practice the pitch publicly or pitch to real investors. Take advantage of them!

- ✔ **National pitch events:** National pitch events are conferences where you can be highlighted to huge rooms of investors, media, and other entrepreneurs. You have to apply to pitch at these events, and they are by invitation only. It's often very difficult to get chosen to pitch at these events, but if you are selected, your deal will be exposed to many investors at one time.

Consider pitching at the annual Angel Capital Summit (http://www.angelcapitalsummit.org), TIECon (http://www.tiecon.org), Seattle Angel Conference (www.seattleangelconference.com), Women 2.0 PITCH Conference & Competition (http://www.women2.com), The Startup Conference (http://www.thestartupconference.com), Disrupt NY (http://techcrunch.com/events/disrupt-ny-2013/event-info/), and MedTech Investing Conference (http://www.medtechconference.com). Or consider any of the countless other start-up and pitch events where you can get exposure to investors on a local or national level.

You may be on stage as the entertainment, but you are getting a lot out of your participation, and the conference planners expect you to pay your own way. So be prepared to pay for your own housing, transportation, and conference admission ticket.

✔ **Accelerators:** *Accelerators* are programs designed to make your company extremely attractive to investors. After being accepted into the program, your company participates for a few weeks to a few months. Accelerators tend to have seed funds associated with them, and companies can graduate with $10,000, $25,000, or $100,000 in investment at program completion. They also have contact lists of investors that they invite to a Demo Day that culminates the program. Companies who get accepted into these accelerator programs have clout from simply being accepted into the program and are shopped to investors almost immediately after the program ends.

Three prominent international groups with this model are 500 Startups (https://500.co), Y Combinator (http://www.ycombinator.com), and TechStars (http://www.techstars.com), all of which are hard to get into.

Handling failure

It's no fun being rejected or pitching to blank, staring faces. But the way you handle failure is probably more indicative of your future fundraising success than any other personality trait. You have to persevere, or you'll never get through all the no's to the yes. The best strategy to get past the natural down feeling of rejection is to plan for rejection in your milestones. Instead of writing "Get funded" as a milestone, write "Get rejected by 35 investors." To depressing? Then write "Talk to 35 investors this month." This mindset acknowledges the fact that a lot of investors won't invest. You still get to check the milestone off your list after 35 conversations, whether new money is committed to your account or not.

Sometimes, if you're met with failure after failure, the best thing you can do is talk with another entrepreneur or a consultant about your company and your fundraising approach. A consultant has an outsider's view and can let you know how things look from an outside perspective. You may be overlooking something that a consultant would find glaringly obvious. And because you're hiring the consultant for her outsider perspective, she doesn't have to have a big price tag or a prestigious name to be helpful. You can choose from the many small, independent consultants whose mission is to help companies build their seed stage business. Just make sure your consultant understands the start-up climate in your community.

Contacting more VCs

Make contacting VCs a priority, and if you have difficulty, try asking VCs outside your industry for introductions to VCs in your industry. Investors who can't invest in your company because they don't invest in your industry are the greatest friends to have. They know a ton of other investors and can make the introductions for you. So make friends with a VC or two outside your industry and ask them for introductions to VCs in your industry. Chapter 7 has more on networking.

You can also cold call VCs. This method of contact isn't ideal, but if it's all you have, go for it. Before calling, though, do your homework and make sure you know the details of the VC firm first. (Having an entrepreneur contact them to hear more about the firm is very off-putting for VCs. Remember, when you contact VCs, offer information, don't ask for information.)

Planning the next funding round

After you're funded, you may have to start planning the next round. Often only 6 to 18 months pass between raises. Spend some time revising your message for the next round. Your company, story, and deal need to be more developed in subsequent rounds; otherwise, investors will wonder what you did with the money from the last round. In other words, your company has to start growing up.

The longer the time that passes, the greater the investor's expectations are for progress. Investors want to see actual progress (product development, sales, and so on) and not just that you hired a bunch of people and loaded up on overhead.

The good news is that after you raise the first round of funding, you'll have more clout with investors and loads more experience at the fundraising process than you did going in the first time.

So good luck and go knock their socks off!

Part V
The Part of Tens

For a bonus venture capital part-of-tens chapter, head online to www.dummies.com/extras/venturecapital.

In this part...

- ✔ Avoid common mistakes that can torpedo your chance of securing venture capital.

- ✔ Get your deal done in the shortest amount of time possible by following advice about what to do before, during, and after your pitch to investors.

- ✔ Find VCs by discovering the places where they're likely to be, developing relationships with people in the know, and becoming involved in events and organizations that can give you exposure.

Chapter 18

Ten Ways to Lose a Deal

You can derail your own deal pretty quickly if you aren't careful. Your own behavior is important. If you are uncoachable, quoting an inflated valuation, or pitching too early, work to change those things. You can keep the people around you positive about your deal by pacifying critics and spreading updates and good news at networking events. Connect with people outside your own city and remember to pitch the whole deal, clearly, to investors who are likely to care about it.

Nobody's perfect, but when you're seeking venture capital, some mistakes, more than others, can cost you the deal. This chapters outlines some of the most damaging mistakes you can make and tells you how to avoid them — or overcome them if they occur.

Being Uncoachable

Growing a company from a team of one or two into a thriving business is hugely difficult. You will learn a ton along the way. Being coachable means having a personality that allows you to say, "I stand corrected." In other words, you can take criticism, constructive or otherwise, and use it or disregard it, while staying positive throughout. Strive to be coachable, especially if that trait isn't one you possess naturally.

People who are uncoachable don't take criticism well or simply don't listen. They are offended by the notion that their company isn't perfect, even though no company is perfect. The uncoachable person resists change and quickly frustrates all investors that he meets.

Having a Critic

You can't do a lot when someone doesn't like you or your company, but be warned, having someone badmouth your deal, even falsely, can ruin the mood around your fundraising campaign very quickly. In an angel meeting of 25 people, if one angel says something less than positive about your deal, the excitement drops, and the deal can die right there on the boardroom table. If a VC asks his advisors what they think of your deal and they dislike it, it's dead. Horrifying but true.

The best way to avoid this problem is to make friends and *don't* make waves for any reason while you are fundraising. Chapter 7 tells you how to cultivate relationships with the people you'll need as you seek capital.

Quoting an Inflated Valuation

Quoting an inflated value for your company is probably the number one reason a deal sours on the investor's plate. When your valuation is too high, investors think you are either greedy or you don't know what you are doing. In both cases, a high valuation can end a conversation. Chapter 10 and Chapter 11 discuss valuation and how to broach the topic without turning anyone off.

Pitching an Idea

At one time, VCs may have doled out $4 million dollars for an idea (or maybe they never did and some people just like to tell tall tales); nevertheless, angels or VCs investing in a concept stage company is not common these days. Now, investors carefully balance the risk versus reward aspects of your deal. If you've accomplished very little and are still a few years away from revenue, VCs aren't going to invest in your deal. It's simply too risky.

If you're not ready for venture capital, you have other options. Chapter 4 describes the other avenues for funding an early-stage company, and Chapter 9 discusses in detail how to set up early investments so that the company will be poised for future A and B rounds.

Being Invisible or Forgotten

Fundraising is like a presidential campaign. You'll have more success if you're more visible. Make sure that you're attending networking events, trade shows, and pitch events so that people in the investment world see you regularly. Ideally, you will have regular updates and good news about your company to share when you are in public.

Be careful not to give the impression that you are pitching the same old deal for a long time. Make sure you are giving a message of progress.

Most of all, stay in touch with investors after you pitch to them. The ball is always in your court. Don't ask for information or the investor's time. Share good news every month though a newsletter or mailing list. It doesn't have to be extensive. Brevity is best anyway. Chapter 17 has suggestions.

Confusing People

As the saying goes, a confused mind says no. People have to understand your deal so well that they can describe it to another person. Everyone has to talk with someone else about your deal before they can invest. Angels have to talk with their spouses; VCs have to talk with the board.

The most effective pitch deck lays everything out simply for the audience. After the pitch is over, people should be able to discuss the deal as though they were discussing the plot of a Disney movie. Simplify everything! The details will come out in subsequent meetings. Head to Chapters 14 through 16 for information on preparing and presenting your pitch deck.

Pitching to Only One Investor

If you went on only one date ever, what is the likelihood that that single date would result in a wedding and a perfect marriage? Probably very slight. Although you may find the right investor immediately (the venture capital version of a high school sweetheart), it's rare. Plan to shop your deal all over your town and other towns.

Having Connections in Only One Town

One of the greatest things about the world we live in is how connected we all are. Use relationships in your hometown or the hometowns of your founders to seek investment from other cities and states. If you have a female founder on the team, contact the few women's investor groups in the country. They are constantly looking for high caliber, women-owned companies.

Use your network to get an introduction to VCs. LinkedIn can be powerful to get connected with VCs in other cities through people you know. You can even try to cold contact them. Keep in mind, though, that some investors are local-only investors. Some will talk to you only if you consider moving to their town. Get the details before you buy a plane ticket. You don't want to have to nod and agree that you'll move to Milwaukee if you had never considered it.

Failing to Study Up on Your Investors

When you meet with an investor, you should have researched him so thoroughly that you know what his favorite dinner is (not really, but you get the idea). When you ask questions, your questions should be highly informed ones about things that you can't learn from the Internet. Investors are very turned off when you don't know what kind of investments they make.

To study up, get ahold of potential investors' portfolios to understand the types of companies they invest in and how much they have been investing. In addition, most VC general partners have a Twitter feed, a website, and a LinkedIn page. From these sources, you should be able to learn quite a bit about the general partners as people before you walk in the door.

Pitching Your Product Instead of Your Deal

When you pitch to investors, you are selling equity in your company; therefore, the pitch has to be about your whole company. If you give the same pitch to investors that you give to a potential customer — one that outlines all the benefits and features of your product — then you've missed the mark.

You have to share with investors all the highlights about your company. They need to know how much you've accomplished, the plan for the future, and how much money your company can make for them. Chapters 14, 15, and 16 discuss the investor pitch in grand detail.

The investor pitch is about money, specifically how you'll make money, how much money you can make, how much money you need to make money faster. If money isn't the central theme of your pitch, you need to revisit your pitch deck and see how you can refocus it. The investor looks at your company as a much needed addition to his portfolio. He sees your company as a whole package with founders, product, opportunity, and exit potential.

Chapter 19

Ten Places and People That Can Lead You to a VC

In This Chapter
▶ Working with investors who know other investors
▶ Choosing your lawyer, accountant, or business banker with capital in mind
▶ Avoiding scam artists

Despite being highly sought out by entrepreneurs, venture capitalists are not easy to find. You have to make an effort to find VCs and get them to take a look at your company. This chapter tells you how. Turn to Chapter 5 for suggestions and strategies on building a rapport with VCs after you find them.

Service Providers

Believe it or not, your accountant, lawyer, or banker may be your connection to future funding. Some firms have good relationships with local venture capitalists.

It's in a service provider's best interest for your company to grow large, wealthy, and prosperous, and the best service providers want to help you do that. An accountant who is willing to go above the call of duty for his client, for example, will take it upon himself to suggest venture capital funding and make introductions to investors when the time is right — definitely something to consider when you're interviewing your next service provider.

Angel Investors

In many communities, VCs and angels are invited to participate in demo days, pitch events, and other networking opportunities that are designed to bring the different types of investors together. Given their opportunities to network with VCs, your seed round investors may have connections to local VC firms. (Head to Chapter 2 to find out more about seed funds.)

When you choose which investors to include in seed rounds, consider their contacts. The best-connected angels have VCs in their contact lists.

Other Venture Capitalists

Throughout this book, we have said that VCs are limited in which industry they can invest in. We've also said that, if a VC firm does not invest in your industry, you have no reason to contact that firm. Here, we're going to suggest you bend the rules a little by telling you that you can contact a VC outside your industry for one really good reason: to ask for a referral to another VC. If you can get the VC to like you and your company just a little, he may be willing to refer you to his friend at another firm.

Online Search

Start with the National Venture Capital Association's website (www.nvca. org). It has a whole section devoted to resources for entrepreneurs. VCs write blogs, tweet, and are otherwise visible online. You can see whether your values match theirs pretty quickly.

You can also simply enter *venture capital* or *venture capital investing* and the name of your state into a search engine to easily access a list of venture capital firms in your area. Be sure you look at the firms' portfolio pages to determine whether their previous investments are real companies that you would like to be connected to. Also do your homework to determine whether the VC firm is respected and established.

Networking Events

Venture capitalists send associates and analysts into the field. A VC office, for example, may ask junior members of its staff to hang out at networking events, trade shows, and other places where they may run across a promising company.

The VC's analyst may be a graduate student intern or a very junior employee. So if a young person asks you about your company, don't blow him or her off. If you play your cards right, your company may be on the analyst's list to discuss further with a senior staff member. Also, some networking events are attended by investors, and some are attended by students, job seekers, lawyers, and so on. Ask around to find out which events are the ones with the highest value to you.

Pitch Events

Apply to pitch your company to investors at organized pitch events. These events happen all over the country and are sometimes called *business plan competitions, investor pitch competitions, start-up competitions, venture competitions,* or *venture challenges.* A single pitch can generate a lot of interest from angels and venture capitalists. As part of the event, you'll also likely get some press and public relations exposure. Sometimes a sizable cash prize is awarded to the winning company.

Pitch events aren't perfect solutions to finding investment. They're a lot of work to prepare for, and if you mess up the pitch, hundreds of people will see your gaff. Also, you have to pay a fee to participate in pitch events. Before you sign up for a pitch event, do some research to see whether companies that participated in the past felt that they got their time and money's worth by attending.

Mentors

Unusual skills are at work in the fundraising process. Companies that successfully raise money often have someone on the team who intimately understands the process of raising money. If you've never raised venture capital, chances are you misunderstand some fundamental points. Mentors can be instrumental in guiding you through those misunderstandings.

More than just coaching, mentors can actually point to the money. Mentors who have raised money in the past know where to find VCs; they also probably have active relationships with VCs. Mentors often act as advisors to the VC's portfolio companies.

Broker-Dealers

Broker-dealers are service providers who act as agents between investors and companies and take a cut of the investment, which can be quite high, for their work. If VCs were not attracted to your company in the past because of things like a messy capitalization table, odd debt structure, or bad partnership agreements, broker-dealers can help you restructure your company to attract VC interest.

Be careful with people who claim to find venture capital for you. You may run across people who call themselves *finders, business brokers,* or even *capital agents,* and perform the services a broker-dealer does. However, if they are not registered with the Securities and Exchange Commission (SEC) as broker-dealers, they cannot legally charge you a percentage fee after successfully helping you get investment. Laws change and are different from state to state, so check with current legislation in your area to be sure that your investment-finding service provider is working within the law.

Incubator Staff

A business incubator is often a physical building where young businesses are invited to rent an office. These groups can be helpful because they concentrate resources in one place and probably provide discounted services and free advice. Your local business incubator may have connections to venture capital. Some incubators are very involved with investment capital — even to the point of having small seed funds associated directly with the incubator (when capital is directly involved, it's called an *accelerator*). At the very least, they probably have all the information about the local pitch events and networking events where you may be able to find a VC.

Incubators are very good at connecting people in the community. Look to your local incubator to find an entrepreneur in residence who can mentor you through the fundraising process. If they can't directly help you find investors, ask them to connect you with someone who has raised venture capital in the past. People who have raised capital know where to find people who invest capital. Incubators are often found near universities. Look to the National Business Incubator Association for more information (http://www.nbia.org).

Funding Websites

A number of websites are devoted to connecting entrepreneurs with investors. Entrepreneurs post their company profiles and share them with investor groups that they think may be interested.

Different from crowdfunding sites (refer to Chapter 4), funding websites focus on getting entrepreneurs' feet in the doors of investors who will invest significant amounts of money. Gust (http://www.gust.com) and AngelList (https://angel.co/) are the most prominent websites where you can post your company profile to find investors.

Many versions of funding websites appear on the Internet, but VCs don't use the majority of these sites to find entrepreneurs. Look through the website before you devote a lot of time into filling out a profile for indications that VCs are using the site.

Index

About the Authors

Nicole Gravagna: Nicole is a leader in the start-up and investing community in Colorado through her work as the Director of Operations in the Rockies Venture Club, Board Member of 10.10.10, and Advisory Board Member of Coalition for a Connected West. She also serves on the board of RAFT (Resource Area for Teaching) and acts as a founding advisor to Alternatives in Science Club, a student organization at University of Colorado devoted to connecting business and life science. You can follow Nicole through Twitter @NicoleGravagna or through her blog posts at RockiesVentureClub.org. Nicole holds a PhD in Neuroscience from the University of Colorado, a MS from the University of Maryland, and a BS from Washington College.

Peter K. Adams: Peter Adams is the Executive Director of the Rockies Venture Club, a non-profit organization furthering economic development by connecting investors and entrepreneurs through conferences (Angel Capital Summit and Colorado Capital Conference), networking events, educational offerings, and facilitation of early-stage investor groups. His role includes creating deal flow of hundreds of firms per year, screening for investable companies, developing best practices for due diligence and negotiation, and providing education for investors in the areas of valuation, term sheets, negotiation, syndication, and portfolio strategies. Peter has over 25 years of business experience, beginning in the 1980s with a technology company responsible for fulfilling a sole-source contract for all personal computers for the Colorado state government, including universities, agencies, and related offices. Peter is a serial entrepreneur, having founded five companies. He has also served over a dozen years as Economics Director and as CIO of an international professional services firm. Peter is also the CEO for BizGirls.org, a non-profit summer camp for high-school girls to learn entrepreneurship, and Omniportraits, a for-profit e-commerce venture. Peter holds a BA degree from Colorado College, and an MBA from Regis University.

Authors' Acknowledgments

Nicole: I would like to thank my husband, Fred, for his unwavering support in all that I do. My family and mentors have empowered and encouraged me to keep reaching farther. The Colorado start-up community has continued to inspire me through my own high-risk journey. And a big thank you to Peter, my coauthor, who held the door to opportunity open for me. I'd also like to thank Jim Keating, for his insightful comments on the manuscript.

Peter: I would like to acknowledge the Colorado Venture Capital and Angel Investing community for their collaboration and helpfulness. I'd also like to thank my family and friends for their support while we were writing this book, and my coauthor who did so much to help get this book written.

Publisher's Acknowledgments

Acquisitions Editor: Stacy Kennedy

Editor: Tracy Barr

Technical Editor: James P. Keating

Project Coordinator: Patrick Redmond

Cover Image: ©iStockphoto.com/David Schmidt